MASTER OF ARTS

After acquiring a BA in English Literature from Stella Maris College, Madras, Tulsi Badrinath graduated with an MBA from Ohio University, USA. Returning to India, she worked for four dreary years at Standard Chartered Bank before quitting her job to pursue her twin passions – writing and dance. Her background in management helps her provide corporate executives with cross-cultural insights while interacting with them through the medium of dance. She is the author of two works of fiction, *Man of a Thousand Chances* and *Meeting Lives*, and one work of non-fiction titled *Madras, Chennai and the Self: Conversations with the City*.

Praise for *Master of Arts*

'Written with sincerity and sensitivity, the book is frank, fair and hugely readable.' – Gopalkrishna Gandhi, former Governor of West Bengal

'Told with sensitivity and an insider's knowledge of the unique relationship between a student and guru that classical training instills in a person. Badrinath describes with rare candour the difficulties of pursuing the art professionally, and even if one has "connections"...things not written about in the art community, for fear of angering patrons, or for the danger of being disregarded for insufficient gratitude at being given an opportunity to perform. It is worthwhile reading for every practitioner and would-be-practitioner of the form.' – *TimeOut*

'Engagingly told, the book is about traditions that are fast disappearing. Time is just one of them. The guru-shishya parampara is another. "When I was learning dance, we would go to class immediately after school," says Badrinath. "There was no fixed time for the class to end. Now, there is constant competition between the mobile, iPad, iPod and computer for your attention. The mind is restless." In her book, however, it stands still.' – *The Week*

'The three narratives, distinctive yet affecting each other, that run through the book, go a good way towards demystifying the male dancer in contemporary society. This book bravely talks of all that a dancer has to go through to get a performance slot, especially one of the coveted December season slots. On a personal level, reading this book has been like taking a peek into the human side of a larger-than-life figure and to hear him talking about his failures as much as his successes.' – *Hindustan Times*

'Imagine thatched-roof cottages and brick walls and the perpetual summer in the lush, green environs of Adyar, Chennai. Now take that and juxtapose it with the sound of ghungroo or small metallic bells tied around one's ankles, two-toned costumes, a cherry tree and the compound, and bamboo frames to let the sea breeze in, and you are transported into the nostalgia of simpler times, of a time forgotten and a world untouched by the encroachment of capitalism and globalisation, and inside Bharata Kalanjali, the dancing school established by the Dhananjayans. Definitely a book worth reading.' – *First City*

'Like many dances, this novel has a double narrative streaming through it... stories of journeys into dance, but generations apart. One is the writer's personal journey into dance and the other is the story of the lives of her teachers, the well-known and remarkable dancing duo Dhananjayan and his wife Shanta. This device of two simultaneous parallel stories, makes for an interesting juxtaposition of perception through different generations. Easy to read and made more pleasurable by the performative writing that relives moments, inner thoughts, and outer identifications of time, place and actions.' – *Indian Express*

'In many ways, the cover [of *Master of Arts: A Life in Dance*] – a mirror with V.P. Dhananjayan looking into a reflection of his son, Satyajit, lining his eyes with kohl – is its central imagery; a peek into the past from the present; an introspective commentary on a world that was, and that is; a narrative that attempts to string together stories that have common links in terms of incidents, issues, concerns or identities. The book's real preoccupation – obsession even – is its hero, V.P. Dhananjayan, the 'Sir', who emerges in all his fierceness, finery, fieriness, and frankness, through every chapter.' – *The Hindu*

MASTER OF ARTS
A Life in Dance

Tulsi Badrinath

hachette
INDIA

First published in 2013 by Hachette India
(Registered name: Hachette Book Publishing India Pvt. Ltd)
An Hachette UK company
www.hachetteindia.com

This edition published in 2015

SRD

Photograph Acknowledgements
The author is grateful to the Dhananjayans for permission to use photos 2, 3, 4, 5, 6, 8, 9, 10 (by Raghavendra Rao), 14, 16, 17, 18, 20 (by Mohan Das Vadakara) from their personal archives; Charles Ma for photo 7; Narendra Kumar for photo 12; B.K.Shafeekuddin for photo 13; Anand Satchidanandan for photo 15 (by Mohan Das Vadakara); Navtej Singh Johar for photo 19 (by Anshuman Sen); Photo 1 and 11 (by Mohan Das Vadakara) – the author's personal archives.

ISBN 978-93-5009-994-0

Hachette Book Publishing India Pvt. Ltd
612/614 (6th Floor), Time Tower,
M.G. Road, Sector 28, Gurgaon 122001, India

Typeset in Minion Pro 11/14.5
by RECTO Graphics, Delhi

Printed and bound in India by
Manipal Technologies Limited, Manipal

FSC
www.fsc.org
MIX
Paper from
responsible sources
FSC™ C104740

Om Gurave Namah

Dedicated to my Gurus
Natya-acharya Sri V.P. Dhananjayan and Srimati Shanta
Yoga-acharya Sri T.K.V. Desikachar and Srimati Menaka
Jyotish-acharya Sri Sanjay Rath

Prologue

He has just shaved to avoid the five o'clock shadow. His face – a fertile field for the many expressions he is famous for – has been prepared with a layer of pancake. Unlike the mineral dyes of Kathakali, this is a colour shades darker than his skin. When blended with blusher it will prevent his face from looking pale beneath the spotlight. Dipping a narrow stick into a pot of kohl and looking at himself in the mirror he now draws it out steadily below his left eye. He uses a brush to paint his lips; the lipstick chosen for the right shade of red rather than any brand value. He draws two curlicues on his cheeks in place of sideburns. His jet black hair has always been thick, thank god, and when combed back sits regally on his forehead. A mixture of oil and water ensures that not a hair moves out of place through the next two hours. Finally, he paints a tilak on his broad forehead.

He knows himself to be Vannadil Pudeeyaveetil Dhananjayan who left home at the age of fourteen, but when he completes his makeup and looks into the mirror, dressed in a yellow silken dhoti, blue cummerbund cinched at the waist with a gold belt, a simple necklace, earrings and armlets, he sees the handsome dancer he has become.

In the kit his wife Shanta has packed for him, he locates his ankle bells, blessed several times over at various temples, and raising them to his closed eyes, invokes the gods. He prays that he remember all that his gurus taught him, that he uphold their tradition and generosity of giving. Tying the brass bells around his ankles, a solemnity and seriousness of purpose descends on him.

From this moment on, his mind leads him into a zone of total concentration. Thoughts flee, save those that he will communicate with his painted face.

Standing in the wings, he knows he has danced innumerable times all over the world. He has won high praise. But every performance is a foray into unknown territory; every performance an encounter with himself.

The musicians sing the praises of Ganesha. Thus begun, the show is underway. And before he knows it, he is on stage, the sound of his bells accompanying every movement of his feet. He is bathed by the lights, but he can only see a well of darkness beyond them. Are there a lot of people? Have the seats been filled? Such anxieties fall away once he starts dancing.

No one knows just how he will develop his ideas through abhinaya. Seated to his right, the musicians watch every twitch of his facial muscles for clues. They are trained to follow him, to support him. When his wife conducts the orchestra he is in safe hands, but even she cannot predict what he will do. It keeps the excitement level high. Something happens within him that he cannot describe.

He feels his own divinity…

Introduction

I remember vividly the exact moment, on a hot day in Madras in 1977, when the dance I had been learning for months came alive for me. What I did not know then, at the age of ten, was that this moment had come into existence because of major shifts in temple mores, social codes and law. It was a reality that had not been possible at the turn of the century – when few men performed '*dasi attam*' (dressed as women when they did) and only women known as devadasis offered their dance in worship to the deities in temples.

Seated on a mat, facing my guru, I was scared. It was the first time I was learning one on one from him, without the protective buffer of my classmates. I watched as he held his left palm open, simulating a lotus leaf, and wrote on it with an imaginary quill. The letter was read, re-read, then folded with care. My guru made a beautiful lotus with his fingers. Its petals were forced open and the letter concealed within, before the flower closed. The letter-writer, a girl pining for Shiva, searched for a messenger and handed the lotus to her. That day, as I made an imperfect lotus with my hands, much smaller than his, something expanded in me.

Encapsulated in that moment, in that thatch-roofed cottage, something marvellous had occurred, something that had no reference to my daily life; a story narrated by my guru's eyes, by his face that changed from *nayika* to Shiva to pink lotus to friend with ease. His expressions reached into me, made me feel each one of them. The clandestine message glowing brightly within the lotus-bud of my fingers, I was taken captive forever by the possibilities of *abhinaya*.

*

My guru, V.P. Dhananjayan, was one of the first men to make a successful career as a Bharata Natyam dancer. By the late sixties, when he made this choice, the dance of the devadasi, variously known as *dasi attam, sadir, chinna melam*, was referred to as Bharata Natyam. Indeed, in making Bharata Natyam his profession, my guru had to create a space for his dance where none existed.

In other parts of India, men had danced for centuries. The young gotipua performed in Odisha and men traditionally performed Kathakali and Kuchipudi, even the female roles. Several generations of Ishwari Prasad's heirs are legendary in Kathak. In the monastries of Assam, for the past five hundred years, monks had danced the Sattriya. However, across Madras Presidency, given the link between *sadir* and devadasis, and the separation of roles between the male and female progeny of a devadasi, *sadir* was performed mostly by women. It is only recently, in the relatively short span of the past seventy years, that greater numbers of men have performed Bharata Natyam as men; without needing to dress as women to appear on stage.

In this development, the legendary Rukmini Devi played a primary if unintended role. Initially, the boys who came to her school of arts, Kalakshetra, as did my guru, majored in music or Kathakali and learnt Bharata Natyam more by osmosis; it was much later that they came solely to learn Bharata Natyam.

As Dhananjayan's student for nearly forty years now, I have interacted with the many young boys who came to learn from him. Battling prejudice (*'Who wants to watch sweaty men dance?'*), and finding innovative ways to earn a living from art, most of these male dancers seemed doomed to struggle as solo dancers, waiting for the right break that would make them stars. Yet, some of them did not give up.

What kept them going? Observing the difficulties that were particular to them, both in acquiring proficiency in the art and in earning a livelihood from it, I was curious about what drew them to dance and held them within its grip. Was it passion alone or the elusive quest for fame, or was it simply – given that many came from low-income families – a lack of education and therefore choice?

My own understanding of the practice of Bharata Natyam derived much from listening over the years to my guru talk about Kalakshetra, its founder Rukmini Devi, and her approach to repertoire, a narrative rich in nuance and detail. Given the oral, intensely personal method of teaching any classical art in India, I discovered that a wealth of knowledge circulated without being captured in print, which is what leads to an anomaly between the world of Bharata Natyam as it exists and its portrayal in academic discourse.

To redress this to some extent, I decided to write about Dhananjayan's journey in dance, about the challenges he has faced in a career that has spanned sixty years, as also the twists and turns in the lives of some of the interesting male dancers I have come across.

Dance, *natya*, was one of the sixteen customary offerings with which gods were adored in Hindu temples for centuries. This resulted in the unique position of the devadasi, the dancing servant of god, who was trained in this specific ritual offering of dance – a sophisticated art form in itself.

Through the centuries, devadasis were dedicated to the temple as children, before they reached puberty by their parents or relatives. The young girls had no say in the matter. I can only imagine the dismay of such children who grew up to find themselves part of a matrilineal establishment with its own rules for male and female children, but set apart from the rest of a patrilineal society; married to god, but allowed liaisons with only too human men, and therefore subject to the slights and taunts of 'respectable' society; wealthy, but only so long as they performed the role they had never voluntarily sought.

Those devadasis linked with the Chola, Pandya, Nayak and Maratha courts, and smaller principalities, in the greater region of Madras, perfomed what was known as *sadir* or *chinna melam*. When offered ritualistically in the temple, there were rules deciding what hour of the day they would be performed and where within the temple complex, as also what sort of musical structure would be used. For example, the *Navasandhi Kauthuvams* were essential to worshipping the protective lords of the eight directions, each performed at a particular place in the temple precincts. During major temple festivals, specific pieces of repertoire were performed in offering. When the devadasis danced at the royal courts or sang in the homes of wealthy patrons, their repertoire was more appropriate to that place and occasion, and less restricted by temple rules.

Over the centuries, it became established practice that while the devadasi was married to god, and therefore always an auspicious presence as a *sumangali* or married woman, she was free to enter into relationships with men. Inducted into these relationships while very young, her liaisons were openly conducted and while the devadasi usually maintained fidelity to one partner, there were many cases where an element of commerce crept into her sexual dealings with men.

There was no dichotomy between the sexual liberty society had sanctioned her and the themes she elaborated upon in her dance.

A devadasi's daughters lived with her; part of a matrilineal system of inheritance. They learnt music or dance and in most cases became devadasis as well. For them, their true wealth was what they inherited in terms of musical styles, knowledge of the intricacies of Carnatic music and the repertoire of particular compositions that they were known for.

When the British took over the Tanjore court, the loss of royal patronage spelt the death knell for the devadasi way of life. Many devadasis made their way to the expanding city of Madras. While not all of them made themselves wantonly available to men, slowly the words devadasi and prostitute began to be synonymous.

With the growth of nationalistic fervour and an increasing degree of westernization, preserving the sacred, exalted offering of dance to the reigning deity of a temple was seen as less important than doing away with the stigma of child prostitution by legislating against devadasis themselves. Dr. Muthulakshmi Reddy who, as the daughter of a devadasi, had first-hand knowledge of the benefits and travails of that life, was determined to end the social stigma and threats to health that the young girls faced. A group of spirited devadasis led by the redoubtable Bangalore Nagaratnamma fought the bill proposed by Dr. Muthulakshmi Reddy, but she won. A series of historical changes led to a ban on the dedication of devadasis, and the offering of dance-as-ritual in temples, in 1947.

Concurrently, in the twenties, an effort had begun to save the art of the devadasis, even as the institution came under approbation from society. Facing the stigma of being labelled prostitutes, *thevadiya*, a corruption of the original meaning of the regal *thevar adiyal*, one serving god, many girls from devadasi families stopped learning or openly performing the dance. Seeking to bypass the unsavoury connotations associated with the words *sadir*, or *dasi attam*, revivalists referred to it as Bharata Natyam.

Chief among these revivalists was E. Krishna Iyer. Trained to be a lawyer, he found himself drawn to the dance of the dasis. An actor in a local theatre group, he began to perform *sadir* wherever he could, dressed as a female. In his fervour to communicate the beauty of the dance, he travelled far, wrote much and as a founder member of the Music Academy, presented the first ever show on a proscenium stage, in Madras, of two devadasis, in 1931.

It was not until I had spent over two decades learning Bharata Natyam that I began to study seriously its history, the role of the devadasis in temple ritual and the early 20th century legislations that resulted simultaneously in the temple gods losing a part of their due and the devadasi her customary way of life. This was not dry history but a living, contentious issue that had direct bearing on my being able to express myself through dance.

My guru's guru, Rukmini Devi, not only participated dynamically in the shift that brought the dance out of the temple to the proscenium stage but also enabled entire generations of girls such as myself, who would otherwise have never been able to dance in public, to learn the art of the devadasis.

To understand a present in which it was possible for me – north Indian, Brahmin, of a family that had a long line of distinguished civil servants, born and brought up in Madras – to state with pride that I was a dancer, to negotiate the circumstances in which dance as a profession currently operates, I had to study the past.

Rukmini Devi, born in 1904 to Brahmin parents influenced by the Theosophical Movement, was to play a major role in the transmission of the art of the devadasis, that until the 1930's had only been performed by women dedicated in the temples. In 1920 when she married, out of caste, a man twenty years older than her, and to further complicate things, an Englishman, she broke several taboos at once. She had to leave Madras to escape the furore caused by her marriage to George Arundale, later President of the Theosophical Society. Learning an art-form, *sadir*, that a swathe of eminent men in public life had taken an oath not to watch, practiced as it was by women equated with prostitutes, was yet another taboo she would break. She once told a friend '...I am not a good girl in the Indian way!'[1]

Rukmini Devi

On January 1, 1933, Rukmini Devi saw the devadasi dancers, Jeevaratnam and Rajalakshmi, perform. Inspired and urged by Russian ballerina Anna Pavlova to study dance forms closer home, rather than ballet, Rukmini Devi knew that this was the art-form she must learn. 'When I saw the dance in the Music Academy, I could see the perfection of technique, the pure classicism of the dance and decided I must learn the dance from Meenakshisundaram Pillai who was their guru.'[2]

The boys and girls of the devadasis were given specific training in the art, to different but complementary ends; to teach, compose and conduct the dance in the case of male children who grew up to become skilled *nattuvanars* or accomplished musicians, and to offer dance-as-ritual in the case of the females. The training of the young daughters of devadasis in the ritual art was entrusted to the *nattuvanars*. Of the village of Pandanallur, Meenakshisundaram Pillai was a legend in his own lifetime. He was no ordinary *nattuvanar*, or dance master, but a renowned guru well versed in music, fluent in three languages – Tamil, Telugu and Sanskrit, and lauded for his skill in fitting movement seamlessly to music. He was known by the calibre of his students, many famous dancers from hereditary devadasi families such as Pandanallur Jayalakshmi and Pandanallur Sabharanjitham among others.

The best of *nattuvanars* were adept in the rhythm-based aspect of the dance; how to pair movement with musical and percussion syllables. They composed music suited to dance and conducted the orchestra with cymbals as the devadasi danced. Meenakshisundaram Pillai himself had a great lineage, as he was a descendent of the four brothers known collectively as the Tanjore Quartet whose compositions carried forward the splendid musical base of *sadir* into the core of present day Bharata Natyam.

The great master of Pandanallur was initially reluctant to teach Rukmini Devi as 'he thought it would be a sacrilege to teach me, a high caste Brahmin lady to perform *sadir*. It was very difficult to break down his resistance.'[3]

It took her one year to persuade him. Meanwhile, she had been learning from Mylapore Gowri Ammal, her first guru, who taught her in secrecy in Mylapore and at times in Adyar.

In agreeing to teach Rukmini Devi, Meenakshisundaram Pillai broke a taboo as well, giving generously of his hereditary treasure of dance. His student was 30 years old, long past the age when dancers were initiated into the basics. Driven by her passion, Rukmini Devi began the long arduous sessions with him and by December 1935, felt ready enough to perform at the Diamond Jubilee celebrations of the Theosophical Society.

Her guru, fearing embarrassment, feeling she was not advanced enough in her practice of the art, disagreed with her about the timing of the debut. Undaunted, Rukmini Devi went ahead to give a spellbinding performance on the grounds of the Theosophical Society. After that, there was no looking back.

Within months, in 1936, she began the International Academy of Arts, later called Kalakshetra.[4] At a time when no students were forthcoming to learn the dance, because of the stigma associated with it, Rukmini Devi had to start with her own niece, Radha. As she put it, Kalakshetra began with 'one tree, one pupil and one teacher'.[5] The main criterion she sought in her students was the willingness to learn. One by one, students came to her, both girls and boys. Initially, the boys who came majored in music or Kathakali and learnt Bharata Natyam by osmosis; it was later that they came solely to learn Bharata Natyam. Muthulakshmi Reddy herself, who had once fiercely opposed Rukmini Devi's idea of teaching the art[6], sent students from Avvai Home, her shelter for destitute women. Artistically mature beyond her years, gifted with an innate sense of beauty and aesthetics, Rukmini Devi did not hesitate to modify what she had learnt to suit the circumstances in which she would be presenting it. Key to this was the choice of repertoire.

A devadasi's repertoire, sung mainly in Telugu, Tamil and Sanskrit, was her chief treasure, not so much the gold and diamonds she owned. A devadasi offered dance in the temples, sang in the royal courts and performed in salons. She sang of *bhakti*, devotion, of yearning for god-as-lover, of the soul's desires. At other times, she emphasized greatly the erotic element or *shringara* in her *padams* and *javalis*.

'*Wait for me, I'm too young for you right now, but once I've matured, I will be yours,*' a heroine might say. Or '*Did I ask you where you went last night? I didn't. Did I ask you about all the marks on your body?*' Or '*You had your way with me. Now, go get an abortificent root, I have no female friends to help me.*' Or '*My body is raw from childbirth, this is not the time to be together. Enamoured of my golden glow, you are begging for sex. If I say no you get offended. Rein in your desires for just two months.*'[7]

Many of these compositions were written by the greatest of bards, Annamacharya (late 15th century) and Kshetrayya (17th century) and Sarangapani (early 18th century). They wrote about life; life in all its aspects fascinated them. There was nothing they considered too low or shocking to be recorded in their poetry. A hero may say, '*At the snap of my fingers, I can get any woman I want. Why are you making a fuss?*' And a heroine might say, '*I let him come once to my bedroom, now see how he's bragging. He winks at me on the road in front of everyone!*' Or '*I can't expect one pierced cowrie in return from him, show him out!*'[8]

In the milieu of the courtesan, where the men came to be entertained in such a manner, songs even more risque, gross, bawdy or erotic than these were presented. All of them fell under the category of *shringara*.

Written by men – interestingly many of the *javalis* were composed by Brahmins – these were all part of the treasured repertoire of the devadasi.

Here lay the crux of the problem that Rukmini Devi faced in the thirties. Having learnt the fundamentals of the dance, she needed the right vehicle of lyrics to carry forth her *abhinaya* and *bhava*, conveying emotions that were her inner truth as well. While there were *varnams* that she could dance to, conveying as they did erotic love or *shringara* addressed to the presiding deity of a particular temple, the *padams* and *javalis* posed a problem.[9] And, as we shall see ahead, these continue to pose a problem to male dancers of Bharata Natyam.

Crude sentiments displayed in some of the *padams* and *javalis* were not to Rukmini Devi's taste. The situations described in others appealed to baser instincts. Some were downright vulgar. Others, such as '*Just ask her how she built this three storey house and got all that jewellery? The fellow who screwed all of those women and gave them riches is in my bedroom now*',[10] were blatantly commercial.

Given the artistic licence to explore raw sensuality and eroticism, the less artistically sophisticated devadasi used explicit, sometimes gross gestures, in some of the songs performed by her. It was her own guru who told Rukmini Devi that certain gestures were not for her: 'My guru Meenakshisundaram Pillai used to make me eliminate the lewd element saying: This is not for you. You should not do it. Here was a *nattuvanar* censoring parts of the songs as unsuitable and these were things he was accustomed to all his life!'[11]

Not a courtesan; dancing away from the context of the temple and the court; charged with the mission of altering public opinion towards the art; she exercised her freedom as an artiste to choose the kind of items she would present. Given the context in which she was trying to effect social change, Rukmini Devi had to be very careful about her choice of lyrics, gestures performed and repertoire. 'I have selected carefully because sometimes people have chosen songs that are rather coarse in words and not suitable for interpretation in the human body...If Bharata Natyam is supposed to stimulate the lower feelings in the audience, then better not to do Bharata Natyam at all.'[12]

It led to the ridiculous misunderstanding and falsehood that she was against *shringara*, the erotic dimension that permeates all human life.

Her own view was, 'It is wrong to say we shouldn't have *shringara*. *Shringara* is love, and beauty. Without which there would be hardly any dance at all. *Bhakti* and *Shringara* must be *one*. You cannot separate the two.'[13]

In emphasizing the spiritual element in the dance, in avoiding those with crude or vulgar lyrics, Rukmini Devi was able both to go beyond the attitude prevalent toward *sadir* then and to find her own personal artistic fulfilment. It was also intimately linked to her understanding of Bharata Natyam as giving visual shape to devotion expressed through music. This choice of the kind of songs that would be presented in a performance defined the Kalakshetra style.

The greatest of Carnatic music *vidwans, nattuvanars* and Kathakali gurus came to Kalakshetra, lived there and helped Rukmini Devi in her work. Tiger Varadachari, Mysore Vasudevachar, Karaikudi Sambasiva Iyer, Budalur Krishnamurthi Shastrigal, Papanasam Sivan, M.D. Ramanathan, Meenakshisundaram Pillai, Chockalingam Pillai, Mylapore Gauri Ammal, Asan Ambu Panikker, Asan Chandu Panikker are just a few names in a long list of renowned artistes who taught there and contributed to her dance dramas. It was a golden period at Kala Kshetra – a sacred place that nurtures the arts – when they reinforced the traditional Indian method of teaching from guru to sishya.

And it was to this Kalakshetra on the banks of the river Adyar in Madras and to this great visionary and aesthete Rukmini Devi that the fortunes of a little boy in Kerala were tied.

1

When fourteen-year-old Dhananjayan, penniless and unproven, boarded a train at Payyanur for Madras in 1953 he did not know that he was embarking on an epic journey. His schoolteacher father, Rama Poduval, relieved at having one less mouth to feed, had borrowed money for a 'half-ticket' to send his son to Kalakshetra.

Dhananjayan was the third of eight children. His father, a schoolteacher and amateur theatre personality was generous to a fault, relinquishing his rights in his own tharavad, his ancestral home, and its verdant paddy fields to his sister and nephews. At times, there was nothing to eat but tapioca and sweet potatoes, which grew freely around the house built of thick mud walls and a grass roof. His father could not save any money; he would either spend it or give it away. On payday, he might return home without his salary, having distributed it to others more in need. He would make ayurvedic medicine to sell, but forget to collect the payment, and so would lose his investment as well.

Rama Poduval would walk to the school where he taught, which was in another town, Trikkaripur. When his mother-in-law Kodi Amma threw him out of her home because he had invited dalits home, he moved with his family to Trikkaripur, famous for the Chakrapani temple. Fortunately, the good that Rama Poduval had done to others came back to him in the form of opportunity.

Among the countless people to whom he had given money, he had once helped T.K.V. Chandu Panikker of Trikkaripur, to set up a tea-stall at a time when the Kathakali maestro was in financial trouble. They met after a long time when they found themselves on the same train. Asan Chandu Panikker, majestic in appearance, renowned for his portrayal of Bheema, Hanuman and Durvasa, to name a few, was approaching eighty by then. Over the course of his long life, he had won many awards, trained many illustrious students including Kalamandalam Krishnan Nair and was now the head of the Kathakali department at Kalakshetra.

As the train rattled from Kannur to Payyanur, Chandu Panikker told Rama Poduval that Rukmini Devi had asked him to look for a suitable boy who would be his apprentice. He had already found such a boy, Balagopal.

By now life's struggles had worn out Rama Poduval. He was beset with troubles. There was the constant pressure of feeding eight children and tiny grandchildren. His mother-in-law had opted to give up her share in her tharavad in lieu of money. So he and his family had been uprooted and worse, her relatives had almost burnt his eldest son alive in a fire and filed a false petition. They were trying to get Rama Poduval arrested.

In the midst of all this domestic turmoil, Rama Poduval grasped at a straw. 'Will you also take one of my sons to her?' he asked.

Chandu Panikker could not refuse. 'Alright, I'll come meet your sons and choose the right boy.'

The four boys were lined up. They were very quiet, unsure and frightened. He asked them a few questions…'What is your name? Do you want to go to Madras?'

The oldest boy was too old, the others too young; Chandu Panikker thought fourteen-year-old Dhananjayan was the right age. He offered to take him then warned, 'But if Rukmini Devi does not take him, I'll have to send him back.'

Rama Poduval did not know how he was going to get the money for the ticket to send his son to Madras, leave alone the return, but he nodded.

After Panikker left, Kodi Amma pored over Dhananjayan's horoscope. When he was born, on April 17, 1939, it had been predicted that he would leave home after the age of twelve; that he would roam around like a nomad and marry four times. Since his nakshatra was Uttrattadi, the same as that of Adi Shankaracharya, Dhananjayan's grandmother had always secretly hoped that he would renounce the world and take *sannyasa*. Therefore, she had insisted on his being taught Sanskrit. Her grandson wrote poetry in Malayalam, he had learnt Kolkali and could sing...his stars were good. 'This is his fate,' pronounced Kodi Amma, 'he *must* go.'

In those days, going to Madras was an event. All of Dhananjayan's friends were excited for him; no one from their village had ever been to Madras before. If strangers ever visited from Madras the villagers used to flock to stare at them out of curiosity. Years later, when Dhananjayan came back from Madras, people from the village came to gawk at him.

Dhananjayan met Balagopal on the train and they instantly became friends.

On reaching Madras, the teenagers jumped excitedly off the train, wondering what the big city would be like. The jutka took them straight down the Marina, and Dhananjayan saw the blue sea for the first time even though Payyanur was on the coast. And so, down the long stretch of road along the sandy beach, with low buildings on the other side, they grew increasingly bewildered, for they had imagined something grander. Their bewilderment turned almost to dismay when they reached Kalakshetra. Why, it was just like their village, with lots of trees, no impressively tall buildings but many thatched cottages.

The lads followed Asan Chandu Panikker through the gates of Kalakshetra, then situated in the wooded grounds of the Theosophical Society, Adyar. It was early in the morning, the 5th of October, 1953, and they were glad to notice other children there, playing. Asan called out to a little girl, the only Malayali girl enrolled in Kalakshetra at that time, with a prophetic request, 'These boys do not know the language spoken here so you take care of them.'

For sixty years now, Shanta, as Dhananjayan's wife, has done just that.

The crucial meeting was yet to take place. Past sturdy tamarind, coconut and mango trees, Asan led them towards Rukmini Devi's house. As they approached, they heard her exclaim loudly to Shankara Menon, her close associate committed to the ideals of Kalakshetra, 'Appuni look here, see who is coming...Rama, Lakshmana and Vishwamitra!' (This prophetic remark was to be echoed later in the evening by the great composer Mysore Vasudevachar as well.)

Asan was apprehensive.

Rukmini Devi said, 'I asked you to bring one boy, you have brought two...send one away!'

Dhananjayan's heart fell but it was Balagopal, short and with a slight squint, whom she wanted to dispatch back to Kerala.

In the morning, though, there was good news. Shankara Menon had persuaded her to keep both boys. Asan had guaranteed that he would correct the squint with special exercises for the eye. And that very minute they began the exercises. They were soon to learn that with Asan night or morning had no meaning when it came to practise. In time, Balagopal's squint vanished.

Two days later it was Vijayadashami and Rukmini Devi conducted the vidyarambham puja, initiating their life in dance. The boys met the staff of Kalakshetra – Jayalakshmi Teacher, who teased them affectionately, Periya Sarada the scholar, and Chinna Sarada (Hoffman) Teacher who was a bit aloof and strict. Kunhiraman – who had been there from 1944 with his father Kathakali Guru Ambu Panikker – took care of them, apart from teaching them Kathakali. As the one who played Shiva to Rukmini Devi's Parvati with aplomb, they looked up to him. Senior C.V. Chandrasekhar was in the hostel with them for a brief while before he left for college. But the girl who had caught Dhananjayan's eye, Shanta, was only a part-time student as she attended school as well – which she hated.

Dhananjayan did not feel homesick. Instead he felt as if he had known all these people from before; as if they were his other family.

Here, over the next sixteen years, as he pushed himself to perfection, Dhananjayan was to discover in himself a masculine but sensitive dancer as he played the hero Rama in the famous Ramayana series, fall madly in love with Shanta, taste success, and also notoriety when he quit Kalakshetra.

2

I clearly remember walking with my mother down the long road that connected my home to that of my future gurus, Shanta and Dhananjayan. My mother bore a tray laden with fruits and flowers, covered with a bright red napkin. I was eight years old, easily embarrassed by my parents who seemed to do things others did not. Why were we carrying fruits in such a conspicuous manner when no one else on the road was?

Traditionally in the South, instruction in the arts begins on the auspicious day of Vijayadashami, when fruits and flowers, among other things, are offered to the goddess Saraswati. In 1975, I did not begin on this particular day, but my mother's friend, Veena Singh, her advisor on the matters related to 'dance class', had told her to take fruits and flowers nonetheless, for this first meeting of teacher and pupil.

Veena and Mohinder Singh were our neighbours, and their daughter Anjali had been a student of the Dhananjayans for a while now. My father Chaturvedi Badrinath and Mohinder Singh were in the IAS, and we were neighbours by virtue of having bought government-allotted plots on the same street in Shastri Nagar, Adyar. When my mother asked me if I would like to learn dance, following Anjali's example, and I nodded enthusiastically, it resulted in our evening parade past the neighbourhood when I wanted to turn invisible.

Soon we were in a large, cool thatch-roofed hall with brick walls, interrupting a class in session. The students, close to my age, stared as we entered with the tray that had ballooned to mythic proportions in my head. I remember being conscious of their impassive scrutiny as Dhananjayan, 'Sir', clad in a veshti and kurta taught me the first steps of a dancer – obeisance to Earth, begging forgiveness for stamping on her. Shanta, 'Akka', arranged for measurements to be taken for the practice costume, a plain cotton kurta and pyjama in the contrasting colours of flag-orange and patriotic green. The fees the first month were twenty rupees and thirty thereafter.

My gurus had impeccable lineage in their training, having studied at the famous Kalakshetra, but a fog of conjecture surrounded them for they had crossed swords with their legendary guru Rukmini Devi, left Kalakshetra, and set up their own institution, Bharata Kalanjali. This daring break with Kalakshetra was seen as an act of rash courage by some, as treachery by others, but it was only many years into the future that I, as an adult, could ask them about the circumstances that led to it.

I soon learnt the names of my classmates and the lone boy in the class, tall Krishna. Thrice a week, dressed in two-tones – red and yellow, pink and purple, blue and mustard – we would climb the branches of the cherry tree in the compound, waiting for class to begin. A sentry perched on the furthest branch would warn us if it was Sir who emerged from his home adjacent to the cottage. It meant he was going to teach us, and then we were in for it. If it was Akka, we heaved a collective sigh of relief, for she had the patience of a saint.

So, thrice each week, after school, we assembled at BK, as Bharata Kalanjali was fondly referred to by us, in the cool interior of the cottage. Shaped like an L, the shorter limb was partitioned from the central hall, creating a smaller chamber where another class could be held simultaneously.

We liked dancing in the dark main hall; in the smaller room our backs were to the door and our impish eyes found no distraction. Here, the exposed brick walls were low, and bamboo window frames between the wall and the thatch let the sea breeze in.

Waiting for class to start, we giggled and chattered only to fall sharply into a V the minute Sir was sighted at the entrance, framed by the oblong light outdoors. Pin-drop silence. Arms akimbo, hands bent backwards at the wrist and placed at the waist. Legs together, feet pointing ahead. The strain of keeping restless skitterish limbs motionless.

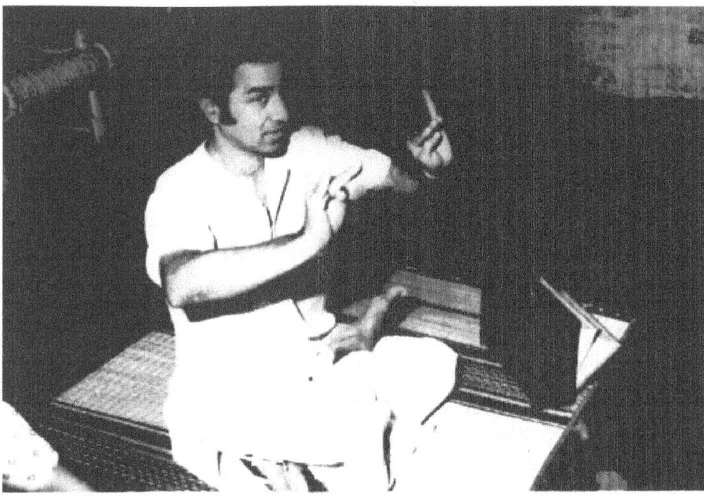

Dhananjayan teaching

Sir, in a white cotton kurta, off-white dhoti, his face set in lines of sternness, would run a stern eye over us as he settled crosslegged on the mat. A rudimentary rectangular block of wood placed in front of him, he grasped a tapering cylindrical stick, *thattu kazhi*, and gave us the basic count. Wood hitting wood, the sound was a military command.

Before actually beginning to practise or learn, the *namaskaram* is a must. In time to come, I could appreciate just how necessary this invocation to Mother Earth was, as some of us stamped anyhow, off beat, hard, and I would imagine Her wincing as the dissonant blows fell on her surface.

Then we'd cluster eagerly around our guru, touching the block of wood, revering it for its guidance, and in a quick, notional swipe, Sir's feet. Seated as he was, legs tucked under him, his feet were out of sight.

Back at our spots, our feet were splayed sideways, knees turned well back and the torso lowered until the knees were bent neatly at a sharp angle. The basic posture, the gauge of style and accomplishment, the *araimandi*.

The first month, I wobbled this way and that, pushing my bottom out for balance, or cheating by not sinking low enough. But the gimlet eye did not miss anything. Muttering, 'No matter how many times I tell you…' he would suddenly stand up and stride over. His disembodied voice snapped from somewhere behind me, 'Sit! And do not get up until I say so!' I could not see him, but I felt the tip of his fingers pressing my shoulders, pushing me down down, down into the hell of a beautiful *araimandi*, holding me there in the burning fire of loaded muscles, until he was satisfied.

Controlling the wobble and the burn, the very first beat. Striking the right foot, *teyya*, then the left foot, *teyyi*. All the while, deep *araimandi*, arms tucked in at the waist, no wobble, spine aligned and head and shoulders straight. Right, left, right, left, finish the count of eight keep going, do not stop or he may make you do another thirty-two, first speed, second speed, third, burning, burning, burning at the back of the thigh, but through it all a strange exhilaration. *Teyya teyyi, taiya teyyi, teyya teyyi….* Over and over, before he was satisfied enough to move to two strikes of each foot.

All the way upto eight.

The spare staccato sound of the *thattu kazhi* has the power still, thirty-seven years later, to make my limbs move involuntarily, racing through grooves that have been laid by practice and repetition, over and over again. It is the one potent sound, I imagine, that has the power to bring me back from the dead.

But at the time, in my eight-year-old world, the sound held joy and menace, reassurance and terror, just as the stick itself became a weapon in his hands, pushing us to perfection by the command: 'Again! Repeat it ten times without a break!' No matter how hard we tried, pulling knees back, sinking low, trying very hard not to stop too early, nothing could change his frown of thwarted expectation into a smile.

Yet, he was gentle while teaching. When he taught something new, the pure intention of transmitting knowledge radiated from him. When he demonstrated how to sit in the *araimandi*, lifting his dhoti out of the way so we could see the impossibly straight line made by his feet, we adored him and were scared of him in equal measure. His feet have high arches, and they rose like the curved spans of a bridge, off the black gleaming floor.

Within weeks, having learnt how to balance while lifting either foot off the ground in basic *araimandi*, it was time to make it more complex by adding the movement of arms.

And now we learnt the other posture that would instantly reveal lineage and calibre, the *natya-arambam* position.

Sir showed us how he wanted it done. Arms spread out at the shoulders, taut, like the wings of a giant bird in flight to paraphrase Nala Najan the American dancer, elbows lifted and hands level with the wrist.

We lifted up our arms anyhow, the way a toddler imitates flying like an aeroplane.

'Hold arms in *natyarambam* and do not drop it till I say so!'

No less torture than the *araimandi*. A new burning now, in the upper arm, where it extended from the shoulder.

Sir walked around the class, adjusting tender limbs, nudging a drooping elbow up with the *thattu kazhi*, or pushing a stiff arm into the contours required. It would be just my luck that he began with the other line of students, so by the time he worked his way up to me, an unseen force had suctioned my arms down to my waist.

Sweat broke out across my forehead.

'*Umm*!' – this sound recurred in my nightmares – it conveyed disapproval and irritation and impatience all at once. I responded to it like a petrified rabbit, freezing, making things worse for myself. 'Where did I ask you to hold it and *where* is it?'

My arms were pushed higher, braced by the *thattu kazhi* under one elbow, so I could not drop them so long as he stood there. But, even though it felt that my arms would fall off, I both shrank from and was thrilled by his attention, and the correct way to hold the position seared itself into my brain. The next time in class, my arms were that much more extended, my elbows held just a tad higher.

In time, this would literally become child's play.

In every class, the focus of attention was on the demanding figure seated on the floor ahead of us. At times he would spring up to demonstrate the movement, cool in a plain cotton kurta, only to return to providing the beat on the block of wood on the floor.

We mirrored what he taught us, the best we could. It was by way of verbal correction and, when that failed, by rearranging our limbs, never touching us with his palm but only the tips of his fingers, that he made us recognize what a position *felt* like. So while we saw him demonstrate and outline what was required, and while we saw what our classmates were doing, we never *saw* our own selves in dance.

There were no mirrors.

Dancing from inside, blind to how it appeared to the onlooker, I only knew the rightness of a position from the way my muscles settled into it. I learnt to read the braille of my guru's expressions, relying on Sir's face as it registered faint approval or disapproval, or frowned angrily, to realign myself in the flight of dance. 'Next! *Tat teyy taa haa, Dhi teyy taa haa...*'

Eight slow attenuated repetitions. Sixteen in the second speed, and what by now felt like two thousand in the third.

Classes lasted an hour, or more if our limbs did not deliver what Sir wanted. At all times, no matter how tired we felt, or if some part of the body ached, while dancing we were to adopt a pleasant expression. While a fixed smile would not do, a genuine smile of pleasure helped.

Drinking water, even in the hottest months, was forbidden. If we felt very thirsty, we could ask permission to drink water. Most times this was an excuse for a break. But it could backfire, and he might say, '*No!* And do not ask until the end of the class!'

Relishing the momentary escape, I would walk very slowly, leaving the dance floor to reach the earthen pot placed near the entrance. Pouring water into my mouth from the stainless steel tumbler held high in the air was a novelty, used as I was to placing my lips on transparent glasses at home.

Two tepid gulps later, it was already time to scurry back to the next *adavu* being practised. *Teyyum tatha, teyyum taa, teyyum tatha, teyyum taa.*

The only other excuse we had, was that of tying and retying our pyjamas. Never mind that the *nada* was tight and it was highly unlikely that our pyjamas would fall. It was a bonafide excuse.

'Sir, pyjama loose-u Sir' – and suppressed giggles all around.

'Okay, go,' and a disdainful pointing of his chin.

At various points in that long, muscle-testing character-building hour, Anita or her sister Sunita, or Sangeeta or Tulsi or Uma or her sister Charu, or Aparna would stand in relief from *araimandi* and head to the little dressing room screened off from the main hall to feverishly undo and retie her pyjamas. We giggled when anyone used the *nada* excuse, because they had squandered the only leeway permissible. Some were brazen – the darn, slippery *nada* just refused to knot tightly – and they just might get away with stopping twice or thrice.

Poor Krishna, barechested, wearing a dhoti drawn between his legs and tucked in at the waist, and a long piece of cloth tied like a cummerbund over that, did not have the *nada* excuse.

For more than two years, we only learnt the basic units of movements, *adavus*. In the language of Bharata Natyam, there are two alphabets. The alphabet of movements-in-rhythm, *nritta* and the alphabet of facial expression or *abhinaya*, aided by *mudras*, specific hand-gestures that convey meaning. When *adavus* are combined, in the same way that alphabets make words, they result in complex variations of *nritta*.

As to *abhinaya*: oh, that stage would take another two years to reach!

3

At the hostel in Kalakshetra, Dhananjayan's day began at 4.30 a.m. While he had to meet the strict schedules of both the hostel and Kalakshetra, Balagopal and he escaped the mandatory PE session, by heading to the 'mirror' cottage. Inside, there was a big mirror along one wall, used by Rukmini Devi, though later she discouraged them from looking at themselves while they danced. Here, the boys practised the movements they had learnt the previous day, in three speeds. If they went off beat, they would soon hear the great veena maestro Karaikudi Sambasiva Iyer tap out the corrections from his cottage next door.

Then they had to walk a long distance to their irascible Asan's quarters to serve him coffee, brought from the hostel kitchen, and ready his bath with hot water. The aroma of filter coffee tempted them daily, forbidden as it was to them. Walking back to the hostel, there was just enough time to bathe and be ready for group prayers.

Prayers over, the boys would rush to the kitchen to fetch Asan's breakfast and then run back to his room with it. Chandu Panikker was temperamental and there was no knowing what mood he would be in. As much as the boys held him in the highest regard, they were terrified of him. If they were the slightest bit late he would scold, or shout, or beat them. 'Even a glance from him was enough to make me feel like wetting my pants,' avers Dhananjayan. 'But the strange thing was that he was severe only with us boys and very gentle and affectionate towards the girls.'

Balagopal (l) and Dhananjayan (r) with Asan Chandu Panikker

At every mealtime, Dhananjayan and Balagopal were in a state of torturous anticipation: would their Asan eat or not? Somedays he would not touch the food they had brought him. If he did not eat, neither could they. If he took his time eating, they would miss their own spartan breakfast of two idlis, or one little dosa or two slices of bread and milk. Escorting him to the class, they then would have to dance on an empty stomach, drained to the point of fainting.

What made matters difficult was that Asan expected both boys to be in joint attendance on him at all times. If one did not come, the other got it in double measure. If they took turns so as to even out the punishment, he took it out on them in class, hitting them,[14] or worse, cursing.

'Asan used to abuse us with very bad words, in class, in front of everyone. Normally I kept quiet whatever Asan did. But if he swore, then

I would burst out saying, "Don't use that word, beat me, do anything, but don't say that." And that would make him even more angry!'

Burning energy, sweating in the heat of Madras, the boys were as thin as reeds. Once Congress leader K. Kamaraj, who happened to be observing the class in progress, remonstrated with Chandu Panikker, 'Are you feeding these boys properly? Why, I can count their ribs!'

At night in the hostel, Dhananjayan's mind would travel back to home. He remembered wistfully how, at the beginning of every solar month, sankranti, there was the great excitement of going to the temple-fair. Everyone loved going to this outdoor marketplace – to buy clothes, or kumkum, or a hairclip – but it was the children who loved it the most. Sometimes his father would actually hand them a few coins, to their delight. It was so enjoyable, so rare! They bought ice fruit, coloured ice shavings, or little books called *Niti saaram* that cost 2 paise and were filled with parables and verses.

In the cold season, there used to be another thrill. His brothers and he would get up early to pluck cashew-nuts, an adventure akin to stealing mangoes. If they went early enough, they gathered the cashews easily, as foxes would have chewed the fruit and left the nut. They sold some of them to bring money home to give to Father.

Naughty and bold for his age, Dhananjayan was frequently punished by being tied to a tree, or by having pepper mixed with mother's milk dropped in his eyes. Climbing trees or making bows, he and his friend, a girl his age named Imbichi, had been free to play anywhere, except near the burial grounds, the railway tracks or the serpent coves, *naga kaavu*, that Kerala is full of. Even so, one day, he had fallen unconscious near one of the serpent abodes after a swim in the lotus-filled temple tank. The family believed a *pisacha*, or angry spirit had attacked him, since it had taken him six months to recover.

That was the first of the three times he escaped death. The second time had been when his brother, Venugopal, pushed him accidentally into an uncovered well. Luckily he fell straight into the waters, not hitting the sides. The water level was low so he stood on tiptoe with his nose above water and instead of crying, had reprimanded his brother! His brother had called out to some villagers who rescued him. They were all amazed that he survived with just a small bruise on his chest.

The Poduval community were skilled in Kalaripayattu, and combined martial art with peripheral activities in the temples. Known as *ambalavasis*, they had a hereditary link with temples, especially the Subrahmanya Temple, where the eldest of the clan was accorded special privileges.

Dhananjayan's uncle, his father's brother, had a wealthy wife, and lived in a two storey house. At his invitation, the family had moved to Annur. Here, Dhananjayan had his third brush with death when he got severe typhoid. He lost a year at school but worse he had to learn to walk all over again. Another classmate also got typhoid and his father took care of that boy as well, without taking any money for his medicines.

'One day, Father set off to school and passed a dead body in the lane. In Kerala it is a lucky omen to see a corpse in the morning. We were scared, I most of all, to look at it, but my father continued on his way, passing through a wooded area, where he saw a bundle of 1000 rupees lying on the ground. There was no way of finding out whose it was. In the evening when he came home, we celebrated as though he had a lakh of rupees in hand! For us, superstition worked…it had come true!'

A few years later when, in a fit of anger, his aunt asked them to leave, his father had to build a shack overnight for his large family on a little bit of land he owned. Though he later tried to strengthen it with tiles, for a long while the family suffered when it rained, all huddled in one room under the dripping thatch.

Hearing of the penurious condition in which they lived, Dhananjayan's maternal grandmother was moved enough to invite her estranged son-in-law and his brood back to Payyanur. They were to stay in her portion of her family's tharavad. It was a share that she fought in court to obtain, arguing the case herself though illiterate.

Dhananjayan was singled out to live away from his siblings, in her home, and she was to have a lasting influence on him.

His grandmother, Kodi Amma was a strong woman, of a very independent nature. When she lost her husband, she did not marry again. Spurning her brothers and sisters, she had earned money from her paddy field and brought up her children.

Boys were not expected to help in the house, but Kodi Amma was a woman ahead of her times. Dhananjayan had to sweep the house every day, tend to the cows and work in the field she owned. The young boy did not protest, he liked climbing coconut trees to pluck the fruit, and making thatch from the leaves. He learnt a lot from her. In summer they planted cucumbers and brinjals. After the harvest, the soil was tilled and vegetables planted.

Kodi Amma was also very strict. She would make her grandson recite shlokas from the Gita every evening. 'Dinner was simple, kanji, rice gruel. I didn't understand the Gita but I had to read a few pages if I wanted dinner! Loudly, so that wherever she was working she could hear it. If I made a mistake, she would reprimand me.'

Early in the morning, Dhananjayan would join his siblings and friends to walk to school, about a kilometre away. He had no slippers, and used to run because of the burning sand. When the bell rang for lunch break, all of them would run home, eat and run back, barefoot, four times a day.

'I was an average student, bad at spelling…to this day I am bad at spelling. I started learning English only in the 6th standard. I was very weak in mathematics. When I reached ESLC, Nambisan, our ex-military headmaster pushed me to improve. He was very strict but affectionate too. The first quarterly exam, I got 10 marks. Next exam I got 40, by the time I cleared the main ELSC exam, which was a big hurdle, I got 90 thanks to him. Few people passed and I was one of them, with a high second class, a hero! Joining government school was very prestigious in those days, and I got admitted to the only one in the province.

His own father, a teacher, had no time to teach him, so involved was he with his own students. If a boy did not come to school, Rama Poduval would walk all the way to his house to enquire about him. At such times he would return late at night and Dhananjayan's mother would not eat waiting for him.

Payyanur was a politically active place, a Congress bastion where the salt satyagraha in Kerala took place in 1930. After independence, Dhananjayan and the other children in the village would sometimes walk around the village waving the national flag, shouting *Mahatma Gandhi ki jai, Bharat Mata ki jai.* At the office of the Congress party, they were served lime juice and biscuits, an incentive strong enough to make them shout louder!

In the month of Vrishchika, the temple festival was held over sixteen days. Relatives and friends from far away would converge on Payyanur, prepared to share whatever hospitality their host could offer. Equally, a guest was never turned away. Dhananjayan would remember the fun they had watching the processions, where the accompanying musicians played the *chenda* and *maddalam.* They were kept busy listening to discourses and trying to catch a glimpse of the Chakkyar koothu that took place inside the temple. They also got to see Kathakali and Ottanthullal in their natural setting

One night, hearing the *chenda*, the speaking drums of Kathakali, Dhananjayan had walked towards the source of the dramatic sounds – a performance by the legendary Chandu Panikker in the heated light of flares. Entranced by the vision of this fantastic creature with reddened eyes, green godly face, high towering crown, silver talons elongating the tips of one hand, and bustling skirts that hid the human figure but not the feet, he was sucked into the story of Balabhadra and Krishna as it spun out over the cool hours of the night. He returned home at dawn, oblivious to the fact that the family had been worrying about his whereabouts. Dhananjayan did not know that his future had already ripened at this point, for Chandu Panikker was to be his Asan, his guru, in Kalakshetra.

*

Back in Kalakshetra, the length of Asan's class varied. If he was in the mood to teach, time fell away. The others' classes would end in time for lunch but the Kathakali classes continued. He pushed his students to the limit and believed in maintaining the integrity of the Kathakali tradition as he had received it.

After three hours of gruelling training, on days when Asan was pleased with the world, they got to serve him his lunch and eat their own. The cooks had learnt to set some food aside for the boys if their Asan delayed them. The famished boys ate, unmindful that the rice was cold, and then ran to their language classes at 1.30 p.m..

After a break for tea at 4 p.m., they attended classes in Bharata Natyam. Usually Jayalakshmi or Chinna Sarada took these classes. Here too, Asan's shadow loomed over them; he was not too happy that they were learning Bharata Natyam and would taunt them the next day in class: 'Oh, this is not Kathakali you are doing, it is Bharata Natyam.' In the evening, they had to rehearse whatever role they were playing in Rukmini Devi's productions. By now, 1954, she was choreographing *Sita Swayamvaram*, the first in what was to be famously known as the Ramayana series.

The boys were conflicted, caught between two giants of equally strong will. Asan wanted them around him and begrudged them the time they spent with Rukmini Devi. There was no question of missing rehearsal with her because these two scholarship holders were there due to her largesse. Rukmini Devi was affectionately referred to as 'Athai' or aunt, since that was how her own niece Radha addressed her. 'We would get Athai's permission to leave, and alternately one of us would serve Asan and come back, even though both of us had to be in the same scene.'

On some blessed days, Asan had to be present to help with the choreography, as Rukmini Devi used Kathakali in her dance-dramas for certain male characters, to enhance the dramatic quotient, and the boys were spared.

4

It is a deep rooted memory in which one terrible part is suppressed – my first performance on stage, at the Music Academy, no less. I remember a white organdie costume with innumerable gold-edged pleats, a long interminable wait backstage before we actually danced, a drumstick tree framed in the oblong of light that was the entrance to our class, and an irate Sir towering over me.

One day, Sir told us that we had to learn something new, different. It was called *pandattam*, or playing with an imaginary ball. Krishna, Anita and Sunita's brother, had stopped coming, so it was just us girls in class. Variously eight or nine or ten years old, we were very excited.

Then began movements unlike any other we had learnt so far. We moved in a position similar to *araimandi*, but all of a sudden our gurus weren't insisting on the knees being pulled back. Elbows fell, arms were lowered; a relief from the rigour we were accustomed to. However, there was an added swaying motion of the torso, circular movements that were entirely unfamiliar.

I struggled with these strange flourishes. Only later did I realize the reason. This little item we were learning was in another style – the sinuous Mohiniattam, not our linear Bharata Natyam at all. I struggled, managing somehow to keep up with the rest of the group.

Sir taught it to us in little digestible bits. Then came the day I could not repeat what he taught. It involved moving towards the right but bending left; when the torso swayed to the right, it was time to move left. Difficult enough; but then there was an incomprehensible tricky bit involving the fists. One fist faced upwards, the other downwards, held off-centre to the left of the chest. As the torso swung right, the fists opened, made a little semi-circle at the chest and reversed positions. I just could not get it. No matter how many times he taught me, his temper rising, no matter how many times I did it, it was all hopelessly clumsy and wrong.

The others had stopped dancing. The focus was on me.

'*Umm*! Do it again!'

My fists were opening and turning anyhow, the body naturally aiming for symmetry so I ended up with both facing in the same direction.

'*Again!*' He was very angry, irritated perhaps that his teaching had not carried through into a visible result. No, it was a mess! The more upset he got, the more nervous I.

'You are not leaving until you get it right! *Again!*' his angry shout echoed off the bamboo rafters, turned me into ice. He stood in front of me, hands on his hips. '*Start.*' He clapped the beat loudly on his palm.

I was trying with all my heart. The sole aim of any session was to please him by responding, in the hope of a smile or the quiet of satisfaction. But today was not my day, my brain and hands had let me down.

This time I must have done something sillier because he suddenly turned on his heel and strode out of the class. Before we could move or react, he was back with a switch, a slim flexible branch broken off the drumstick tree outside.

Thwack!

No man had ever hit me.

I did not know this was possible.

An only child, my father's darling, I had only ever received hugs and kisses from him. My mother hit me, occasionally; a smack across the face.

I did not cry, I did not squeal in pain, or say anything. But when I reached home, my mother only had to look at my face to ask, 'What happened?' And then, gathered in her arms, the shock flowed outward in sobs and tears. And a red weal appeared on my left leg.

My parents discussed the incident in grave tones at dinner. The next day, my mother accompanied me to class and had a little talk with my flustered guru, letting him know that what he had done was unacceptable. She left and I had to face him alone.

Seated on the verandah outside his home, he swept me onto his knee. Sulking, I kept my head lowered.

'I hit you and you complained about me?' His tone was affectionate and teasing. 'You are like my own child, just like Sanjay, you and he are almost the same age. Ten years old. I did what any parent might. Now run along to class and concentrate.'

In the years to come, Sir and Akka would refer to this incident with some amusement. I was the only student he had ever hit and, if only in this regard, it made me special.

I remained uneasy in his presence for decades after the stick lashed my leg. It is only now – he in his mellow seventies and I, in my forties – that I can talk to him without quaking inside.

The rehearsals continued. Miraculously, my hands and feet co-operated during the tricky bit. We were measured for the costumes, our parents contributing fifty rupees each, and soon we had gold-covered bangles and *jimikki*-earrings and a necklace to match!

On the day, Sir and Akka did our makeup, assembly-line. After Akka had swept my hair to the side in a bun over my ear, and encircled it with jasmines, I had to sit on a mat facing Sir.

He held my quivering chin, to steady my face. 'Look up and don't move.'

I tried not to squirm as he moved closer, drawing a kohl-pencil under my eyes with motherly care. He then applied a yellow dash of sandal over a big red bindi on my forehead and frowningly appraising his handiwork called out, 'Next!'

When we clustered around the mirror in the green room, we saw six exotic Malayali girls who seemed to resemble us.

After a long, interminable delay and infinite good behaviour on our part, we were finally on stage. I still remember what it felt like. There was no fear, because we did not know that there was anything to be scared about. Used to dancing without water, we did not feel thirsty. The dancing-space and wooden floor were different from what we were used to. I danced under the lights, looking out at a great darkness.

We acquitted ourselves well. But, in a photograph taken on that day I see that while everyone is leaning at a particular angle, I am the only one leaning more acutely to the right!

My mother still has that costume wrapped up in mothballs. When I look at its dimensions, doll's clothes as it were, I realize how impossibly tiny we were.

5

Did Dhananjayan regret having had to leave home, at so young an age?

'I had no choice! *I have come here, I have to learn*, that was all I thought. But the minute I started learning it kindled everything in me that was dormant. I loved the poetry, the music, the descriptions of nature. And our progress was so quick! Within six months we were on stage.'

In the brief time he had been there, Dhananjayan had already acquired a reputation for being outspoken. It had its origins in a 'theory' class related to the *Abhinaya Darpanam*. The teacher began by saying, 'I am going to teach you *Abhinaya* Dh*arpanam*. Repeat after me.' The other students obeyed her, but not Dhananjayan.

'Why are you not repeating it?'

'I won't say it.'

'Why not?'

'It is not correct, it is wrong.'

Such cheek, a little chit of a boy, not even paying fees, barely a week old at Kalakshetra, speaking this way – the teacher, naturally, was upset and called scholar Periya Sarada to her aid. In Malayalam, Dhananjayan said to her, 'I will only say *d*arpanam.'

Sarada, a stickler for pronounciation, had to agree with him; it was the soft *da*, not the aspirated *dha*.

'I was very adamant, I don't know why I was like that, and I would talk back, so that was a problem.'

This perception – that he was bold, arrogant – was to come between him and Chinna Sarada when she taught him a puppet dance, rendered without facial expression. Reserved at times, he was a quick learner with tremendous, perhaps precocious, self-confidence. What otherwise would be pleasing to any teacher, an ability to grasp things quickly and re-present them well, was read by her as the arrogance of a big ego.

So on hearing that Dhananjayan had been cast as the young Rama, and Balagopal as Lakshmana in *Sita Swayamvaram*, she remarked tartly, 'Oh, the arrogant boy gets to play the hero.' They were going to perform with with their seniors, their teachers, and had to be brought up to that exacting standard. Who better than Chinna Sarada to drill them both in the basics and the advanced moves for the dance-drama?

Dhananjayan and Balagopal were set to a rigorous regimen. They were made to do rounds of the mirror cottage, an hour spent just on the bobbing walk – *kulukki nadai* – where each step is preceded with a deep bend and upward spring at the knee. It was an unforgettable lesson.

Next came *taa-teyy-teyy-ta* and *di-di-teyy*, where the arms came into synchronized play with the feet. Chinna Sarada was very strict, a perfectionist. She taught them how to retain precision of placement, even at high speeds and whittled their movements. Whatever Rukmini Devi had asked them to do the previous day, she would make them rehearse and perfect: posture, *mudra*, expression, everything had to be just so. Soon, though they were primarily Kathakali students, they were thorough with their Bharata Natyam *adavus*.

In the evening they had to be ready to dance for Rukmini Devi, retracing for her the scenes she had choreographed. They admired her, but were scared of her as well. Extremely punctual, she would arrive a few minutes before she was due. Everything was tidied and made ready for her; the edges of the mats aligned properly. Anyone who came dressed in sloppy costume, whether veshti or sari, would be publicly chastized; there was a way to speak, a way to stand, a way to conduct oneself, as a dancer. Nothing was casual in dance;

every movement had a beginning and a final position in space that it was heading towards, a definition. *Mudras* were to be held firmly, regardless of how involved one might be in one's *abhinaya*.

When she was composing her dance-dramas, Periya Sarada and Chinna Sarada were considered Rukmini Devi's right and left arms. When her creative energies were flowing, Rukmini Devi could get impatient if someone did not grasp something quickly or give her the desired result while trying out a movement. The dancers had to be alert. A mistake could result in their being replaced by someone less annoying and more responsible. Chinna Sarada would make tangible what Rukmini Devi conceived of in her flights of imagination.

Periya Sarada with her encyclopedic knowledge would offer possibilities suggested by the verses, 'We could also do it this way perhaps...' At times, Rukmini Devi was short with her, cutting her off mid-suggestion but Periya Sarada always responded with patience and good humour. Later, Rukmini Devi would often come around to the very version suggested by Periya Sarada.

For the boys, this was the focal point of the day. Dancing, as Rama and Lakshmana, under Rukmini Devi's direct supervision, thrilled them.

'Athai would fix or change certain things according to the dancer's personality. By then, the standard of the dance also improved because the students practised more. She could do more complicated and sophisticated movements, knowing we could perform it. When we were all together, we enjoyed how she conceived her ideas spontaneously and changed her choreography depending on the dancer in front of her. Sometimes, the very next day she would change something and the teachers, especially Chinna Sarada who had to drill us and make us ready for the next rehearsal, would get upset by this, as they had to undo everything!'

Dhananjayan recalls: 'Sometimes the teachers would make it more sterile than what she had visualized. Then Athai would come and watch up to the point she had composed and say, "Don't be so stiff!" Chinna Sarada Teacher wanted everything extra firm and proper but

Athai wanted it to be flexible. It was very beautiful the way Athai and Sarada Teacher worked together. We learnt from both, so we got a new dimension and had the freedom to evolve our own way of doing it.'

Dhananjayan and Balagopal owned the third scene in *Sita Swayamvaram*. They described the forest they passed through while accompanying Vishwamitra. The gigantic mountain ranges in the distance, timid deer making love, an angry elephant charging towards them…it gave the boys scope to develop their *abhinaya*. Kunhiraman portrayed the sage so well that he was called Vishwamitra afterwards. All three characters performed in the Kathakali style, and the scenes were visualized by Asan Chandu Panikker.

When Rukmini Devi wanted a particular Kathakali effect to be introduced into her dance-drama she would ask Chandu Panikker to demonstrate it and then decide whether to render it in Bharata Natyam or retain the original Kathakali *mudra*. The entry of Rama and Lakshmana, *patra pravesham*, was inspired by the *kalaashams* in Kathakali, only adapted to Bharata Natyam using *adavus* and *tala* patterns. The *thirashila*, or curtain, integral to Kathakali was a novel introduction to the dance-drama format.

'Asan's contribution to Rukmini Devi's dance dramas was tremendous. She utilized his talent to the maximum. Later on, certain characters came alive when done by Kunhiraman Sir…Dasharatha, Guha. I was always Rama, so I didn't have much scope, I had always to be *sattvika*, good,' laughed my guru in amusement.

Sita Swayamvaram premiered in 1955 and was a huge success. People came just to see Rama and Lakshmana in the third scene. On the first day, their *kulukki nadai* alone earned them spontaneous clapping from the audience. 'Balagopal had a talent for acting. Everything he did would impress the audience. Sometimes, it was not relevant or correct but people loved it. It was in his blood. He and I, we always improvized in this scene! There was no song, only verse and the *maddalam*-beat to accentuate our *abhinaya*. It was a big hit!' Dhananjayan smiled at the memory.

The hours the boys had spent in the mirror cottage bore fruit. It earned them the praise of E. Krishna Iyer who used to come and watch classes at Kalakshetra and talk to Chandu Panikker, despite knowing no Malayalam.

Eminent Tamil writer Kalki Krishnamurthy was greatly appreciative. 'Darlings Rama and Lakshmana, your *kulukki nadai* itself is enough to soothe our eyes,' he wrote in his *Kalki* magazine.

Even Rukmini Devi paid them a compliment, backhanded though it was, 'Oh, just because your picture came in the paper, do not let it go to your head.'

6

During the day I attended a convent school, happy in my blue scalloped pinafore worn over a starched white shirt, my long plaits secured with white ribbons. Through my school years I was watched over by Christ, from his crucifix placed high above the blackboard. I recited the Lord's Prayer with gusto at assembly, scrupulously maintained my Moral Science long notebook, and prayed feverishly in the chapel before every exam.

Studying in English, following a secular syllabus, there was much that was lost of Indian thought, literature, its world-views. Hindi, as the second language chosen, gave me some exposure to Kabir and snippets of contemporary poetry.

At home, we did not have television, even after Doordarshan started broadcasting in colour, and we rarely watched movies, books being my family's form of escapism. But in BK, there was a richly populated universe that revealed itself, parts at a time, in every class.

Speeding to BK after school, I inhabited a completely different vernacular at dusk – filled with clouds carrying messages of love, cupid's five-flower scented arrows and peacocks who lent Krishna their feathers. Various 'bee-loud glades' appeared and faded: Ashokavan where Sita was imprisoned, sylvan Vrindavan where Krishna and Radha dallied, or the many gardens where damsels pined for their lovers. Ganesha's tiny mouse, Vishnu's fiercely loyal Garuda, Devi's lion…they all dwelled here.

It was as though the cottage were an enchanted grove where the characters found in my cherished *Amar Chitra Kathas* came alive.

In Bharata Natyam, the ideas expressed in a particular 'item' ride on those contained in the verse or poem set to a raga. The text defines the areas the dancer will venture into. While one can expand upon an idea or use many metaphors to convey a basic idea, one cannot introduce ideas, situations or characters that are not supported by the song. Through *mudras* and facial expressions, the dancer makes visible the musicality of a poem, conveying emotions and meaning. All imagery was drawn from nature.

None of it was *visible*; it had to be imagined first and then projected.

The first item we learnt that had an element of *bhava* in it was the *shabdam, aayar sheriyar*. In narrating the mesmerizing effect of Krishna's flute on the *gopis*, the deer who heard it, we learnt basic descriptions. We had to conjure coral lips, curly locks, Krishna's radiant face, lotus eyes, pearl drops of sweat and playful *gopis*. Leaving behind layers of my everyday self – school life, home, parents, books, exams – I was rapt within the music, the words, this Krishna whom I hadn't seen but whose aplomb I had to adopt, lifting the mountain Govardhan as he had, with great ease.

As the ragas changed and musical variations spilled into the class, Sir became Krishna's little dancing self, briefly.

'Imagine his small hands and tiny fingers holding a *big* flute. How do you show small? See...'

And having seen and imagined, we could go on to essay our own version. Only, our flutes turned out to be bent, or short, or twisted. He sang that one line several times.

Trying to teach city girls pastoral tropes had its own share of frustrations for Sir. 'Carry the pot on your head, like this. Before you actually dip it into the river, you remove the debris on the surface. Thus...gently.' We would watch him – the way he reached the river, swished the water, and then dipped the imaginary pot sideways – with utter concentration. Far easier to admire him than to imitate what he had done! 'Now you can fill your pots.'

Six containers of various sizes and shapes crashed on the riverbank.

'I must see a deep shining river in front of each of you! I see a muddy *puddle*! Okay, now lift it up, onto your head. It's heavy, my dears. You have to make it look like there's a *lot* of water inside. You look like you're carrying paper pots.'

A good thirty minutes would vanish in getting the swaying voluptuous walk of a *gopi* carrying a pot of water right.

'Sangeeta! *Do!*'

Watching others get into trouble was loads of fun!

'If you carried a pot like that, there'd be no water left by the time you got home! Hold it straight! Haven't any of you seen women carrying pots of water?'

Sangeeta tried valiantly.

Irritated, fuming at her inept handling of the pot, his hand flew close to her cheek, just stopping short of a slap. Instantly, her eyes glazed with unshed tears.

'Walk up and down twenty times. Start!'

As whoever was 'caught' stumbled on, we froze, inwardly relishing both our temporary safety and her discomfiture. His temper flared suddenly, when someone did not pick up something fast enough, but subsided just as soon, and he would forget transgressions by the next class. Today her; tomorrow me. It all depended on one's luck that day.

Changing mores bring other frustrations. I happened to be in class recently while Sir taught the same piece to a group of juniors. After the *gopi* fills her pot, comes a passage where she dresses up for Krishna: 'And you need to plait your hair like this. See, she has long long hair. Bring all of it over your right shoulder. One strand over another, all the way down and tie a knot and fling it back.' He surveyed the class, and commented wryly, 'Of course since all of you have short hair, you have *no* idea what it is to plait hair or weave flowers into it!'

7

The boys in the hostel were a mix of students who studied at the local Besant Theosophical High School or at Kalakshetra. Dhananjayan was awarded the merry task of waking them all up at 4.30 a.m. for PE, even while prankster Balagopal slept on.

Some of the younger kids who were bullied felt safe with Dhananjayan. 'I used to guide and protect them, even from Balan! Parents were fond of me because of this. I would make them sleep near me, because sometimes they would wake at night and cry and the others would get upset.'

During the rains, the thatched roofs of the hostel cottages leaked. Snakes dropped from the roofs into the rooms and everyone panicked. At such times, Dhananjayan would remember the night his redoubtable grandmother had lain rigidly in the dark, waiting for the cobra winding its way over and across her body to slither away!

It was an interesting mix of children from different backgrounds. At the time, admission to the local Besant Theosophical High School was much sought after, and a lot of the students went on to achieve success. Many families from Andhra, rich from agriculture, would send their sons to this school. These affluent children had money to spare and could afford luxuries like Binaca toothpaste, Pears soap and tickets to the monthly English movie screened on campus. Other children made do with what little pocket money they had.

Dhananjayan and Balagopal had none.

'We used to wait for the movie on Saturday. There was a small entrance fee, 4 annas, which we did not have. We were the only poor kids, me and Balagopal. Sometimes the other boys would pay for us or the headmaster Krishnaratnam would let us in free. Once there was a movie, *Living Desert*, that everyone was talking about. We did not have money so Shanta took us, paying the one rupee ticket for both Balan and me.'

In the hot summer nights, the boys slept outside the hostel, near a huge tamarind tree. Ghost stories were swapped, each designed to scare by describing spirits that supposedly resided in the dense branches of the tamarind. Some boys, prone to sleepwalking, would awake to find that they had slept beneath the tree and would yell in terror while the others rolled in laughter.

After a few months, Dhananjayan and Balagopal were sanctioned two rupees a month. 'The hostel warden Padmasini would never give us our money. We had to fight for it. One day, I told Rukmini Devi's mother. Rukmini Devi pulled up the warden, who got angry with me for telling her. We felt we were treated shabbily because we were poor. Maybe I should not have spoken out but I was very vocal about my feelings, and that was a black mark against me. Nobody dared say anything in front of Rukmini Devi, except me.

'If I disagreed with Rukmini Devi I would tell her. The teachers who never raised a voice against Athai thought I was wrong to do so. I think Athai appreciated it in me, she admired my capacity as a creative artist and would often say, "Do your own version."

'If someone snitched to her about people, she would start finding fault with them. I would try and help the person in trouble and stand up for him. Unlike the other teachers who, if Athai saw the sun and called it the moon, would say "Yes, Athai", I was different. If a *mudra* was not suitable I would say, "No, Athai, it is not appropriate. If we do this here instead, it would be better." No one liked my being forthright with her.'

Later, the two rupees became five, but even then the warden would make them beg, or give it a rupee at a time, which was humiliating.

*

During the term holidays, parents would come to collect their children and take them home. No one came for the two boys.

'Balan and I would look at each other and then cry in the mango grove. Sometimes Asan would go back to Trikkaripur but he could not take us, so we were left in the care of the cooks. Nothing else made me cry, only the thought that we were so poor and not able to help our family while the other boys had no such worries. Even Balan was not as poor as I; he was better off, his father had fields.'

Once in a while Krishnaratnam, the headmaster, would buy them a ticket back for the summer holidays, or miraculously, Dhananjayan's father would save the money for it. Having brought him home, when it came time to send him back, Rama Poduval had to scrabble for money once again.

The year the boys turned sixteen – old enough to warrant a full ticket priced at twelve rupees – Kunhiraman who had accompanied them back to Madras thought they could still get by on a half-ticket. The ticket conductor asked him how old the boys were. Putting his cherubic good looks to best use, Kunhiraman deadpanned: 'Thirteen.'

'Hmph,' retorted the conductor. 'Thirteen indeed! Evidently they sprout moustaches at thirteen these days.'

Once, the boys in the hostel went on strike demanding white rice instead of the healthier red rice that was served. For Dhananjayan and Balagopal, constantly hungry, it was unthinkable to complain about the food: 'There was a bias towards Brahmins, we felt it, but we could not say anything because we were poor, second class. Moneyed people were treated better.'

Over at the girls' hostel, there was a bigger subversion. A Sri Lankan girl, whom Balagopal had a crush on, and Sanjukta (later famous as *the* Odissi dancer Sanjukta Panigrahi) found the vegetarian food – no onion, no garlic, no fiery spices – too tame, even though the masala dosa they got once a week actually had onion in it.

An ayah would smuggle in non-vegetarian food for them, stuffed inside a loaf of bread. Once, a pious vegetarian got whiff of the forbidden aroma and told the teachers. Shanta happened to overhear and sped to the hostel to warn her friends. They ate as much as they could of their supplies and buried the rest beneath a jasmine plant outside. The teachers could not find anything. The next morning, the girls woke to discover bones strewn near their hostel door. The three campus dogs, Andal, Mohan and Susheela had excavated a jasmine-scented feast for themselves!

Among the many benefits of living on the Kalakshetra campus, the greatest perhaps was the opportunity to interact with the distinguished personalities who visited the campus: the Dalai Lama, C. Rajagopalachari, C.P. Ramasamy Aiyer, the Maharaja of Mysore Jayachamaraja Wodeyar and Martha Graham to name a few. At night, the Tamil pandit Vishwanatha Iyer told them stories from the Kamba Ramayana and the youngsters would fight to sit crosslegged in the front rows. In this atmosphere of learning, it was a simple matter of running across to the homes of the great musicians Mysore Vasudevachar or Karaikudi Samabasiva Iyer, to play the tambura for them as they sang, or just sit and listen. A lot of the intricacies of music and dance came to them by this kind of wonderful osmosis.

Inspired by Rajaram – Mysore Vasudevachar's grandson, who was of the firm opinion that 'boys must study' – Dhananjayan wanted to appear for the matriculation exam in 1959. Mostly everyone thought he was wasting his time, while others thought he was doing it just to impress Shanta. No scholarship holder had ever attempted it; none of the other dancers, except C.V. Chandrasekhar who was attending college, were that interested in studies.

Teacher Sundari admitted him into the matriculation class, which was held in English. Dhananjayan's English was weak, so everyone tried to dissuade him from appearing for the exam saying he wouldn't pass. He was good in science, though algebra was like quicksand.

Rehearsals continued throughout and there was no free time in which to study. The cooks, taking pity on him, would secretly give him some coffee to stay awake at night.

'When I was about to write the matric exam I went to take Athai's blessings. "You are not going to pass, so why are you going?" she exclaimed discouragingly. But I passed with 60 marks in English. It was a *big* thing! I did not even attempt algebra, but I got 98 in the other two maths papers, so I passed with high second, losing a first class by one mark! Athai was surprised; she never thought I would pass. I went deliberately to show her my results.'

Needless to say, Rajaram – the only person to have encouraged Dhananjayan – was very happy.

8

It was only after four years of strict training, that we arrived at the *Ela varnam.*

A *varnam* is the *piece de resistance* of any performance. Lasting from thirty to ninety minutes, it is the test of a dancer's skills as both *nritta* and *bhava* are presented.

The order of items in a performance of *sadir* was codified by four gifted brothers, Chinnaiah, Ponniah, Vadivelu and Sivanandam, known as the Thanjavur Quartet attached to the Thanjavur Court, in the early 19th century. Their oeuvre still comprises the major part of the Bharata Natyam repertoire today. Increasing in complexity, the sequence of *alarippu, jatiswaram, shabdam, varnam, padam, javali, tillana,* collectively known as the *margam,* charts the standard progress of a student of dance.[15]

The theme of *Ela varnam* went thus:

Why deceive me O lord, why don't you protect me?

Some lotus faced beauty poisoned your ears about me and you registered it in your heart. Don't you have even a tiny bit of compassion, O lord?

Dhananjayan Sir wanted our faces to brighten into a wicked beautiful face as *she* filled his right ear with untruths, while the lord paid attention to it with his left ear. I remember long hours spent as Sir tried to extract from us the desolate expression required for the heroine's plea for a 'tiny bit of compassion' and the love-laden reproach in her address 'O lord'.

It was all so unfamiliar and yet it all made sense. As he sang in Telugu – a language I did not know – I tumbled into a world of unknown emotions and situations. Handsome heroes, heartfelt love, intrigue, recrimination, absences, broken promises, delayed arrivals, jilted hearts. What possible experience could I have of any of this, at age twelve? Yet the sheer human drama of it was attractive.

It was a strange anomaly where we were quite innocent of the kind of 'knowledge' displayed by the heroines of certain *padams* and *javalis*.

In many of the songs, the basic love triangle was an inevitable theme.

'*This* is love,' Sir would say, hooking one little finger below the other in the *kilaka mudra*.

Somehow, as his neck moved imperceptibly from side to side and the interlocked hands moved forward, his downcast eyes and tender smile created the feeling of love.

At such moments, one stood stockstill, grateful.

Or, there was the hand flowering open near the heart. This was a more blatant expression of love. The eyes spoke, unashamed in their declaration of desire. If it was a hero, he held his gaze. If a heroine, the eyes were lowered in a sudden fit of shyness. If it was a villain, the brash eyes held carnality and arrogance as well.

Arms encircled space, denoting an embrace. One was the sought after embrace by a lover, the other was the *nayika* herself yearning to secure him within her arms.

And, there was the kiss. The fingers of one hand bloomed open into the lotus face of the beloved, and here was the other hand become a bee, buzzing close, close, close until it drank nectar. The hero kissed, the heroine allowed herself to be kissed. Her enjoyment was always conveyed with a hint of bashfulness.

Manmatha, the god of love, had an unerring aim and delighted in tormenting the gullible human heart. Born of the mind, he was invisible, formless. Here now, in *Ela varnam*, the heroine was pleading distress as a stream of pointed arrows, the innumerable unseen arrows of love pierced her.

Though barely an adolescent, it was not difficult to imagine myself in the situation, feeling all those feelings the heroine was going through. It also allowed me to be the lotus-faced vamp, and fleetingly, this easily misled lord.

I loved it.

I took to it like a duck to water. Somewhere in the juncture between music and mood, words and meaning, there was space for me to dance with all my being, combining all those energies in one purposeful flow until it streamed from my face towards the invisible audience.

9

Asan Chandu Panikker, as was the guru's custom, would never utter a word of appreciation, but he had other ways of making known his approval. He might tell Dhananjayan's peers to follow him in the expression of a certain line or he would scold his seniors in Dhananjayan's presence, saying they were useless. They were all collectively terrified of him, and did not really expect praise.

Asan taught Dhananjayan a *padam* '*Baale Variga*' from *Krimeera Vadham* that was considered *his* signature piece. In this very slow *padam*, Yudhisthira in an abiding state of sadness expresses his love to Draupadi. It was physically demanding, as the dancer had to sit in one position for an hour and fifteen minutes, and elaborate on Yudhisthira's many conflicting feelings.

Finally, when he judged him ready, Asan made Dhananjayan perform it in class. Addressing Draupadi as a beautiful woman, filled with love for her, Yudhisthira spoke with regret at having made her suffer. They were kings, kshatriyas, and instead of giving her a palace to sleep in, he had made the forest her home. Disgusted with himself, for having put her in that position by playing dice, he was full of suppressed anger at his inability to stop his wife from being humiliated in full court. Through it all, the main abiding emotion was *shringara* or love. Dhananjayan gave it his best hoping to impress his Asan, but was disheartened when he got up and strode away without a word!

Later, he heard Rukmini Devi exclaim, 'Asan said you did well! I will come and watch it tomorrow.' The next day, when he performed the same *padam* for her, she wiped her eyes with her handkerchief, and sniffed a lot. When he reached the end, she protested gruffly, 'I am not crying! I have a cold, that's all!' In his heart's store of cherished compliments, albeit unspoken, Dhananjayan would rate this the highest.

Asan was getting older, but the boys continued to train under him and were completely immersed in Kathakali. Their Bharata Natyam classes were stopped, but because they were not paying fees, they had no say in the matter. They also travelled extensively, performing *Sita Swayamvaram* and other productions.

In 1959, fortune smiled on Dhananjayan again.

He applied for a Government of India scholarship for Kathakali students. Only students trained in Kerala were thought to be of the calibre required and people tended to dismiss the Kathakali section of Kalakshetra calling it Bharata Natyam Kathakali. Over thirty students from Kerala Kalamandalam appeared for the interview as did Dhananjayan, supremely confident of the might of his Asan's training.

The judges were the eminent Guru Gopinath and Thekkinkattil Ramunni Nair. They asked Dhananjayan to present a *padam* and he chose to do Bhima from *Kalyana Saugandhikam*. A visibly moved Guru Gopinath stood up and declared, 'This boy is getting the scholarship.' There were others awaiting their turn, so the government officials were annoyed at this premature disclosure. Guru Gopinath stuck to his decision.

He asked Dhananjayan to wait for him. The twenty year old was in the seventh heaven. Taking him home, Guru Gopinath introduced him to his wife and gave him tea. Dhananjayan was overawed by him. Such a great man; such vocal appreciation of a younger man's talent.

Back in Kalakshetra, Dhananjayan ran to Rukmini Devi's house with the good news. Her casual reply was: 'Oh one can't believe them. They will say such things, but wait till the letter comes to be sure.' But even her cynical response could not dampen his joy.

The scholarship was a boon. Of the 250 rupees he got a month, Kalakshetra took 50 rupees as fees and 75 for the hostel. The joy of paying fees! Of no longer being a second-class citizen! 100 rupees was dispatched to Payyanur, and over time the thatched roof over his family's head became a pucca roof. Rama Poduval could now contribute money to his mother-in-law's household!

Many sudden changes were made to the syllabus at Kalakshetra. To acquire the diploma, one had to pass an examination. Examined by Dr. S.K. Nair, an expert in literature and Kathakali, Dhananjayan got very high marks in Kathakali and passed with distinction. Dr. Nair was so impressed by him, he took to teaching Dhananjayan the nuances of *padams* at his house in Mandaveli on Sundays.

Dhananjayan had passed the matriculation exam despite all odds, and had achieved a high distinction in his Kathakali exam and won the GOI scholarship. He must have tempted the fates, for now there were skirmishes with his teachers Chinna Sharada and Sundari who wanted him to appear for an exam in Bharata Natyam.

'We haven't been taught, I can't take the exam!' protested the boy already branded as outspoken. 'Not in Bharata Natyam, we don't even know the repertoire, we haven't learnt *varnam* or *tillana*! Examine me in the content of the dance-dramas, *any* character.' He spoke for Balagopal as well.

'Then we can't give you a diploma.'

'I don't want a diploma.'

Such arrogance!

He was summoned by Rukmini Devi and Shankara Menon. To his consternation he discovered that Athai had no idea that their Bharata Natyam classes had been stopped. The teachers were reprimanded.

The boys refused to appear for the exam; proof of their high-handed behaviour; how could he be given a diploma? Rukmini Devi who liked them both did not intervene.

The great Carnatic vocalist M.D. Ramanathan spoke on Dhananjayan's behalf. 'Give him a bad character certificate if you must, but his hard work should be rewarded with a diploma. Look at the roles he has done…Rama, Manmatha, Aniruddha! Plus he has done the best in theory.'

Eventually, Dhananjayan received the distinction diploma along with Shanta and Krishnaveni.

10

After our first performance, Dhananjayan Sir continued to present us in public. Obviously, we were not yet ready to perform Bharata Natyam so he taught us folk dances, simple to do, but requiring hours of practice to synchronize our movements.

These came with their own share of amusement, such as the time we had a show in our own BK cottage, performing for some guests. We were to do a *pinnal* or 'braid' *kolattam*, a Tamil folk dance. Ribbons tied to the roof at one end, fell to the ground. There, the other end was tied to a painted stick we held in our hands. The ribbons would plait themselves as we wove in and out of a moving circle. A mistake could prove fatal as the plait would go awry, entangle and knot itself. First we learnt the various interlocking movements and then came the day when we practised with the sticks and ribbons. Looking up, a rainbow braid had been magically woven above our head!

Finally, the show! Dressed in our best silk *pavadais*, the long skirts trailing the floor for some and hanging close to the ankles of those who had suddenly shot up, we looked the way Sir wanted little girls to look like – flowers in our long plaits ending in a *kunjalam*, kajal in our eyes, big bindis, a showy necklace and lots of bangles.

Things were going well. The colourful plait had come into being, visible in the air. Suddenly, one of the girls felt her skirt's *nada* coming undone. Instinctively, preferring modesty over achievement, she stopped and tried to retie the *nada*, blouse lifted under her chin. The rest of us, not knowing how to deal with this unforeseen calamity, bumped into each other and stopped. The plait was in danger of becoming an irreparable tangle of ribbons and Sir gestured to us to end, rather than risk further chaos.

The Calamity Jane did not last long at BK. But for those of us who continued there, it was an early invaluable lesson – how to deal with the unforeseen and unpredictable on stage; how to manage mistakes, of one's own creation and by others; how to exit gracefully after a less than stellar performance.

Foreground Dhananjayan (l), author Tulsi Badrinath aged ten (centre) Sangeeta Vijeyasarathy (r) dance with lamps

Of all the challenges Sir continually threw at us, nothing was designed less in our favour than the dance of lights, or *deepanjali*.

A row of dancers enter the darkened stage, each carrying a glowing diya. The wavering lights acquire a beauty of their own, and the dancers manipulating them are but shadowy presences. It made for a dramatic beginning to any show. It was also an example of what might be enjoyable for the audience being traumatic for the performer.

While there is the phrase 'dancing on eggshells', there is nothing that adequately conveys the exaggerated care with which we bore a shining brass plate in our flattened palms, with the diya placed in the centre. Anything could happen – it could slide, the little candle inside could topple, the brass plate might fall, clattering on the floor, and of course worst of all, the flame could be blown out. And through it all, one had to remain poised and smile confidently.

The problem lay in the fact that the tiny flame was vulnerable to the slightest change in the flow of air. It did not require gusts of wind to douse it, nor a passing breeze. Just waving it in the air while dancing could extinguish it. There is nothing so forlorn as being the only one in the group carrying darkness aloft, on a dead wick. One had to go through all the motions, feeling like a complete failure.

It did not help that Sir took it as a sign of moral decrepitude if the diya-light blew out. One could be sure of a yelling, and there was no way of avoiding it by remaining on stage!

Time passed and we crossed into adolescence. As our bodies grew and breasts began to appear, the next rite of passage took place. We were now ready to wear the sari, discarding our kurta-pyjamas. The dance practice sari is half the width of a normal sari but of the same length. Usually in two contrasting colours, it has a distinctive plain, narrow border.

I was around twelve when Akka whisked me into the changing room, and there behind the bamboo partition showed me how to wear the knee-length sari, tucking it into baggy pyjamas rather than a petticoat. As though she were dressing a lightweight doll, she moved me this way and that, bringing the long pallu over my blouse, around my waist, and pulling it tight. All air was sucked out of my stomach. Extremely conscious of this elevation in status, I appeared in front of my friends, engulfed in five yards of green and yellow cotton. How was one to dance in it?

As it turned out, pleating the sari for dance class, sometimes in a great hurry, resulted in a lifelong ease with wearing the full-length version. It was practice not only for real life, but also practice for the time we had to change costumes backstage and rush out for the next item.

Many years later, a tiny battery operated bulb became available and it replaced the candle inside the diya. While it made life easier, its steady light is not a patch on the warm golden flicker of unpredictability.

11

Although situated in the grounds of the Theosophical Society of Madras, Kalakshetra was a separate institution, begun in 1936. While many Theosophists were involved in its activities, it was never run by the Theosophical Society. After George Arundale died and a new President took over at the Theosophical Society, it was made clear to Rukmini Devi that all her activities connected with dance and Indian art and handlooms and education, to name just a few, were not welcome there. It took her many years and the help of those devoted to her dream, to arrange for an alternative place and relocate.

In 1963, Kalakshetra shifted to its present campus in Thiruvanmiyur. Getting the place ready was a group effort in which all the dancers willingly participated, the boys pushing the road-roller, the girls carrying sand and pebbles to help with laying the road. Lunch would arrive in a bullock-cart, the crackle of potato chips, sambar and curd-rice tasting like manna after all the work in the sun.

Here, a concert section was created, separate from the teaching section. Designated staff performing artist, Dhananjayan was given charge of the concert section. 'So I started arranging Bharata Natyam solo programmes. Outside Kalakshetra, whenever we had a programme I would include boys in it and we got a good response from the audience. Rukmini Devi always insisted that there be no trace of femininity in our movements and our Kathakali training helped us in this. We were second-class citizens otherwise, but *on stage* we were equal and in the reviews, the males got the limelight and the appreciation.

'Athai used Kathakali in her *Shyama* of Tagore, where the boys performed it without the elaborate costume. This gave us the idea that we did not need the costume for every show. That's how I did the forest description later without the Kathakali costume.'

Dhananjayan expanded on the way Rukmini Devi blended the two styles in her dance dramas, 'Sometimes even if Asan was not there she would ask us to show how a particular thing was done in Kathakali and she would do it in Bharata Natyam. That is, Athai would have the word to word meaning for a particular composition but there were certain stories we knew from the Kathakali repertoire, and Athai would have seen it and ask us to do it. Watching the description of the peacock, in a Kathakali *padam*, she would say "Keep the idea and do it with Bharata Natyam steps."

'When she choreographed certain scenes, especially when we started doing the Ramayana, she would encourage us to use our imagination. Since we were doing Kathakali, we could do a lot of things on our own. We had a lot of stories, lot of story-oriented training unlike Bharata Natyam which is song oriented. We would demonstrate and she would take it as a base and interpret it in Bharata Natyam... not blindly but taking into account many factors. She maintained the integrity of the two styles.'

In 1963, Dhananjayan was appointed a teacher with a salary of 139 rupees. 'By the time I paid 40 for Hostel and 60 for stay, and PPF all I had in hand was two rupees. I could not afford to buy Binaca toothpaste...I made do with mango leaves or neem sticks or tooth powder. Getting a cake of soap was a big thrill, if someone gave me one I was so happy. So we boys, Kunhiraman, Balagopalan and I, we got together and decided to cook for ourselves. It cost us only 20 or 30 rupees compared to the hostel fee. Kunhiraman Sir was the main cook, we were his assistants. When I was a little boy, my grandmother used to make me cook rice, make dosai, do all that at the age of nine or ten. Very unusual for a boy! That's how I learnt cooking before I got married.'

Meanwhile, Shanta had left for Malaysia, to stay with her parents. In love, but yet to commit to each other formally, they had been corresponding. Shanta was teaching Bharata Natyam there at the Sarada Sangam with Uma Sambandam, whose husband was the health minister. Uma Sambandam wanted to bring Dhananjayan over as well, offering him many lucrative opportunities and government support.

There was a need for a really good school of dance there and Dhananjayan could have made a lot of money to support the endless needs of his large family back home, but he never thought of leaving Kalakshetra. In his way of thinking his life and identity were entwined with that of Kalakshetra.

12

When the fair good-looking Krishna abruptly left class, I was curious as only a ten-year-old can be. Why had he left? Was it possible to quit BK with such ease? Did he not *like* learning how to dance? How come his sisters continued, while he did not? He had to focus on his studies, they said, but then the rest of us managed to study and dance, didn't we? Unwittingly, he planted the seeds of this book by that long forgotten act of his.

I became slowly aware that the number of boys learning dance in BK was much lower than the girls. Those who came to learn were different from us in so many ways: older, for example. Because of this, class at BK was not a co-ed class as one might have in school, where boys and girls of the same age and more or less the same economic background studied together. Drawn to Dhananjayan, male dancers came and left periodically, while our classes proceeded evenly.

One such, Richard Frasca, was an American with dark curly hair who came to Madras to research *therukoothu*, the regional theatre form. He was part of our class when we were learning the basics, the sole adult student. He sweated so much when he danced that a spray of droplets flew around him, landing on the floor and making it slippery for everyone. Richard spoke Tamil fluently. That, coupled with the mat of black hair on his chest, could have fooled people into thinking he was Indian. He returned to his country after a while.

Then, for a long time, there were no boys in our class.

Sadanam Unnikrishnan, a thin young man arrived at BK in the early 80s. Though he did not learn in our class, we did get to dance with him in the variety shows and dance dramas. Years later, he said in an interview[16]: 'It was poverty at home that took me to Gandhi Seva Sadanam Kathakali School in Palakkad at the age of nine.' After eight long years of training he reached Kalakshetra where he had been invited to teach Kathakali. 'The salary offered was Rs 300 a month. Instead of accepting it, I became a student of Bharata Natyam. To earn a living, I started a mobile library and in the evening I distributed the magazines to readers living around Kalakshetra and earned up to Rs 400 every month. This was sent to my mother at Pattambi. She thought I was drawing a handsome salary at Kalakshetra.'

Of this, we had no idea. He was older than us; our interactions with him were limited to the hours at BK. We adored this gentle and very good dancer as our senior. In 1984, he flew to London to dance in Dhananjayan's path-breaking production *Jungle Book – Adventures of Mowgli*. When he settled down there, we missed him. Thereafter, we saw him rarely in Madras.

Jayachandran, also from Kerala, joined around the same time as Unnikrishnan. He had a lithe, hairless body. I was very intrigued by the fact that his ribcage showed clearly when he lifted his arms in movement. He learnt alongside us sometimes when we had graduated to learning more difficult items. In 1987, he headed to London to study at the London Contemporary Dance School. He took to contemporary dance and made a name for himself with his group, Attakalari.

One fine day, we did have a boy of our age in class. His name was Karthik and he had joined along with his sister Uttara. Shy in the presence of girls, he always wore a *banian* while dancing. Chiefly, I remember the hugely embarassing moment when, intent on completing a *tillana*, I was on the left side crossing to the right and he on the right, crossing to the left. Bang! We collided and I recoiled as if stung! It was bad enough to have crashed into someone, but a boy? Mortifying! It took me a while to get over that. He was in school at that time and it seemed a foregone conclusion that he would leave in a while to pursue higher studies.

I now see a pattern in these early memories. While many girls from middle-class and affluent families were encouraged to learn dance, their brothers were not. If at all they were to be exposed to the arts, then Carnatic music was a more appropriate choice for them. The negative perception of boys who learnt dance being sissies, or turning out effeminate, was at work here. Most importantly, there was the clear understanding that this was not a highly paying or high-status profession for men. The male children of middle-class families were already being chanelled towards becoming engineers or doctors or running the family business.

Through the years, sadly, this disparity in the socio-economic background, with a few exceptions, of the boys and the girls studying at BK has not changed.

13

In 1964, the committee organizing the Edinburgh Festival visited India in order to select established troupes to dance at the 1965 Festival. They came to Kalakshetra and were so impressed by the Kathakali that they invited the troupe to represent India.

Within Kalakshetra, there were those who felt the institution was best represented by its dance-dramas or Bharata Natyam, not Kathakali. Already, between 1963 and 1965, the Kathakali section had achieved greater recognition and dancers were being invited to perform in many plays. Some of the teachers were not happy. In their thinking, Kalakshetra ought to be known for Bharata Natyam, not Kathakali.

Dhananjayan was jubilant. They were going to tour Edinburgh with his childhood idol Kalamandalam Krishnan Nair. Asan Chandu Panikker was now in his nineties and a bit frail so the great Krishnan Nair had come all the way to Madras six months in advance to train them. He delineated *abhinaya* and *manodharma*, creative flights of self-expression, in a way that opened up so many exhilarating possibilities in their minds. He taught them new stories to perform. One of these, *The Pregnant Deer* was to seal Dhananjayan's reputation for powerful yet sensitive *abhinaya*.

Kunhiraman and Balagopal and A. Janardhanan (Chandu Panikker's son who joined Kalakshetra in 1958) and Dhananjayan set to work, making costumes, compressing stories to suit the interval

Dhananjayan in Kathakali costume, *Katthi vesham*

of time required by the Festival. They stayed back over summer at Kalakshetra, for which they were not paid. Asan Chandu Panikker was not well. He came by now and then to see how his students were doing. Stage director, Paul Storm, an ace at lighting, helped with the technical aspects.

Krishnan Nair taught Dhananjayan *kari vesham* in *Narakasura Vadham*. Humour is the essence of *kari vesham*, most difficult to communicate with the stylized codes of Kathakali. Dhananjayan admired him greatly and inspired by his teaching, excelled while performing the role. When his friends and fellow dancers told him 'You do it exactly like him' they meant it as the ultimate compliment; they all wanted to emulate him. Rukmini Devi said the same, though with a tinge of sarcasm, 'Not bad, you performed it exactly the way *he* does it, not like your Asan,' – forgetting momentarily perhaps that Krishnan Nair was Asan's student.

The difference lay in the creative genius of the two men. Asan Chandu Panikker taught from within the tradition – exactly the way he had received it from his own guru. Krishnan Nair had a flair for expanding the scope of what he performed, unafraid of pushing the boundaries of tradition. He had amalgamated what he learnt from other gurus, and his acting skills enhanced his presentation, taking it to another level altogether. That is why his name was synonymous with Kathakali.

As they had with their Asan, Dhananjayan and Balagopal served Krishnan Nair, and willingly ran errands for him. A simple man at heart, he spent the early hours of the morning on ablutions and rituals, even though he might have taught them late into the night. No one was to disturb him at this time. The young lads were privileged in being able to trace the invisible link between those early hours of meditation and the man as artiste and teacher.

'His life was about his art and nothing else, the entire focus was on performing and teaching. He was very easy to look after, had a quiet sense of humour and he was very friendly with us though we gave him all the respect due.' Dhananjayan's face lit up as he remembered those intimate moments with the one of the greatest Kathakali dancers of all time.

'He did not see us as his students and treated us as junior associates because we had learnt under the same guru. He would narrate incidents to us that helped understand what it was to actually be a professional dancer. He told us about a time when two famous Kathakali Asans, Pattikkamthodi Ravunni Menon and Kunju Kurup had an ongoing feud. It spilled onto the stage when they performed together and wherever the story allowed for improvization they would each try to outdo the other. In the process, they lost track of time, so much so that junior artists waiting in the side wings did not get a chance to perform!'

Krishnan Nair too had been born in a poor family and had struggled early in his career, succeeding entirely on the strength of his talent. Dhananjayan could relate to him, especially when he talked about the tough time he had had under Asan Chandu Panikker who was younger and even more vigorous then.

Once, the Asan had got so furious with him in class, he had hit Krishnan Nair with the wooden stick, *thattu kazhi*. Krishnan Nair had jumped to avoid the blow, and broken his leg. Asan was instantly contrite. Krishnan Nair was touched by the depth of concern he showed, a side he had never seen of his martinet-guru. The leg took a long time to heal and he could not perform one entire Kathakali season. Hearing that his student was dejected and ruing the financial loss, Asan Chandu Panikker had visited him at *his* house and reassured him with the spiritual force of his blessing, 'Whatever you have lost in this one season you will gain multifold in the years to come.' My guru's eyes brimmed with tears, and his voice choked as he narrated this story to me.

'Krishnan Nair taught us little nuances that would embellish our portrayal of a character. These were discoveries he had made and perfected and he was incredibly generous in sharing it with us. For example, in the overtly stylized Kathakali, *shringara* was conveyed with a grave demeanour but he taught us to do the same thing in a gentler way. I incorporated a lot of things he taught me in my performance.'

After months of strenuous rehearsals, and painstaking preparation and packing of costumes and the Kathakali headgear, they were raring to go. It was the first time that Krishnan Nair was going abroad. It would be cold in Edinburgh as winter was approaching. They got themselves achkans to stay warm and look smart at the same time.

Rukmini Devi left for the Festival, travelling with the renowned Carnatic musician, M.S. Subbulakshmi. The next day, the Kathakali troupe had loaded its luggage onto the bus and was about to leave for the airport when news arrived that an Indo-Pak war had broken out and all flights had been cancelled.

Krishnan Nair was devastated. He slumped heavily and did not move for two days. In private, he sobbed like a child. Fate had dealt him a nasty blow. 'Look at my luck, I cannot go abroad but if I return to Kerala, I will be humiliated by everyone for not achieving what I had set out to do.' The boys did not know how to console their hero. Soon, he left for Kerala. Years later, he did travel abroad.

When they heard, some of the Bharata Natyam teachers openly expressed their glee at the Kathakali team's misfortune: 'It was their *shaapam*, curse.'

1965 marked the height of an age when Kalakshetra was also known for its Kathakali. 'We were fully trained to be Kathakali dancers. I was good in every role, all the characters, but because I had a good physique I did *pachcha* and *katthi vesham*. Asan decided what we would do. Balan specialized in *stree vesham* because he was short. I thought and everyone thought I will be a full-time Kathakali dancer.'

Fate decided otherwise.

14

The train pulled away from Madras Central and we were off, occupying twenty seats in the second-class sleeper section. The time had been carefully calibrated – the tickets had been checked, the mridangam and veena carefully stowed and protected by a barricade of hard-topped suitcases, friends had paired up and the musicians had already changed into their lungis.

The rattle rhythm of the train thundered towards a show: makeup, costumes, and the indescribable thrill of dancing on stage. But all of this lay a day away, and judging the right moment some intrepid one would ask the question, and we would settle down to hear the love story we had heard in parts so many times before, for in the hearing of it we saw our own future brightened by the promise of romance and in seeing the visible outcome of it, we heard the haunting melody of abiding love.

'So how did Shanta Akka and you get married?'

'How did you know she liked you?'

'How did you propose?'

Somewhat stunned at our own audacity, we paused, not knowing when his temper would flare suddenly if he perceived a question had crossed a line. But he was in a good mood that day and soon we were spellbound, the darkness bunched at the window, the breeze whipping our hair into knots and the dim yellow lights of the open compartment throwing shadows on his handsome face. Akka sat next to him.

'She was the first girl I saw on 5 October 1953, in Kalakshetra playing in the Theosophical Gardens, near Bharat Samaj. I still remember the exact spot in the mango garden. Shanta was wearing a *pavadai* skirt-blouse with dots. I thought she was a very nice girl. "Take care of them" Shankara Menon had told her.'

Akka elaborated: 'Mainly because they did not speak the language. And I thought, *Oh two boys here to learn dance*! It was quite an exciting thing! There were hardly any full-time male dancers at Kalakshetra, the others were older. These boys came in wearing shorts.'

'In class, she would explain things to me if I did not understand.' His eyes twinkled: 'She was my senior, by one year. Sometimes she would make us practise.'

'But soon they overtook us, because they were full-time.'

'You were part-time.'

It was touching to watch them jog each other's memory at the same time as they delved into it for us.

'We would meet for morning prayer, for lunch. Then she would go to school. Sometimes we were in the same Bharata Natyam class in the evening. We were in a big group together. Kolkali, Payattu, Asan taught all of us after six o'clock...I started getting attracted towards her. Of all the girls, she was a good girl. In front of us, she would not laugh a lot or talk a lot. I was very strict, reserved and chivalrous of course. I had an image in my mind about how a lady should be. *Roopeshu lakshmi*...I had learnt as a child.' Interrupting himself, he asked her the question we were all dying to ask, 'What did you feel at that time?'

Akka smiled, searching for the right words: 'I always felt that he was a very balanced person and I admired the way he conducted himself. As a student, he was excellent. It was so nice to see him dance. Almost overnight after his arrival at Kalakshetra, he was performing. We were awestruck. It was the talk of the town, everyone came to see the two beautiful boys.'

'Admiration slowly became feelings. We did not express it...'

'...We were too young.'

'Boys and girls did not mingle freely in those days. Teachers would be watching us; they were very strict. In class we were friendly, but no touching, we stood at a distance.'

'No *question* of touching.'

'My friend Balagopal was a bit of a flirt,' Dhananjayan chuckled.

'Little? He was quite flirty! They had very different natures but were such close friends. Individually they were different, but together on stage they were fantastic. They went everywhere together.'

'The first time people realized I had feelings for Shanta, was when we were touring north India, 1956-57.'

'In *Sita Swayamvaram*, first time.'

'We were traveling all over Calcutta, Patna, Ujjain, Gwalior, Udaipur, Delhi...I would take care of Shanta, give her hot water for her bath. The weather was very cold. We were staying in an elementary school dormitory. Only benches to sleep on. I had no bedding, only a bedsheet and dhurrie. Some people had a holdall...'

'I had a holdall!'

'I used to wake up early and heat the water, to make sure that she got the hot water. Then they would all tease me, "Oh, you are heating it only for Shanta!" While crossing the Ganga at Patna in a boat, I sat close to her.'

'Made sure he can see me wherever he sits.'

'Under the pretext of holding the umbrella over Rukmini Devi, I would be near Shanta. I didn't know if she felt the way I did...I used to say, "I will teach you swimming" and hold her hand and lead her into the water. That was the beginning, everything blossomed on the tour.'

'Uma, who played Sita, left and M.S. Rama was made Sita. When *she* left, Krishnaveni performed that role...' prompted Akka.

'...Yes, I exchanged garlands with four Sitas, so they interpreted that as the four wives in my horoscope...Krishnaveni was like me, we liked improvizing on stage. In the forest scene, while describing Sita's beauty I often changed what I did. I would ask Rukmini Devi, "Can we do it this way?" and when she agreed we would try it, but other teachers resented Athai accepting my ideas. On the other hand, Shanta would not budge an inch from the set choreography...then Shanta became Sita, and our romance began!'

'By then I had realized that he was very interested in me. Friends would come and tell me, "Oh Dhananjayan loves you, he likes you." I was happy but scared, I was shy to show my love, I did not know how to react, but I liked him...'

'You liked me but not in *that* sense,' he spoke blithely, knowing that their story had a happy ending.

'I...I felt something special but I did not even want to tell my friends.'

'I would tell the other girls, "Be like Shanta! Don't laugh immodestly, laugh like her, only Shanta is the perfect girl."'

'The more they told me, the more silent I became. I felt very... very scared, in fact. *What will happen? What will people say?* I got scared. *Why is this happening to me?* It was a very funny feeling. In fact I would cry. I did not want this to happen to me. I was getting into that age, adolescence.'

'During this time she developed a problem, she had boils...'

'I had a kind of eczema, boils on my head. I was so sick, I was sent home. There they shaved my head, and put me on heavy medication and were unhappy that I had not been looked after at Kalakshetra.'

'There was this rumour: *Shanta is not going to come back*. That was a big blow for me. I was feeling very sad, uncomfortable, that she will not come.'

'But I did come back.'

Some of us grinned, hearing clearly the two silent words, *for you*.

'But she came back after two months as *mottai* Shanta – no hair – and all the boys would tease her. When they did that, then I would get angry...annoyed...and fight with them, "Don't call her *mottai*!" And they would needle me, "What is it to you if we tease her?" Then she became Sita in *Sita Swayamvaram*. We were always together, holding hands...'

'Putting a garland around each other's necks.'

'I used to stay close to her and try and be funny with her.'

'Yes, he would get naughty. There was a small stool, hardly any space to sit, and we had to share it. I would sit as far away as possible, one leg sticking out and he would say, "Don't be scared, don't be scared."All my teachers were around me, dancing, this side Chinna Sharada Teacher, that side Jaya Teacher. They all sensed something was going on and their eyes were on us. That is why I was so scared, I did not want to sit near him. When he held my hand, my hands would tremble, it was *so-oo* difficult.'

'I would say, "Why are you scared? Nothing wrong in holding my hand. Don't be silly." After the rehearsals, we had to roll up the mats… I'd try and touch her or hold her and…'

'I would run away. He would get upset and say, "Why did you go?" If he so much as held my hand, I would not talk to him for months together.'

'If I do something like that, *fin-nished*, she would not talk to me except if it had to with the dance.'

'I wouldn't talk,' affirmed Akka. 'Then my friends would say, "Dhananjayan is feeling bad, why are you not talking to him?" I had some very encouraging sakhis! I kept my distance. I felt I should not be so open about my love for him. I never said "*I love you*" to him. My friends would say, "He loves you Shanta, don't you love him?" Some kind of pride did not allow me to say that he was special.'

'Once, in Coimbatore, during *Sita Swayamvaram*, my sorrow or depression over her was visible while performing. So she said, "You are not doing properly." But I was trying to show her my real feeling towards her. I was morose. Then what did you say?'

'"*Lousy* Rama*!*"'

'*Lousy* Rama,' he laughed, mimicking her.

'He remembers it this to this day. "You called me *lousy* Rama."'

He laughed in amusement. 'One day after the show, when we were in Bombay, as we came off the stage, I placed the long *navaratna* necklace that Shanta had given me as Sita, back around her neck. Padmasini Teacher got very angry and said: "How can you do this?" She scolded me and I shouted back, "*I like her, I am going to marry her.*" I didn't know what it meant, but I said it boldly. Balagopal and others, they all egged me on.'

Thrilled by his daring, we turned to Akka and chorused, 'What did you do?'

'I was trembling and again I did not speak to him for months. Athai got to know and called me to the office.'

Happy to have escaped *that* disgrace, we exclaimed, 'Sir did it and she called *you*!'

Shanta took on Rukmini Devi's stern demeanour. '"What is this I hear...that Dhananjayan is very fond of you? What is your feeling?"'

'"I like him."'

'"But I hear that you are always trying to be close. You know that your parents are not here, they have left you in my care, I am responsible."'

Akka continued: 'After *Sita Swayamvaram*, when we were doing *Vanagamanam* and *Paduka Pattabhishekam*, they had thought of casting me as Sita, but among the teachers some felt that they should not encourage our romance this way, however Athai wanted me to do Sita. Krishnaveni and me, we learnt the role together, and till the last day of the performance we did not know who was going to actually perform. We had no jealousy between us.'

Now young Rama and Sita, now young Shanta and Dhananjayan – we hastened to keep track of the various layers of their story. The older Shanta, seated in front of us, turned to Dhananjayan and reminded him fondly: 'You had to tie a sari around Sita.' She explained to us, 'Sita, the princess, does not know how to wear the coarse garment of bark, she feels very uncomfortable and Rama ties it for her. It is *such* a beautiful scene. I get goosebumps thinking of it. I was feeling so shy, so awkward because Asan was there.'

'Asan showed me how to tie it! I was hesitant to touch her. Asan ordered, "*Do it!*" Gave me a nice slap!'

'You had to put your arm around Sita's waist to do that.'

'Asan had no patience for such shyness. He was very angry with me for being reluctant. I can never forget it.'

Dhananjayan picked up the thread again. 'There was an audition. Athai called her entire family and they voted for Shanta but Athai vetoed it because Padmasini Teacher, among others, was against it, so at the last minute Krishnaveni became Sita.'

'It was a last minute decision because of Chinna Sarada Teacher and Padmasini Teacher. Were you heartbroken, sad?'

She looked directly at him, 'No, no, I somehow felt...I knew it is because of this.'

But Akka had not emerged fully from the scene in Rukmini Devi's office. 'Athai asked me, "What is your feeling?" and advised me, "We believe in the practice of universal brotherhood."'

A Greek chorus erupted in the train compartment, '*Universal Brotherhood!?*'

A rare grin appeared on Sir's face: 'She used to say all this in English. When she said that, we used to laugh. So many other things were happening at Kalakshetra – other romances, affairs, it was like a joke.'

'I was in tears. I cried. I knew Athai liked me and I consoled myself with that thought.'

'Then in 1962, she went back to Malaysia.'

We gasped. This was the period of separation in their romance, when Shanta went away to stay with her parents. She had left everybody guessing, including Dhananjayan, as to her real feelings for him. Rumours had been rife in Kalakshetra, that her parents, unhappy with the budding romance, had sent for her; that the obviously well-off Shanta could not marry the penurious Dhananjayan; that she would get married soon and settle down in Malaysia.

'Athai asked me, "Why are you going? Not happy?" "I want to see my parents. They say they have never been with me, so they want to spend time with me before I settle down." "Okay. Go but come back." No one could understand why I left.'

'When she was about to go, 1962, April 18th...That's when I embraced you in the puja hall the first time...'

To hear Dhananjayan say this was to be taken into that private sphere which was theirs alone. We had never seen our gurus hold hands, or be intimate with each other in public. I held my breath, dying to hear what happened next.

'He came up behind me, like that, just hugged me! Ahh! First time, and I was …'

'She was leaving Kalakshetra and going. You remember that day, don't you?'

'Yes, yes, *of course*.'

'She sent me a photograph signed *Your loving sister*. I still have that photo!'

The chorus protested, 'Akka!'

'So that nobody should think anything. I was so scared.'

'After Shanta left, my thoughts were always fixed on Shanta. I used to get some letters from her. My letters were opened and read and I got angry and yelled at Padmasini Teacher! She complained about me to Shankara Menon. He pacified me.'

'All the letters were plain letters. I knew they would be read.'

'My letters were very poetic…'

'Very exciting for me to receive his letters. Father did not know, but Mother knew, though we did not discuss it. When they asked my views on a good proposal they were considering, I cried and ran into another room. Mother followed me. "Why are you crying? Is it because of Dhananjayan?" I shook my head. Mother said: "If you do not tell me how will I know?" Then she talked about real love and infatuation. "Do you think you really love him? He comes from this background where he has a lot of responsibilities and will you be able to deal with that?" I said "Yes!"' Akka paused: 'At that time, in 1963, Kalakshetra was visiting Singapore–Malaysia and I was asked by Rukmini Devi to participate. Mother said, "So when Dhananjayan comes, let your father meet him and we will talk about it." Father agreed.'

'Her father was very strict and stern-looking. I was so scared, but when he talked…very loving and understanding.'

'After my parents knew about it, we were okay about it. Now we could let people know we are in love, we are going to get married.'

'Our close friends knew. While travelling in the night train, they encouraged us to sit together openly, hold hands on the journey between Singapore and Malaysia. Athai was blissfully unaware.'

'At the airport, Athai said to my mother, "Mrs Menon don't worry we will take care of her. There is nothing between them. She will be safe."And my mother laughed to herself. She did not want to say anything...I remained in Malaysia and he returned with the troupe to India. I never doubted his love for me. Honestly, I did not worry about how it will happen. I knew this is the man for me, the man in my life. It all came together beautifully. In 1965, Athai wrote to me saying that I was wasting my time in Malaysia. Then she wrote again saying that the troupe was going to Australia and she wanted me to return to Kalakshetra. In February 1966, we went to Australia. I was asked to perform as Sita. When she invited me, it was as though she knew about *us*.'

'Anyway when we toured Australia, for four months, there we were introduced as engaged to be married.'

'That was later. In the beginning, openly, he would come near me. One day, I was shivering with fever so he gave me his overcoat. Athai was sitting next to me in the bus and she always had sinus problems. The *moment* we reached the hotel she called for me, and lambasted me, "So many of us were feeling cold and why did he bring a coat especially for you?" She did not know about us. Like a child she burst out, "I was running fever, I was also sick and had a cold, and he is not taking care of *me*."'

'Then slowly she realized...something was going on, again they are together. Shanta's mother wrote to her – *Treat them as engaged.* Athai got a shock, but then the issue was taken care of. Then on she would complain to Shanta about me! "He's eating all sorts of things. Tell him not to eat apples and prunes, it will upset his stomach."'

'So, *when* did you get married?' we cried in unison, unable to bear the suspense.

Akka gave us the details we craved for. 'In 1966, my sister and her future husband were coming from London to Bangalore for their wedding, so my parents suggested we also have our wedding at the same time, as we were coming from Malaysia.'

'I did not have any money at that time. I was penniless. As soon as we came back from Australia, in May, I had to rush to Kerala when my sister died in childbirth. My family did not have much money, and we had no time either, so we went to Guruvayur to get married.'

They sang in joyous tandem, '1966 August 24th.'

Newly-weds Dhananjayan and Shanta with Rukmini Devi

'I had no new clothes for my wedding! Everything was done by Shanta's family. They made the ring. What they gave, I wore. Girl also they gave!'

His appreciative audience giggled. He continued, 'A day after Rukmini Devi came back from the US we had a small reception at Kalakshetra. I borrowed 600 rupees from one of my old schoolmates,

C. B. Venkatesh, and returned all his money in instalments. We had a small tea party under the banyan tree, with a vocal concert by Seetharama Sharma.'

Shanta echoed his words. 'Under the banyan tree, we had our wedding reception. Rukmini Devi put her arm around me and said, "You should always be here with me."'

Within fourteen months, Dhananjayan would leave Kalakshetra but that story would be told later, for now the train was sliding into Delhi central station and we were busy lining up our suitcases and stage properties near the open door.

15

The slow fuse lit in 1963, when Dhananjayan was put in charge of the concert section, resulted in an explosion in 1967.

'Before our Australia tour, in the summer of '65, we were asked to do *Usha Parinayam* in the Thiruvananthapuram palace. Nobody was around, as it was summer. Athai asked me, "How will we manage to do this?" I said, "We will get everyone to come back and rehearse and do the show." I sent telegrams to everyone and they came. The programme went off very well. When we got back to Madras, we heard that the musicians like Seetharama Sharma, K. Krishnamurthy had been paid extra but not us. We were not given anything.

'I went to the office and asked Sundari Teacher and she was evasive, "I don't know anything. Ask Shankara Menon." He also gave a vague answer so I went to Athai. She pretended that she did not know anything about it. I said, "We have worked hard, we should also be paid." Finally they sanctioned an amount, much less than what they paid the musicians. We were given a stern warning: *This is the first and last time. It is being given just this time. Don't ask again.* We were given 15 rupees. I told my colleagues, "Do not accept it, it is not right. The musicians were given almost a month's salary whereas we dancers undertook to do it, we slogged, 15 is not enough." Shankara Menon summoned me, "Why are you behaving like a trade unionist?" I did not even know what it meant at the time.'

In 1966, when Kalakshetra was invited to the Adelaide Festival, Dhananjayan was responsible for putting the show together. Rukmini

Devi, in her early sixties by then, had a soft spot for him, and his increased proximity to her was resented by others.

There were certain times when she was upset with Dhananjayan for not having reported minor incidents to her. One of these flared into a skirmish. K. Krishnamurthy, chiefly a mridangam player, had also played another percussion instrument, the *maddalam*, during the dance-drama. He was Dhananjayan's mridangam teacher, and resented being told by his junior to play the *maddalam* for a TV recording as well. He then stopped playing it on stage. After a couple of shows, Paul Storm enquired why there was no *maddalam* accompaniment as rehearsed. Dhananjayan was equally mystified.

While the next show was going on, they saw Krishnamurthy talking to Rukmini Devi, having left his place with the rest of the orchestra. In the interval, Dhananjayan asked Rukmini Devi what the problem was. Usually, no one spoke to Athai on matters such as these, for she was prone to snap, 'Are you the Director or am I?' but Dhananjayan was unafraid.

She replied, 'I believe you had some misunderstanding with him and you offended him.'

Dhananjayan, never able to rein in his tongue, responded, 'Even if I am at fault, you are the director of the Kalakshetra troupe. He should listen to you. We saw you talking to him when he should have been playing. Ask Paul.'

Rukmini Devi got very upset. 'Are you saying I am telling lies?'

'Yes, you are telling a lie.'

When angry she would speak in English. 'Dhananjayan called me a *liar*! He told *me* I'm a liar.' Understandably, she was agitated and her voice rose high. For the rest of the tour, she did not speak to him.

Otherwise, the tour was a great success. On their return to Kalakshetra, Rukmini Devi told the other senior teachers and her family members of this confrontation. No one had ever spoken to her in such a fashion. How *dare* he! It marked the beginning of the end.

The concert section was doing well, and rehearsals, the key to the success of Kalakshetra productions, were intensive. The teaching section resented perhaps the attention and praise commanded by the concert section. They did not like the blunt way in which Dhananjayan spoke to them.

Some took it upon themselves to report to Rukmini Devi every minor clash in the ongoing rehearsals, but Dhananjayan did not want to get the others into further trouble. For instance, the singer Seetharama Sharma did not come every day for the musicians' rehearsals. Or, if asked to repeat certain lines so that Kunhiraman could perfect his part, he would get upset and enquire, 'How many times do I have to keep singing?' He had time constraints as he took classes outside Kalakshetra, while the dancers had all the time to spare.

Athai would question Dhananjayan, 'I heard that in rehearsal today...'

He would evade the issue, 'No, no problems at all, nothing happened.'

'You are not telling me.'

'There is no complaint, we have settled it. I don't want to bring every little thing to your attention.'

'But I should know.'

'Better I take care of it, I will handle it, it is not a problem.'

Out of the blue, Dhananjayan received a memo informing him that he was no longer in charge. Vasanta Teacher, unfamiliar with all aspects of the concert section, took over from him. Dhananjayan continued to help her. From his perspective, the 'boys' were getting fewer chances to perform and were being limited to Kathakali. The 'girls' alone were performing Bharata Natyam. Dhananjayan brought this to Rukmini Devi's notice.

Meanwhile, there was the ever present problem of money. No one seemed to have any money in hand to spend freely. They were earning a princely salary of 150 rupees as Kalakshetra staff but they could not imagine ever performing for anyone else. The teenagers Balagopal and Dhananjayan had grown up; their needs were different.

Dhananjayan, now a married man, had two homes to support. Shanta and he lived in a single room cottage on the Kalakshetra campus.

'Shanta did not know anything about running a house, not even how to boil water. I taught her how to cook!

'We all felt we should ask for more money. In October 1967, I arranged a meeting and we agreed we needed more money, our salary was not enough; we were not able to manage. Kalakshetra was also charging us for our quarters. We decided to write an appeal to Rukmini Amma. Balan, Kunhiraman, Krishnaveni, Kamalarani all of them, they made me bell the cat. Shanta and I were married by then...I represented both of us; she did not sign. So, I wrote down our points – raise our salary, give an ex-gratia per performance, reduce the house rent which was taking almost 50% of our salary – they all signed, and then I took it to Athai. That was a big shock to her, because it was the first time something like this had happened in the history of Kalakshetra. Athai was in her office. I gave her the appeal. "What is this? What is this?"

"Please read it at your leisure and give a reply."'

After a few days, Rukmini Devi replied. She held Dhananjayan responsible for the letter though it was signed by everyone. 'She said, "You were a scholarship holder..." all that old history was dragged out. "Kalakshetra has no money to pay, why have you formed a group trade union against us?" I was really offended but I kept quiet. I was branded as the outspoken troublemaker. "He was always arrogant, this is his latest misdeed." I had no right to speak, as far as *they* were concerned...I was under their protection, a scholarship holder was not supposed to ask for anything. After all they had taught us everything, looked after us so many years...Until then, no matter what they felt, everyone kept quiet in Kalakshetra, even Shanta, no one ever voiced their thoughts frankly.'

I held my breath as Dhananjayan narrated what happened next. Scared that I might irritate him with some thoughtless question, I remained silent.

'Rukmini Devi and Shankara Menon asked each one of the dancers and musicians to meet them. When face to face with Athai, they quailed. No one had the guts to go ahead with it. They backed down,

"We have no demands. We did not do anything, he did everything." But they had signed. "*He* asked us to sign; we did not know what he had written." Now the entire blame was on me. I was pulled up by Athai, very sternly, "Why are you doing this, making a group? You are from Kerala and have communist blood, that is why." "It is everybody's demand, Athai, they have all signed," I replied. "I have two families to look after, one in Payyanur and now here." "No, everyone I talked to swore they had no demands, only you." Then she changed her tone of voice, spoke persuasively, "You are a very good artiste, you've been like my right hand." She paid me lots of compliments: "Don't tell anyone but I will give you extra money. I will give you 100 rupees extra." I was put off, "No, everyone should be given, I cannot accept it." "I cannot afford to pay everyone," stated Athai.

'Actually, I found out later that some people were already being given extra money, that is why they were quiet. Or maybe she had made them the same offer she had made me, so they backed off. When I said "No" on just grounds, it aggravated her, she said, "What will you do?" I said, "If everyone is happy with their pay, I will go." *I will go*. Just came out of my mouth, "I will leave Kalakshetra and find work." That was another shock to her. She did not really expect me to go. In the past, so many times she had said that after her I would look after Kalakshetra, and take it forward. That too was a cause for jealousy, as some of the teachers did not like Athai saying this publicly, while introducing me to visitors. My friends would make fun of me, "Oh, Athai said you are going to be the next *director*?" All those memories were flashing in my mind as Athai replied, "If you are going, then you should give me three months notice."

'I stuck to my position. I had already passed the BA exam by correspondence and I thought I would get a job outside. "Yes, I will give you three months notice."

'Immediately she demanded, "Then you must teach all your portions to the others. All that you know you must teach them."

'I was forced to give the notice and spent three months working, without pay, teaching Janardhanan and Balagopal all that I knew, mainly the part of Rama in the Ramayanam series and Usha Parinayam.'

Dhananjayan recounted without rancour the exchange of words that rocked his world and changed the course of his life, but clearly it was burnt deep into his memory.

The couple continued to live in the staff cottage on campus. Dhananjayan now had to brave the world outside the cocoon that was Kalakshetra. He got a job at TTK & Co., at a salary of Rs 300 a month, double what he was earning at Kalakshetra. Rukmini Devi uniformly increased everyone's salary by Rs 50. His fellow artistes thanked Dhananjayan, who reacted sardonically, 'You ditched me and *all* of you benefited, except me!'

Shanta, who had trained many students in the three years she was in Malaysia, and had left it all to return to Kalakshetra and Dhananjayan, was struck by the irony of it all. 'See what happens. He leaves first and I am still there in Kalakshetra. He never persuaded me to leave. "You stay," he said. I had the lead role in *Shakuntalam*, the dance-drama Athai was still choreographing then. One day, Athai called out to me...she was in her car, and she made me sit beside her on the back seat. No one could see us. "How come he let you stay? Good. At least some good sense prevailed in him."'

Soon, Shanta too would follow her husband out through the gates of Kalakshetra.

16

One of the chief features of the devadasi's preparation for her role in the temple rituals was her training in music. It was this musicality that was expressed through dance. Her ensemble of musicians, led by the *nattuvanar*, had a singular, developed approach to music, and she herself saw no division between the terms singer and dancer. They were synonymous. To dance meant *really* knowing how to *sing* the song.

This is best exemplified in the life of Balasaraswati, granddaughter of the famous *vainika* and musician, Dhanammal. Her mother Jayammal who sang for her concerts, and her brothers – part of the group of accompanying musicians – were all highly skilled musicians in their own right. When she danced, she was making visible the lyrical flow of musical wealth in her family, wearing the garment of mellifluous notes. She is the only dancer honoured with the prestigious title of 'Sangeeta Kalanidhi' by the Music Academy in Chennai.

When *sadir* was renamed Bharata Natyam and disseminated to anyone who had an interest in learning the art-form, one of the features that could not be replicated was this hereditary background, with its immersion in music and its keen appreciation of how music was to be used as a setting in which the gem of dance shone.

Sir had always insisted that we learn vocal music and had arranged for classes at BK. Here, I was to learn my first lesson, albeit of a different kind than my classmates. When the teacher asked us to sing sa-re-ga-ma, 'This is easy,' I said to myself and belted out what I knew. The teacher listened carefully and then said, 'No, we sing it differently.' I discovered later that I had learnt the notes in the Hindustani style, whereas here we were learning the time honoured beginner's scales of Carnatic music set in the raga Mayamalavagowla.

While learning Bharata Natyam, since my gurus sang as they taught, and provided the rhythm, it was possible in the early stages to dance without having any prior exposure to ragas.

It was when I was asked to teach a junior, as my gurus were out of town, that all the gaps in my knowledge were revealed. Seated on the floor, facing the student, *thattu kazhi* in hand, the first requirement was to *sing*, not so much my knowledge of dance. And to sing meant to deliver the emotion required for the dancer to emote, it meant meaning-laden variations, it meant sticking to the amorphous shape of the raga. Outside, I was learning the basic series of notes with my music teacher, but in BK I had to deliver a capsule of musical knowledge that was not mine yet. I taught, hampered by my clearly perceived inadequacy. It took a long time before I could sing with some confidence. As for the complex system of *Carnatic talas*, it was an ignominious struggle.

Periodically, as we ventured into rhythms and cross-rhythms, Sir would ask us to stand still. 'Call out the percussion syllables, can you do it to *talam*?' he'd test us. Simultaneously clapping the *tala* or coded rhythm cycle, we had to enunciate the dialect of the mridangam. *ta-ding-gina-thom, taka-ta-ding-gina-thom, taka-dhiku-ta-ding-gina-thom…Clap, finger, finger, finger, clap, flip, clap, flip*: the hand continued doggedly marking the eight-beat while we called out cross-rhythms. On the last beat, the last spoken syllable, we arrived in sync.

Whenever Sir would ask us to demonstrate our grip, or lack of, over rhythm and pace, he did it by rotation. One student would call it out loud and the next one would start. It was nervewracking, watching the number of people ahead of me diminish.

Suddenly it would be my turn.

I usually messed it up, having heard both the right and the wrong demonstrations, all of them jostling in my head.

Some rhythm patterns were easy to call out, some complicated, I found all of them challenging. Where my feet sailed over the most devious of cross-rhythm traps, my tongue tripped, fumbled, and played tricks. Saying the syllables out aloud was not a problem, neither was maintaining the beat, but to do the two together was akin to jugglery for me.

Once class was over, it would remain stuck in my mind. The next day, at odd moments, I'd try to get it right. Going over and over this irritant as it were sometimes yielded a beautiful pearl of synchronization, but alas, at those times Sir was not around to witness the miracle!

In the current system of training, it has become possible for many children to learn the art, the dance alone, as something separate from music. Dance to them, or to those who teach them, is the complex system of Bharata Natyam movements set to various ragas, rather than an organic expression of a fine philosophy of music.

Among the many things lost when the devadasi system was dismantled, was the milieu of individual training, an ambience, a closed culture which nurtured an inherent understanding of musical phrases suitable for dance.

The dance flowing with the music, each aiming towards the expression of the same thing, they created something larger in the process – *sangeetam*, a confluence of song, instruments and dance.

17

All of a sudden, the air crackled with rumours of Dhananjayan ill-treating Shanta. *Arrogant, bad, ungrateful, money-minded, one already knew all those things about him, but do you know the latest? He is harassing her as well. No one can talk sense into him, he argues about everything. So brash. She's a nice girl...tch tch...so unhappy now with him. Shouldn't have married him.*

None of their close friends believed any of this. The first person who actually acted on the rumours was Rukmini Devi's brother, Yegneshwara Shastri, who asked Dhananjayan, out of concern, if there was any truth to what he had heard. The next one to ask was her sister Dr. Sivakamu Amma. Clearly, someone in Rukmini Devi's close circle was spreading this canard.

By now, Dhananjayan and Shanta were expecting their first child. She was hurt by the rumours but he felt they ought to ignore them. Soon, several people, including her teachers, began to enquire about her welfare. When Shankara Menon asked, 'Are you happy, my dear child?' Shanta began to wonder. The couple realized there could be only one source, a thought too shocking to entertain.

The rumours spread outside Kalakshetra.

One day, Kunhiraman reported a recent conversation with Athai. She had talked about the demands made by Dhananjayan and his resignation. It was a big shock to her, after all that she had done for him. 'Please look after Shanta, she is a nice girl, she is suffering under him,' was the request she made of Kunhiraman.

Hearing this upset Shanta a great deal. 'Why are people saying all this and now even Kunhiraman has heard it, you *must* go and ask Athai. Enough is enough.' Seeing Shanta in a rare state of anger, Dhananjayan told her it might be better if she went. He had already left Kalakshetra and did not fancy another confrontation with Rukmini Devi. But Shanta insisted.

The rehearsals for *Shakuntalam* and the art festival were in full swing. Shanta had the lead role in the dance drama. Dhananjayan, once the hero Rama, had speedily been demoted to the relatively minor role of the fisherman in *Shakuntalam*. He approached Rukmini Devi during a break. Having tea with Shankara Menon at that time, she was affable, '*Enna pa*, what is it? Come, come.'

Dhananjayan spoke quietly but firmly, 'This is a very serious matter. You are like my mother. I have been hearing this rumour for a long time now and it is not true. Please do not tell people such things. If I am wrong in my behaviour, correct me. You have every right to advise me but please do not spread these rumours.'

Rukmini Devi frowned, 'No, no. I did not say such things, you are unnecessarily blaming me.'

'Kunhiraman Sir told me. Yesterday evening you told him this.'

Taken by surprise, she declared, 'He is lying.'

'It is not him lying. It is *you* who are lying.'

'I am not lying. I am a great person, you cannot accuse me of lying.' She spoke in English now.

'If you are great you should behave like a great person,' replied Dhananjayan in English. 'If you like I can bring Kunhiraman Sir.'

Rukmini Devi did not favour the idea but Dhananjayan insisted. 'If he says that you did not say anything, I will apologize to you.'

Dhananjayan marshalled a recalcitrant Kunhiraman – 'No no. Please don't take me to Rukmini Devi' – and produced him triumphantly as witness. In her commanding presence Kunhiraman was reduced to silence. When she questioned him, 'What is this, Kunhiraman, are you carrying tales behind my back?' Kunhiraman, caught between loyalty to a friend and tremendous awe, reverence and respect for his benefactor, remained silent.

She turned to Dhananjayan, 'I gave you loin cloth, slippers and now you are telling me I am a liar?'

They began to argue and Dhananjayan raised his voice in frustration and anger. Shankara Menon, whose primary role was to protect Athai, stepped in, 'Don't shout! You…*get out.*'

Instantly, as though cold water had been poured on his head, Dhananjayan calmed down. 'Yes Sir, I am getting out,' his hands folded in a namaste, he returned home to the cottage.

The next morning when Dhananjayan was dressing for rehearsal, tying the final knot around his veshti, an office-peon arrived with a note from Sundari Teacher enquiring whether or not he would be present at the rehearsal. 'Sometimes I think I was a fool. So naïve, so dedicated to Kalakshetra. I was ready to leave for the rehearsal and along came this note. What was the need for a note? That really upset me. It never occurred to me to *not* attend rehearsals. I told Shanta, "*Because* they have asked me, I am not going." I boycotted the *Shakuntalam* rehearsals from that day on, so they had to find a substitute for the fisherman.

'Even though Shanta was playing the lead role, she was not given any complimentary tickets. On the first day of the show, I bought a ticket, 10 rupees was a lot of money, for a front seat and Shanta's mother also bought one. It was houseful and when a distinguished person came, I got up and gave my seat. I stood at the back. One of the teachers posted as an usher came up and asked, "Why are you standing?" "I gave my seat to someone." She was embarassed, "Athai asked me to find out if you have bought a ticket." I gave her the ticket, "Go show it to Athai. As if it were my own home, I have given the guest my place." Later I told Shanta about the incident. We decided that we would move out of the campus.'

18

Periodically, Sir and Akka would disappear on a performance tour and leave us in the charge of a substitute teacher, a short wiry young man who took us through our paces valiantly. Like monkeys let out of a cage, we behaved atrociously with him. Water drinking and *nada* tying became rampant; worse, we took all sorts of liberties with our *adavus*.

Swinging hips, bending legs when they should be straight, dropping elbows, keeping the entire body slack instead of taut and poised, we refused to cooperate with him. It was bad enough our beloved gurus had left us, how could they expect us to adjust to someone else taking their place? We would take giant strides while dancing to end up close to him; with no further space ahead we had the perfect excuse to stop. We delighted in his plea, 'Go to back! Go to back!'

We were happy when our gurus returned, both gifted in their ability to teach. There was something about the way Sir taught that imbedded itself in the mind and the heart. Mostly, through painstaking repetition, he laid our foundations right. His hands opening out into a beautiful flower, he could make us smell its fragrance with the power of his expression. The beauty of the flower was the sum of many individual movements, fingers fluttering open in a blossom, the eyebrows rising and falling rapidly, neck extending both sides in a gentle *attami*, and a smile pushing into his cheeks.

He loved depicting animals. The elephant, the tiger, a peacock, the pregnant deer in his signature Kathakali piece, Ganesha discovering he had an elephant's head when he regained consciousness, all of them came alive in front of our eyes. 'You should observe animals, the way they move,' he'd advise us. 'I have observed all of them closely, that's why I am able to do this.' As for us, he thought we did monkeys rather well, and cast us as Rama's army of monkeys building the bridge to Lanka!

Distance was another concept that he wanted reflected in our eyes. 'Look beyond you, behind me, through the wall, all the way to the Bay of Bengal. Standing there, you should be able to make me feel that you are looking kilometres away.' I would try, but my gaze hit the wall and rebounded.

When Vishnu and Brahma challenge each other to find the beginning and end of the fiery lingam that is Shiva, one flies up up up into the skies, and the other digs down down down into the netherworld. Just looking up or down, he wanted those skies and the netherworld to appear in our eyes. Easier understood than done!

'Hold your *mudra* properly!' was a frequent admonition. Meaning was conveyed through *mudras*, the words of the song, facial expression and the body language. If the main vehicle, the *mudra*, were not held properly, then everything else was secondary. To say that in the rush of expression, overcome by feeling, one held a *mudra* slackly was no excuse at all.

Similiarly, the foot established a certain equation with the ground. 'Strike your foot, don't wipe the floor with it!'

In any class, his refrain was 'Sit more' referring to the *araimandi*. This was a must; an *adavu* implied *araimandi*. To do them 'standing' was of no account. On a good day, for him, he would make us freeze in a position, and woe betide anyone who broke out of it. Or he would mock our feeble attempts at *kulukki nadai* and tell us the story of the 'mirror' cottage.

When he told us stories of the time he was a student, he was already grander and more polished in our imaginations than a student our equal. We were in awe of him for having dared to dance in front of his guru Rukmini Devi, and proud that he had done it so well.

It is not always that a great performing artiste is a great teacher. I remember being constantly proud as a child that I was his student. Girls at school who studied from female gurus would sigh and say, 'You learn from Dhananjayan Master? So*ooo* lucky you are man!' And so one day, when my father introduced me to Rukmini Devi, I felt the same pride welling as I told her that I learnt dance. She bent down kindly and enquired from whom. I stated proudly, 'From the Dhananjayans.' I did not understand then why her smile froze.

When I think of how tedious it can be to transform raw clumsy potential into graceful dance, I marvel at the energy he poured into us. Due to the long time required to ripen into a Bharata Natyam dancer, it is a paradox that at the young age at which one joins, the guru cannot possibly predict whether one will continue to dance or not. In the face of that uncertainty, it seems to me an act of ultimate generosity to invest so much of oneself in teaching a little child. All the more reason for Rukmini Devi to have taken it to heart when Dhananjayan and Shanta left Kalakshetra.

Equally, it is a matter of great luck to get the right guru. By the time one commits with an adult understanding to one's love of the art, it is usually too late to repair a poor foundation.

19

Just how much luck is required to get a good guru was made even more apparent to me when I met Charles Ma at the 2011 Natya Kala Conference in Madras.

'In Bangalore, there are no good gurus,' stated Charles categorically when I spoke to him. 'Everything's in bits and pieces in Bangalore. They'll take a *ta hata jham tari ta* from this style, *tat tai ta ha* from another.' Born and brought up in Bangalore, Charles used to party like crazy. 'I was a rogue. I'd do drugs, smoke and drink, party until 2 in the morning! My parents were very cool.'

Charles offered these details as a way of saying he was not the typical Bharata Natyam dancer. In that construct, Bharata Natyam tends to be associated with a conservative, middle-class Tamilian morality, where the pleasures of smoking and drinking are by default 'guilty', to be indulged in on the sly. Some even argue that Bharata Natyam is monopolized by Tamil Brahmins.

Twenty-eight year old Charles is of Naga-Assamese blood on his mother's side – 'I cannot trace their lineage', and Nepali-Chinese on his father's side – 'My grandmother is Nepalese and grandfather ethnic Chinese'. To this he adds the south Indian influence, having been born and brought up in Bangalore.

I wondered how the pub-hopping, brazenly outspoken boy with slanted eyes became a dancer. Charles read my mind: 'Jiving at parties I used to dance from the inside. Cool people, older women, college girls would flirt with me, I'd be kicked about it.' While studying Mass

Communications at Christ College, Charles decided to participate in college culturals. 'I was doing filmy stuff. I saw some seniors doing contemporary dance. I wanted to join them. They snubbed me. It made my blood boil. I am *very* competitive.' He began to learn Bharata Natyam in 2002.

Charles Ma

That decision was to cause an upheaval in his life – ('I was 18, what did I know? Parents were not south Indians. It wasn't my culture') – bring him to deep despair at times – ('I would cry') – as well as propel him into the exhilarating discovery that, 'Intrinsically I was an artist.'

Charles had an aversion to the men he had watched performing in the classical style. 'I thought *Oh oh, they're effeminate boys, O god, looks like a girl, look at him sit*...It's true, 96% of them are gay or effeminate or hidden gay.' He decided that he would 'dance like a man' or not at all.

When his teacher Vidya Shimladka left Bangalore Charles was at a crossroads. It did not help when a 'friend' made a thoughtless remark:

'*Tchaiyy*, you ehn? Look at your chinky eyes! Bharata Natyam dancers have big big eyes!'

Charles went into a tizzy. 'That twisted me, so I went into Odissi. I went to Nrityagram in 2004. While doing the *tribhangi*, they said I look spastic. I practised it so many times, I got frustrated. Then I realized I was born to do Bharata Natyam.'

After these hits and misses, Charles joined Poornima Ashok who runs the dance school Nrityanjali. He loved what he learnt but 'my mind and heart were fighting. I am a soft-featured oriental boy. I'd worry, *Damn am I looking effeminate?* I'd fret over colours, *No no change this colour*. A male dancer will be careful not to wear certain colours. I looked white as a ghost when I wore makeup.'

At the same time in college, his '*hatta katta*' footballer friends would appreciate his efforts; they said he was 'dancing like a man'. His sensitivity about the issue proved to be a pressure point: 'One day, for a performance Poornima Ma'am wanted me to wear pink lipstick and her daughter's *jhumkas* to dance. "If I am going to look like a woman on stage, I don't want to dance," I said. I left and went guru hopping. I do weird things, the spirit is very free. Silly things.'

He found a teacher, who promised an *arangetram* within a year, if he paid her one lakh rupees. To Charles's shock and dismay, the one lakh did not buy him the right teaching. 'My *arangetram jatis* were off the *tala* framework. At the rehearsal the mridangist told her so. The violinist was teaching the vocalist just before the show how to sing the Revati *tillana*. I knew things were wrong as I was doing it. I could not hear the music. The stage was messy, I slipped twice. I was a laughing stock.'

The *arangetram* really announces to the world that a dancer has completed his period of study and is now ready to present his art to the world. It is real, it is critical. It marks the transition when the hidden obsessive training is now taken into the public domain.

The dancer Lakshmi Vishwanathan made the useful distinction, in a private conversation, between Gurus, a vanishing breed of the stature of Ramiah Pillai or Meenakshisundaram Pillai, and teachers, lesser mortals who transfer what they have learnt but don't have the artistic capital to do much more.

When a dancer begins learning, he relies completely on his teacher's wisdom, and reputation. He is not in any position to assess what he is being taught for accuracy and authenticity. Therefore, when the teacher is incompetent, or sub-par, it is a betrayal of sorts.

The *arangetram* in 2008 did not just cost a lakh. Charles spent 30,000 hiring Chowdiah Hall and another lakh on his blue and white costumes, jewellery and other expenses. His parents struggled to fund half the *arangetram*, and Charles earned enough with his choreographic work to make up the rest. Sadly, it was a wasted expenditure.

'It was a *big* flop. People say you should not talk about your guru like that. She no longer talks to me. People said "His career is finished." They said I had no *tala* knowledge, when it wasn't of my doing.'

There is something that is both refreshing and disarming in Charles's candour. Not many dancers would admit to a failed performance. What did he feel at the time? 'My parents didn't know. Everybody said "fantastic" to them…"A few *tala* slip-ups but he will improve." *I* felt let down by my guru. There's a burning, and you work so hard, so I felt bad.'

In the small community of dance, no matter what the circumstances are, to openly badmouth one's guru, as Charles had, is simply not done. It would make both musicians and other gurus wary of working with him.

'People don't like me in Bangalore. I went from guru to guru.' Already Charles had been vacillating between wanting to dance and the steady money that an office job provides. 'Then the roadblocks came. Gurus bitching about me. Musicians not talking to me. Musicians bitch about other dancers all the time: "What a pathetic dancer." I am sure they bitched about me.'

Charles continued to practise, alone, for hours. He realized he had to continue learning in order to become a dancer. 'For me it's a burning. I have to do it. It was an addiction. It was not the fame. Now what to do? I went to Poornima Ashok and said, "I want to learn properly from you from the beginning." But I also told her, "No *jhumkas*," so now she does not interfere with my makeup at all.'

In the traditional way of Guru–sishya training, when the guru is worthy of the name, the item taught is received as a gift. Its choice, appropriateness to one's level of skill, the way it is 'set' within the music – these are all the prerogative of the guru. It is an outward flow of grace that reaches the student with the many nuances and intricacies that are part of the lineage of the style. A student might have many doubts, which are answered, but will hesitate to question the actual structure of what is being taught.

Charles had no such hesitations. 'We Bangaloreans are intelligent and sharp. We ask questions. Why is the Kalakshetra style like that? Why do you hold your hand like that? I'm observing everything and swallowing it...what suits my body, what doesn't. I was unlucky with gurus but I have been with so many I now know what is good and bad and what suits my body. I am short, so the Vazhuvoor style is good for me.' Finally, teacher and taught were able to arrive at an understanding.

Charles practised hard, retracing all that he had learnt. He set off to Madras to participate in the dance competition at IIT Saarang. 'There were fifty dancers and one effeminate boy in jazzy tissue. I wore a simple costume. I was shivering...*I'm not going to make it.* I hit stage and I knew I performed well. I won the first prize! It was a walkover! I beat a famous dancer's daughter, Dhananjayan's student, I beat them all!'

Charles' thirst for learning finally brought him to Chennai, for master classes with acclaimed dancer Priyadarshini Govind. 'To date, Priyadarshini has been my biggest influence. I don't imitate anyone. It is *my* journey, and the goal was always to make it mine.'

At the end of a ten-year journey in the world of dance, he has this wisdom to offer: 'For any male dancer who says "I will live on passion and fresh air." You damn well can't do that. You need luck.'

20

Dhananjayan and Shanta, expecting their first child, vacated their staff cottage at Kalakshetra. They took a small house on hire in Shastri Nagar still within the umbilical radius of their alma mater. Shanta's grandmother furnished Shanta's marital home with basic furniture. Now, her parents moved in with them to help with the baby.

If Shanta's parents had any doubts about their son-in-law, it was related to his finances; would he be able to support both his family back in Payyanur *and* the one he was beginning with Shanta? Recently, his sister had died leaving five children who had to be looked after.

'If we got 100 rupees, about 70 would go home and I would get 20 for housekeeping. I did not ask for luxury, I was prepared for that. Just a decent lifestyle. When I became pregnant, he constantly felt the need to earn more,' recalled Shanta.

'As far as my immediate family was concerned, no one had any problem with him being a dancer. My sister liked him a lot, admired him as Rama. Outside, there was a stigma. Automatically people think if a man learns dance he is effeminate. A student's mother nudged me and whispered, "Male dancers...they are a little *odd*, aren't they? How is he?"'

When Sanjay was born in 1968, Rukmini Devi was the first person Dhananjayan informed. 'We wanted her to come home and bless the child. She came with Shankara Menon but did not talk to me, only to Shanta and her mother. She liked the payasam at the feast so Shanta's mother sent some home with her. I took some pictures of her holding the baby, but when they were developed there was not a single proper picture of her with Sanjay!'

Far from the natural beauty of the forested enclosure that was Kalakshetra, Dhananjayan now encountered the crowded urban landscape of Madras – the metropolis as imagined by the villagers he had left behind in Payyanur. Dhananjayan would leave early in the morning, walking about 4 kilometres to Adyar to take bus No 5. It took him about 10 kilometres away, to the commercial hub in Parry's. 'I learnt a lot about business, correspondence. I worked directly under the Chairman, T.T. Narasimhan. I had learnt typing in the Kalakshetra office, so now it improved. He would dictate, a colleague took it down in shorthand, and I typed it up.

'In the corporate set-up, I was able to understand how the world of commerce worked...administration, dealing with the bank, how to make documents, exports, typing, paperwork, later I was involved in the marketing of some new toothpaste, so I learnt all that. It gave me another type of exposure and work and maybe I would have done well there if I had stayed long enough. All my colleagues, they knew I danced, they knew the whole story.'

He would take the bus back from his office in Parry's, to teach Bharata Natyam from evening till night. The open roof of the small house was converted into a classroom with the help of coconut thatching. This school was called Bharata Kalanjali. Katherine, an American who later married Kunhiraman, had studied at Kalakshetra and wanting to learn more, came to Dhananjayan. She stayed with the couple in their new home as a paying guest, bringing in additional income.

Shanta was still teaching in Kalakshetra. Shanta recalls, 'If Sir were late from his job, I would take class for Katharine 'Keki'. Once Athai reprimanded me: "You work in Kalakshetra. How can you take class outside?" "I am only part time in Kalakshetra, I am helping my husband, at home," I replied.'

In 1969, Asan Chandu Panikker passed away. While he had seen Dhananjayan do exceedingly well as Rama in the Kalakshetra productions, he did not live to see the heights his protégé achieved. 'We went to his house in Payyanur, to see him when he was sick. Both my father and guru did not live to see my success – that came in the seventies. That is my life's main regret.'

21

In 1970 the famous Swiss choreographer Maurice Bejart invited Dhananjayan to dance in Belgium. He had to ask for leave at TTK, which was not granted at first. 'Somehow I managed to get leave. I needed a visa and RBI clearance, a very difficult task. I tried getting it done in Madras but could not, so I had to go all the way to Bombay. They gave me a big send off, with garlands and everything. It was the first time I was going abroad as Dhananjayan the dancer, not as part of the Kalakshetra troupe. If I got the visa, I would leave the country from Bombay. On reaching Bombay, I had a very rough time. I went from pillar to post, but was not able to get the visa and so I had to return to Madras.

'After I had been at TTK & Co. for a while, some retrenchment happened. T.T. Vasu, the Chairman's brother, was quite a personality. At the time, dramatist Cho Ramasamy worked there too, as did P.N. Kumar, who acted in Cho's drama company, and he demeaned us three with this derogatory label "Koothadi." So…he wanted to relieve us first of our jobs.

'It was actually a blessing in disguise, because when he said "Go" I took it coolly. By then I had already established contact with hotels, tourism department, and was giving short programmes, lecture demonstrations for tourists with Kalakshetra artists who had graduated. Now, I plunged full-time into dance.'

The number of students at BK was increasing, many of them 'foreign students' who had finished the one or two year course at

Kalakshetra and wanted to learn more. The couple got busy with teaching. Money trickled in. Then came a lucrative offer.

Mr Pathar, a juggler in a circus, had watched a group performance the Dhananjayans had put together, and approached them. He wanted to present a dance show in the intervals, between acts. He offered them a tour lasting six months, travelling around the world with his circus, and good money.

Wanting to share this piece of good fortune, Dhananjayan sounded out his friends at Kalakshetra. Some wanted to leave, others wanted to supplement their income. 'So they secretly collaborated with me.'

Earlier, when he was still at Kalakshetra, when the Indo-Pak war broke out, Dhananjayan had wanted to collect money for the jawans. There were many students at Kalakshetra from different parts of India, and Dhananjayan had the brilliant idea of getting each of them to contribute a folk dance from their respective states. Until then, the folk dances presented by Kalakshetra veered towards the classical, but Dhananjayan had put together a programme of typical folk dances – Kashmir to Kanyakumari – with the rudimentary steps and unique movements used by villagers. The fund-raiser had been a hit, and he handed over Rs 5000 to the jawan's fund.

'I used lots of different instruments. Until then, only the mridangam was used in Kalakshetra for folk dances. It caused a stir in Kalakshetra: "He's using the *tabla!*" Rukmini Devi also came to watch.

Dhananjayan had an idea that the folk dances with their colour and energy would make for an ideal presentation. He decided that it would be called '*Aikya Bharatham*', based on a line from poet-patriot Subramania Bharathi's poem on Indian unity. However, dream all he might, there was a harsh reality to be faced.

'We had no costumes and no money to make them! A Mr Khan, Pathar's friend, gave us the money to buy fabric for costumes. We made them at home, at a minimal cost. Shanta's mother stitched through the night. Shanta and our teacher Pushpa Akka went shopping for the jewellery, beads, bangles. Some bellmetal necklaces and hip-chains for the *garba* and *raas*, we got through friends from Chandni Chowk in Delhi. Kunhiraman Sir was an ace at hand-crafting and painting and everything he did was perfect. He made feathers for the Naga costumes, painted beads and bells the right colour...This was the Kalakshetra training! We were so excited, we practised very hard and there were rumours we might even perform at the White House! We were ready, the costumes were ready and our passports had been sent for the visas.

'Somehow, Kalakshetra got to know something is brewing, that dancers were sneaking out and performing to earn some extra money. All the artistes were called back, they were scolded, and overnight they withdrew from the troupe. They ditched me! It was a very big shock, not only for me but for the organizers. It was an international tour. There was no time to find other dancers and train them, we had to cancel the whole thing.'

Mr Pathar and Mr Khan were businessmen first; they salvaged their loss. 'They took the costumes away. Of course, they had paid for them, but the labour was ours. *It was devastating.*'

As it turned out, all of Dhananjayan's hard work did not go waste. In fact, it seemed like a run-up for a much better opportunity.

'Soon after, we got an invitation from Malaysia Singapore Airlines to tour South East Asia. Operating between Chennai and Malaysia–Singapore, they wanted to have a cultural exchange as part of publicity.'

Again, Dhananjayan had to find dancers. This time he chose those who had already graduated from Kalakshetra. Pushpa Shankar, Gayathri, Ambika Buch, Adyar Lakshman, Mythili Raghavan, Narasimhachari and Vasantalakshmi. Still, he was back to square one when it came to a crucial component.

'*We had no costumes!* I had no money to make all of them again. So I went to Mr Pathar and Mr Khan and literally begged them for the costumes, because they had no use for them. They said, "You have to pay Rs 10,000 for them." For me, to get such a large sum on loan was very difficult. I could not borrow, nor pay. We had no savings.

'Shanta's father was very strict in money matters. He gave me a loan, but on the condition that I repaid him after the tour. I also pledged whatever jewellery Shanta had and gave the bundle of currency adding up to 10,000 to Pathar. We had our costumes and we did the programme.

'It was a very *big* success. First we had a big show here with a Malaysian troupe and then we travelled all over Malaysia and Singapore and Borneo. We earned enough money to pay the artists, repay the loan and have some left in hand. It was the first time we made some good money.'

Shanta was still part of Kalakshetra. News of their performances must have reached Rukmini Devi. It led to the final cut of the umbilical cord.

'I had to leave because Athai said, "I heard you are dancing with Dhananjayan? You cannot do that." He was my husband, my partner, and she called him "Dhananjayan" as though he were some stranger. The real problem was that Rukmini Devi was easily swayed by other's opinions. She loved to be praised and Master was the one person who told her things as he saw it. He was the only one to cross swords with her so it sometimes seemed as though he were talking back. Some of the teachers there found it very easy to praise her and colour her opinion of him, they felt threatened by him perhaps. He was a big part of Kalakshetra at that time, a pillar you could say.

'By then, he and I were giving small shows outside. We needed musicians and Adyar Lakshman Sir helped us a lot. He had a complete music unit, with his sister Nagamani who sang and his brother Gopi playing the mridangam.

'Athai did not like me performing Kalakshetra items outside. But that was *all* I knew! It was not as though others who had graduated did not perform the same items...but in my case, she directed her anger and frustration and regret that things had turned out this way with Master. So she said disapprovingly to me, "How can you perform these items outside? Then will you also perform Mysore Vasudevachar's Ramayana? When you perform, who sings for you?

'I was already in tears by now. I could feel them falling as I replied, "Adyar Lakshman Sir."

'"No, you can't do that. If at all you arrange your own programmes, the musicians have to be from Kalakshetra."

'How could that be? It was eating me up. I told Dhananjayan it is better for me to quit. Our school was growing slowly. What I earned was nothing much, just the satisfaction of being there and teaching. One fine day, I wrote a resignation letter, and that was that.'

Dhananjayan's father, Rama Poduval, passed away in 1970. His chief regret in life is that before he could help him in any substantial way his father passed away. 'I think he knew that things will work out well. I wish he was alive when we had accumulated some money but he died.'

22

Teenagers now, we were elevated to performing a series of folk dances from across India, with pairs of 'boys' and 'girls'. The 'boys' on a given day might include Sir, his younger brother Mohan, our substitute teacher Janardhanan or the Kathakali artiste, Krishnan, all grown men. In stage shorthand, they still were 'boys' or male, paired with their female 'girls' partner.

The 'variety' show was called *Aikya Bharatham* and depending on the length of time available, we presented folk dances from Orissa, Assam, Nagaland, Punjab, Gujarat, and Tamil Nadu. It was immensely exciting because now we were dancing alongside our seniors. In the traditional system of training, there is a hierarchy established by the length of time one has learnt. They were the batch who had joined before us, and I, an only child, finally understood what felt like to kowtow to elder siblings who were always ahead, no matter what. How could one beat their stories, such as the one about Shobana falling asleep as a little girl on Sir's lap and he carrying her home after class, or the fact that Sumati was their First Student? They were the chosen!

Being part of the BK troupe gave me a solid foundation of stage and greenroom experience. Here was a safe (relatively, there was always the post-performance rap sheet called out by Sir) way to perform on stage – folk dances by their very nature being less formal – and garner the experience that would enhance my Bharata Natyam debut.

Aikya Bharatham was in great demand at conferences, presentations for tourists and at weddings. For us teenagers, to be chosen by Sir alone was a great honour. Additionally, it promised an evening of great excitement, a 'show', and the venue of a five-star hotel, usually the Taj or the Connemara just added to the sheen.

The Taj at Fisherman's Cove usually gave us two cottages in which to change. We gave so many shows there, on the open air stage that we began to think of those cottages as our own.

Elsewhere, since we required a greenroom with mirrors, usually the Bharata Kalanjali troupe commandeered the restrooms nearest the conference hall. These were often side by side which ensured easy access.

Too easy at times, such as once at the Taj Coromandel when Richard Frasca dashed into the 'girls' bathroom in nothing but his underwear, clutching both ends of his lungi wide open, pleading with Akka to help him tie it. The girls screamed at this assault to their virginal eyes and Richard seemed dazed by this reaction!

While we were doing our makeup, Akka would recall some hilarious experiences...On the tour of Australia, Paul Storm, the Kalakshetra stage manager, disregarded the elaborate code of knocks they had set up for entry to the dressing rooms. He would repeatedly burst into the girls' dressing room saying 'May I komm in?' and enjoy the sight of mortified girls in various stages of undress.

For an *Aikya Bharatham* show, there was an assembly-line precision to the preparation backstage. The costumes had to be laid out in the order of presentation, and since Indian women love jewellery and all the different states have their own distinctive pieces, special care had to be taken with the accoutrements. For the men, this included the false beards they would need for the bhangra.

Akka, punctilious and exact when packing the costumes, once forgot the beards. Fisherman's Cove was a forty minute drive away, and in those days the bumpy roads often made it longer. There was no question of returning for them. The tiny fishing hamlet nearby would certainly not stock false beards. You could not do a bhangra with turbans and no beard; the men would not look like Sardarjis! It was a catastrophe on a major scale! What to do?

Even as Sir steamed in the background, Akka used a long three-strand switch of synthetic hair to make three individual slings of hair, wrapped a hair net around each and voila! It was long enough to give the men their false moustache as well. No MBA, as I was to learn in Business school, can teach one disaster management as effectively as the performing arts.

As soon as we reached the venue, we were each to do our own makeup. The eyes were the most difficult to do, and took me the longest. I would draw one eye well, but would fail in trying to draw the other eye symmetrically. The tail would be at a different angle, the line thicker, and I would have to wipe it off and start again. Sometimes if I got very late, Akka would seize the eyebrow pencil and in seconds give me beautiful matching eyes. She also gave me a tip: draw the left eye first, the right is always easier to do.

Akka was unflappable backstage. Turning into a goddess with many heads and a hundred arms, she would do one girl's eyes, supervise the hairdo of another, tweak a third's sari, all the while laying out the costumes and giving us instructions. With the same composure, she would lead the orchestra, giving the musicians their cues.

Inevitably, one of us would have forgotten to pack her hairpins or safety pins, false hair, lipstick, and there was frantic borrowing going on all the time. We had three high-necked blouses of our own – mustard yellow, bright red and emerald green. Akka had spares in her makeup case for all emergencies, but not bringing your own blouse was tantamount to treason.

There were ten or more of us girls required for a variety show, as one group danced while the other changed costumes. In the six or seven minutes that an item lasted, I had to rush to the restroom or the cottage, peel off a wet costume, drape the next one on my sweaty-sticky body, throw on multiple necklaces, change earrings, shove bangles on my wrists, jostle at the mirror with others to check my appearance and emerge flushed, ready to charge into the next item. There was no time for stagefright!

While the Gujarati skirt was the easiest to wear, and it neatly served two items, the *garba* and the *raas*, the *santhali* costume which involved several revolutions of the sari around the body was the toughest to drape. One of the seniors was deputed to help us. After a show, the hundreds of pieces of jewellery, the costumes would all be carefully counted and packed. Used, used and reused countless number of times, they were the core of the BK stage properties.

Sir insisted that no food or drink would be served to the audience during the performance, so that we had their full attention when we began. He also ensured that we were fed well before, to have the energy to dance. There was no question of dancing on an empty stomach.

I have the fondest memories of the soft inch-thick bread the sandwiches at Fisherman's Cove were made of, and the chilled 'phoren' Coke served aboard the enormous liner, QEII. After the show, we would tuck in ravenously at the best of spreads laid out for the guests.

Twirling in a lyrical *garba* or stomping vigorously in the *bhangra*, I enjoyed most the vibrant colours we wore. Released from our rather boring practice saris and white dhotis, here we were serially transformed by clothes, now a village belle from Odisha, now a magnificent Naga warrior. And while flying around the stage, swirling in and out in the *raas*, who should one encounter but Sir, almost unrecognizable in his short Kathiawar kurta and curving moustache! It required bravery of an altogether different sort to partner him, all the while maintaining a joyous smile.

Once at Music Academy, he crept, turbanned and bearded, into his seat in the darkness, before the *bhangra*. When the drums throbbed, he got up and began jerking his upraised arms to *Balle Balle Ho*, exhorting the audience to clap along. The *bhangra* was an absolute favourite with any crowd, Indian or foreign, and the peppy beat soon had everyone tapping their feet. When he leaped onto the stage, the audience gasped thinking an overenthusiastic Sardar had breached the barrier!

23

'Please do not leave Kalakshetra, there is no life for male dancers outside Kalakshetra.' This was the advice given by Mohan Khokar, one of Kalakshetra's earliest male students,[17] to Dhananjayan. When circumstances resulted in Dhananjayan leaving – despite never having intended to – he took it as a challenge: He would demonstrate that it was possible to make a career in dance and succeed outside Kalakshetra. However, it was easier thought than done. There were many impediments along the way.

First, to step into the great unknown beyond the gates of Kalakshetra was daunting in itself. Then came the choice of disciplines. Two roads branched out in front of him, Kathakali and Bharata Natyam. Of the two, the more demanding was Kathakali. Dhananjayan had been fully prepared by an exacting Asan to meet the rigorous standards of that art-form. He had the looks and radiated a certain innate goodness in *abhinaya*, a quality of peaceful *sattwa* that earned him the '*pachcha*' roles of the gods, his face painted 'green' and wearing the large circular crowns as Rama or Vishnu. However, one could not be a solo Kathakali dancer; it required a group, in order to present the plays. That would mean returning to Kerala, but Dhananjayan and Shanta were happy in Madras and already had a few students.

The great Guru Gopinath, whom Dhananjayan admired a lot, had paved a unique path when he drew from his training as a Kathakali dancer to create his own style of dance, Kerala Natanam, way back in 1931. However, Dhananjayan was too steeped in Kalakshetra's aesthetic to shift to another style.

Could he make a living from Bharata Natyam then?

In the late sixties, there were no male dancers in Bharata Natyam whose path Dhananjayan could readily follow. The one world-famous Indian male dancer, whom everyone had heard of, Uday Shankar, had evolved his own unique style. Ram Gopal, who had studied Kathakali, Bharata Natyam and Kathak from the best of gurus, had shifted base to London, and drew from all these disciplines in his presentations. Bhaskar Roy Chowdhury, born in Madras, was to find his fame and fortune in America. They had all established their careers outside India. Would Madras, the part 'outside' Kalakshetra, offer him any scope to perform?

It was a bleak scenario.

The earlier patrons of the arts, royal families and moneyed zamindars spread across the fertile lands of the Madras Presidency, had dwindled. In the city, Carnatic music was kept alive by self-financing associations called sabhas. Funded by rich industrialists and wealthy Madras-based professionals, these were primarily associations of the lovers and connoisseurs of Carnatic music. It was only lately, with the growing social acceptance of Bharata Natyam, that they had started presenting dance performances as well.

'In those days people paid to watch *natya* performances. When Balasaraswati or Kamala or Vyjayantimala danced, tickets would be sold out. Most of the sabhas...The Music Academy, Sri Parthasarathy Swami Sabha, Sri Brahma Gana Sabha, Indian Fine Arts Society... earned much of their annual revenue from Bharata Natyam performances,' explained Dhananjayan.

Certainly, the ambience, the location and indeed the audience at these sabha performances were very different from the mostly male audience that a *sadir* performance would have attracted in a salon.

While women did attend dance performances at sabhas, it did not necessarily translate into an audience that wanted to watch a man dance. The established sabhas were not particularly interested in presenting a male dancer performing Bharata Natyam. In their thinking, if a young nubile girl danced, at the very least, her lissome body would be on display even if she had no great talent.

The Music Academy, long considered the premier sabha, 'did not recognize us at all. They do not have a tradition of inviting male dancers nor couples. Its Secretary, T.S. Parthasarathy, who was a great admirer of ours and helped us a lot, said, "My hands are tied because of the policies."'

Might a woman's presence alongside his make him more acceptable to the organizers of shows?

Dhananjayan was married to a dancer who shared the same foundation and training from childhood. Each trying to establish an individual career in dance did not seem a viable proposition. It seemed inevitable that Shanta and he would dance together, with all the experience that Kalakshetra had given them when it came to precise co-ordination on stage. Today they are known as The Dhananjayans, the dancing couple, but at the time they were courting in Kalakshetra, did they ever dream of this?

'Never!' confessed Shanta. 'I *never ever* thought that we would leave, and establish ourselves as a duo!'

The dancing couple

24

Past the gate, I first had to cross my gurus' home to get to the safety of the cherry tree. A modest three-bedroom house, similar to those in the neighbourhood, it reinforced the sense of BK being home. To us children, it also obscured to a large extent the fact that Sir and Akka were still trying to make ends meet. Akka's father had built the house for her in 1976. He expected the young couple to stand on their own feet, but this was his solid gesture of support. Akka told me one day, 'People would say, "Oh, her father gave her everything." But he too had worked hard to earn that money. Apart from the roof over the head, we have had to work very hard to provide for our family.'

On the verandah outside, I might pass Sanjay, their elder son, swotting from his books. One look at his woebegone face and it would be clear he had been ordered to study. Sanjay learnt vocal music and the mridangam while Satyajit, born in 1974, took to dance. I might also come upon Sir sitting on a cane chair, and totter past him, fearing he would catch me for anything at all. My bindi might have fallen off, I might have unthinkingly worn a puff-sleeved blouse, perhaps I had forgotten my bangles, or had parted my hair to the side...

I remember always dithering if I had to ring their doorbell. I saw it as an intrusive act that could result in Sir opening the door and scolding me for having disturbed him. He never did, but that irrational fear still holds strong. Recently, the Dhananjayans have added a security feature to their gate that involves ringing the bell and then waiting to be buzzed in. At age forty-five, I've stood in the hot sun staring at that dratted bell, trying to muster the courage to press it. I thought it was just me, but my friend Sangeeta assures me she dithers too.

There was no division between home – a place to retire to after interacting with the world – and their place of work, the studio cottage.

Satyajit recalled, 'I grew up in a dance class with the sound of *teyya tei* around. That was life. And then I was told to go class. As part of a natural progression: "Now you are six years old, so you will dance." And I started learning dance.'

If the rap of the *thattu kazhi* was to be heard at all times inside the house, the sound of music often spiralled late into the night sky as stop-start rehearsals dragged on.

'I used to hate the late rehearsals,' declared Satyajit. 'One o'clock, twelve o'clock. I remember my brother once screaming out of the bedroom window: "Stop it! It's late, he needs to sleep, he has school tomorrow." I loved to perform but not the rehearsals. The lone *thattu kazhi* rehearsals were never for me. I liked the ones with the full complement of musicians, though.'

Sir and Akka generously offered every suitable space in their home to us. I have danced on their roof, in the main hall, in the upper storey added later on. When one of the bedrooms was cleared of all furniture and classes held briefly there, it felt cramped compared to our cottage!

Perhaps invaded isn't the right word because it was always open house, and they were not fiercely protective of their privacy. We roamed about happily, raiding their fridge for cold water when we became older and dared, or dressing for performances in the spare bedroom.

Parents, students, in-house musicians, musicians searching for work, old students and *their* students, spouses, children...on any given day more than fifty people might traipse through the property, most headed for the studio, some entering Sir's home, not all with the sort of trepidation I had.

'That's my parents' life. They love all that. If I was exposed to the same environment, seeing my parents take class day in and day out, then I would have believed this is all there is.'

When Satyajit moved to his own flat for a while after his marriage to Anupama, his classmate at BK, 'I enjoyed my privacy! Not so many people coming and going!'

Over time, the cottage lost its thatched roof, acquired a second storey and a cement roof, as the Dhananjayans's fortunes rose. I still practise in that classroom, the cement flooring renovated with tiles that give the illusion of dancing on a wooden surface. The cherry tree was chopped down— the courtyard had to be paved— and is mourned to this day by us monkeys.

Like the cottage, the house too changed in shape and size when all their hard work paid off. Sometime in the eighties, when they added a second storey with a distinctive Kerala tiled roof, they shifted their living quarters upstairs, and one of the rooms downstairs was converted to Sir's office. It was here that parents seeking to admit their children met him, it was here that we ran excitedly to tell him about some inconsequential development in our lives.

Sir speaks often of the administrative skills he learnt, helping out as a young boy at the office in Kalakshetra, and later in his brief stint at a company. It helped him take care of all the correspondence, paperwork for visas for the entire troupe at times, publicity handouts and of course the perennial income statements. I frequently saw Sir pecking away at his typewriter, shifting later to Mac, and got a sense of the multiple roles a dancer juggles with in the course of a performance. Sir and Akka had divided their areas of command. He took care of the money angle, travel, stay, and dealing with the organizers. Akka visualized, shopped for and designed the costumes working closely with a specialized tailor, trained new musicians, and headed the orchestra.

Before a show, a fully made-up Sir was visible backstage attending to all sorts of minor issues. A shawl thrown over his costume, one might find him marking centre-stage with an x, or checking the spotlights, or upbraiding a tardy musician.

On returning home after a show, no matter how tired, Akka would unpack the sweat soaked BK costumes and air them on clotheslines strung inside. Those that needed to be washed were set aside. The next day, one would find her ironing them so that they were ready for the next show. They always gave off a whiff of sandal; Akka stored the innumerable sandalwood garlands they received in the costume cupboards at home.

Meticulous in her attention to the little details, Akka was a living demonstration of how such care resulted in incident-free performances. The image of the creative artist, too immersed in flights of fancy to pay attention to mundane details, had no play here. The place to be creative was while dancing. But to get to that point, one had to be practical, organized, thrifty, careful, diligent, steadfast and focused. Everything, even one's home, was sacrificed at the altar of a higher purpose.

As the couple began to be invited to various cities, increasingly they spent a lot of time away from home. In India, thanks to the discount offered by the railways to performing artistes travelling third class, Dhananjayan saved much money but it necessitated inhabiting trains for hours and hours. While Shanta's mother and aunt ably took over the reins of the household, it did mean that both children spent long spells without the company of their parents.

When his son Samartha was born, Satyajit enjoyed his new role as a father. 'I am also very involved with my family. I can't say that about my parents. I have never regretted that they were not around. They didn't spend time with us, it's just an observation, not a grudge. We never leave Samartha with anybody else.'

25

'After the South Asian tour, the Tourism Department gave us a lot of help. The director, Shivamani Nathan, knew us from the Kalakshetra days and she would sometimes bring important visitors to watch us dance. We were more accessible than Kalakshetra, and it was more intimate here, not so formal. That gave us a lot of opportunities. Once, Air India and the Tourism Department were doing a promotion. It was a multivision project, very hi-tech for those times. When the French photographer saw Shanta he wanted her as the model. Not me, just her! Westerners have always loved her looks...very thin and with high cheekbones, it's their idea of beauty. It was a *big* event in our life, a milestone, a landmark. We were given a contract *and* money. They shot photographs for over a week at many locations. I sang, Shanta had to keep dancing – the photographer said "Do not stop!" – and he kept clicking. He made almost 15,000 slides. It was a new experience for us, no freezing in a pose!'

Shanta provided a significant detail, 'I did not even have a proper costume at that time; had to make one overnight! It was Sunday, I ran to the only shop open. I could not afford a Kanjivaram. I bought one in art-silk, mustard with small green checks, a nine yard sari...the mustard border looked nice. The Kalakshetra tailor quickly stitched it for us. We travelled for the first time in an air-conditioned car!'

Fond husband Dhananjayan resumed the anecdote: 'Suddenly Shanta was everywhere. In the Air India brochures, calendars, and a life-size poster outside every Air India shop, so everyone admired her. Money also, they paid very well.'

'Shivamani asked us to present small programmes for tourists. The Tourism Department did not have much money so sometimes we performed for free, but we also learnt how to present shows for smaller gatherings. So, a lot of connections and contacts came through her and that is how we got noticed by Chandra of Travel Corporation India. He often had groups of travellers visiting Madras, for whom we danced. And sometimes, they asked us to do bigger shows for which they paid more. Lakshman Sir helped us a lot and of course we had to share what we got with him.'

'Slowly the hotels started approaching us for such programmes. During that period, a European gentleman who was selecting people for a festival came to Madras. We had to put up a show for him, but we did not have a proper place, so we danced at Adyar Lakshman Sir's studio. He then went away and we did not hear from him. Suddenly, after six months or so, we got a letter in French. It was an invitation from Theatre de la Ville in Paris; we had never heard of them! They had chosen Hariprasad Chaurasia, Birju Maharaj, Shivkumar Sharma, and from Madras, Shanta and myself. They wanted to present only classical artistes. Alarmel Valli, a teenager then, was included as well.

Dhananjayan (l) with Jean Mercure centre and Birju Maharaj (r)

'We spent one month in Paris, at a small hotel within walking distance of the theatre. During the rehearsals, we had a problem with the musicians – because there were no visible mikes in the hall! They had concealed mikes, so it was technically superb, but all the musicians refused to play. I told their technicians, "Bring some dummy mikes. Just place them in front of the musicians." The musicians gave a sound test and then they said, "This is fine. See it needed the mike." When it was over, I called all of them and said "No wires, see! These mikes are dummies! Now, we will sing, and you sit in the seats at the back and listen." Once they heard the sound quality, they stopped grumbling!'

'The first day, the show opened with Birju Maharaj. I did Kathakali without the full costume, *The Pregnant Deer*. It was a big success! They celebrated with champagne and I was horrified when they offered me some. That was the first time I touched alcohol.'

'During that one month, we had three shows, six days a week, only Sunday off. All the six days were houseful!'

Reporting about it from Paris for the *Times of India*, Dileep Padgaonkar exclaimed,[18] 'Paris raves about Indian arts fete'. He quoted Rene Sirvin of *L'Aurore* who wrote, 'Absolutely authentic, extremely refined, a spellbinding spectacle' and praised 'the admirable expression of mobility' of the Dhananjayans.

But while they were getting these rave reviews, they were dancing on almost empty stomachs!

'Food was a problem! We South Indians were mostly vegetarian. Alarmel Valli's mother had brought along rasam powder. We asked for hot water and a lemon to make rasam. The waiters spoke only French, so we used all our *abhinaya*. "We want lime, hot water," the waiter did not understand. He brought hot water, but no lemons. We were showing an imaginary round thing in our hand. He brought eggs, then he brought onions, one by one he brought all sorts of round ingredients, potatoes, and soon we started laughing. Then Shanta said "Wait!" She mimed cutting something, tasting it and screwing up her face as the tartness hit her tongue. "Ah!" he exclaimed, "*Citron!*"

The whole month, we managed on hot water "*citron*" rasam, rice, yoghurt! We learnt a few French words.'

'The show was such a big success we had to extend our tour for another month, travelling to Holland, Switzerland, and all over France! One particular waiter at a hotel we stayed in, he knew every *mudra* and expression because he watched the show every day. He became a great admirer, he would tell us, "You did it differently today!"

'1973 was a great year! From that time onwards we started getting many invitations to dance and started producing shows. At BK, one student became ten, then slowly ten became a hundred.'

26

Sometime in 1984, when I was seventeen, V.R. Devika, one of my seniors, casually asked Sir, 'Don't you think it's time for her *arangetram*?'

Sir glanced at me consideringly, and then nodded his head, 'Why not.'

It was a great compliment; he thought I was ready.

The *arangetram* is the formal debut performance, of the entire *margam*. Unlike today, where parents expect to see their children complete the *arangetram* within a certain time, back then that decision was the sole prerogative of the guru. I had been learning for about ten years now, intensely, seriously, happily but without any aim in mind. In the manner that everyone eventually had an *arangetram*, I thought hazily that someday I might too.

My parents had entrusted me to the care of my gurus, and as long as I wanted to continue learning, they were happy to send me. They had no particular idea of what my training ought to consist of, nor had they any great ambitions for me in any direction. That they had a daughter who had some talent in the arts, who *danced*, was in itself a surprise, and its own reward.

Primed by Aunty Veena as to what the *arangetram* would entail – booking a hall, payments and gifts to musicians, the delicate matter of *guru dakshina* to both Sir and Akka (they would neither demand nor indicate a sum), costumes, tailoring, invitations – my mother agreed on the date with Sir, Jan 6, 1985.

In all the excitement of choosing silk saris to be made into costumes, the delight of acquiring my own set of sumptuous temple jewellery, no one had told me what exactly it meant in terms of training. An entire month of two hour sessions with Sir, at five in the morning!

Alone with him.

If there ever was a time to run away, this was it.

Never bright eyed in the morning, I would somehow wake at that unearthly sanctified hour and trudge to class in the chilly pre-dawn of December in Madras. Sir would emerge from his home, stern, remote even, and I would scurry to unfurl the mat for him, feeling like a lamb about to be slaughtered.

But what he taught in those hours, with a heart full of giving, was the essence of *abhinaya.*

To my secret joy, I was doing the *varnam* which had the message-in-a-lotus episode, *Ati moham konden.* As the grandeur of the raga, Shankarabharanam, slowly prised my day open, I was a girl who bore great love for Shiva. A girl who found ways to send lotus-messages to him, even as she hid her love from the world.

'Your gaze *must* follow your hands. Your mind will automatically follow. When *bhava* or emotions are expressed with complete involvement of the mind, then only can *rasa* or enjoyment be created,' Sir would often say, expanding on the meaning of a famous verse.[19]

'What that really means is that *mudras* can only do part of the work. If you use your eyes well, then it increases the magnitude of what you are trying to communicate. But that will only carry you so far...when you do *abhinaya* with complete involvement, with all of your being, that *rasa* will be felt by even a person in the very last row of the audience. You must be able to touch *that* person sitting so far away with your *abhinaya.*

'See, she is tormented by cupid's arrows. Here is his bow, made of sugarcane. These are the bees with which it is strung, and here the five flowers he shoots. Open out your *mudra* into a beautiful flower. Now when he shoots it, it should look like the arrow will penetrate your heart, not fall limply. And when it hits you, what do you feel? Delight, love, pleasure, longing? Or are you dead, because it is a real arrow?'

He talked, he demonstrated. I listened, watched and tried stringing cupid's pliant bow with angry buzzing bees. A lumbering Cupid with a mangled bow, that's what I felt like, but outwardly, miraculously, it seemed that I had done what was required of me. If he did not scold me, it meant I was half-way okay.

Slowly, I awoke to the spaces within the music, the way time paused long or briefly, the curves and glides the notes took and the corresponding feelings they created in me. Slipping into the grand architecture of Ponniah Pillai's 19th century *varnam*, I found my way to the many transient emotions that would evoke this *nayika*'s state of intense longing in love.

Time was fluid, I learnt. In the now, full of fear that I must not let down my guru, I was also conversing with the Timeless One, Shiva. In the now, I was simultaneously a soul longing for grace and a girl educated in modern times. In the now, why did I have the strangest feeling that I had known all of this before? Using my body, I was transcending time by losing track of it.

Sir's face was my only means of reckoning, the mirror that reflected his reactions to my valiant efforts. Seated in front of me, his hair just a tad tousled, his eyes spoke. As he frowned, scowled, knit his eyebrows, hit the stick sharply to draw my attention to a mistake, yelled at me, was impassive, withdrawn, let slip the rare glimmer of a smile, I sight-read my way to accomplishment.

27

A dancer's repertoire showcases his skills. Each item presented on stage needs to be chosen with care and for a reason. Having decided to project himself as a Bharata Natyam dancer, Dhananjayan had to create a core repertoire.

Balagopal and he, as boys in Kalakshetra, had not been encouraged to dance the solo Bharata Natyam repertoire. 'We were considered mainly Kathakali artists, who were taught Bharata Natyam so as to dance in the dramas. While I had done minor items in class which were male oriented, there were no suitable songs for boys. Only *Rupamu joochi*, a *varnam* in praise of Shiva. We did that *varnam*, dropping the line *suma shara mulache* where the *nayika* complains of being struck by the flower-arrows of Cupid. The *padams* were *Natanam adinar*, about the vigorous dance of Shiva, *Nee Uraippai Hanumane*, or the *ashtapadi Vadasiyadi*, where Krishna cajoles an angry Radha. Balan and I learnt items such as the *tillana* on our own initiative which did not go down well with some of the teachers. But *because* we were doing every possible role in the dance-dramas, the technical grounding was very strong. We could learn *anything* later on.'

It meant that Dhananjayan had to find suitable themes and choreograph them in a way that highlighted his strengths as a dancer. Rukmini Devi's objections to Shanta and him using the repertoire learnt at Kalakshetra served as an additional spur to creativity. Dhananjayan, already used to doing impromptu variations in his performances, now concentrated on crystallizing his approach to choreography.

'When we started performing on our own, outside, the Bharata Natyam repertoire was limited to the time-tested margam. The standard presentation from *alarippu* to *tillana* was becoming a little boring for the audience. So I thought we must develop a new repertoire. I came up with Natyanjali which has all the *adavu* patterns, basic *tala* beats and major *mudras.* A three-in-one introduction to Bharata Natyam, the way the *todayam* is a foretaste of Kathakali. For the audience, it was something exciting and different, with the *jugalbandi* between the percussionist and the dancer at the end. Initially Kalakshetra criticized me. They said he has changed the traditional *margam* but people liked it.

'We started doing many new combinations of movements, such as in the Hindolam *jatiswaram* I choreographed in 1968. In *Nrittaswaravali*, instead of the usual *jatiswaram*, we used a lot of cross rhythms.

'Then came the choice of *varnam*, the centrepiece of a show. I thought to myself...I am a man, what can I express best? I did not want to do the *varnams* with the *nayika bhava*, from the heroine's point of view. I always felt that, even when we were learning them in Kalakshetra. Athai did not want us to do *Manavi* or *Sakhiye*, the prevalent *varnams* with the *nayika bhava* or lovelorn *shringara*-in-separation. These were traditional *varnams* performed by the devadasis who were women and the words were suitable to that context. She thought *shringara pada varnams* were not very appropriate for boys but she did not venture to choreograph anything suitable for us. That is why we used to do *Rupamu joochi*, with more of *bhakti*, as men.'

Turaiyur Rajagopala Sharma, a gifted musician had composed an Atana *varnam* suffused with Krishna *bhakti*. When he approached Rukmini Devi with it, she said it was not suitable for Bharata Natyam, as some of the words came too fast, packed together. 'So she rejected it. I took it as a challenge! The beautiful thing was it had all the Krishna stories in it...*natyam bhaktivivardhanam*...so I could bring *bhakti* in with this item. When I did it, I deviated from the usual kind of composition required in *varnams* where different interpretations of each word were done, not much of *sanchari*, the extended depiction of an idea or situation. So I used *sanchari* to depict the stories related to Krishna that could be easily understood by people and I decided to call it *nrityopahaaram*.

'When I announced it in place of the *varnam*, people came out of curiosity...*what is this, what is Dhananjayan doing?* The stories were liked a lot by the connoisseurs but the famous critic Subbudu remarked, "Oh, Dhananjayan is doing *abhinaya* for *swaras*," but when I explained it is not so, I am using the musical notes or *swaras* to communicate some ideas, then he said, "That's good."'

What Dhananjayan had done was link body movements that mimicked activities such as swimming or playing with a ball with plain musical notes (instead of pairing notes with abstract body movements known as *adavus*). It became so popular with the audience, this *varnam* was a regular feature in their performances. With time, the criticism dropped away. Other dancers adopted the idea.

However, there was a core issue facing Dhananjayan, just as it had faced Rukmini Devi in the 30s, related to the genre of musical compositions called *padams* and *javalis* that belonged to the devadasi repertoire.

The traditional corpus of songs performed by the devadasis expressed feelings from a feminine viewpoint. To enter any one of the situations in these *padams* is to first take on the role of a woman, and then within that role, portray convincingly the specific character demanded by the song. For a man performing Bharata Natyam, there is the added challenge of the instrument of a male body.

This was the two-edged problem that faced Dhananjayan when he left Kalakshetra and tried to build a repertoire suitable for a man. It continues to be a factor that every professional male dancer grapples with when putting together a repertoire: the corpus of traditional songs that explore *shringara* are heroine-predominant.

Dhananjayan has strong views on this. '*If* at all I do such a piece, I *must* do it as though I were a female doing it. As a character, you have to do it that way. I cannot do a heroine in a *padam* in a manly way. That would be incongruous! Nowadays at Kalakshetra, they do teach some *viraha* items, dealing with the pain and longing born of separation between lovers...Kshetrayya *padams* such as *Bala Vinave*...but when the boys do it, it looks like a *bhakta* or devotee doing it, not like a female *nayika* doing it. They are just taking the words and interpreting it like a man...they do not change themselves into a *nayika*. So the *sambhoga shringara*, the expression of sexual fulfillment, does not come through I feel.'

In his role as guru to hundreds of girls, children when they started learning from him, Dhananjayan had to decide whether or not he would teach them many of these pieces. He had left Kalakshetra; he no longer had to follow Rukmini Devi's views in this matter. On the other hand, would conservative middle-class parents continue to send their daughters to him if he taught such items? Dhananjayan decided to align with the Kalakshetra perspective, finding it to be consonant with his own views on emphasizing *bhakti* or devotion.

As Nataraja, photographed by Raghavendra Rao

So, 'For the second half of the programme...I did a lot of Thyagaraja and Swati Thirunal compositions. In Kalakshetra, they never chose to perform Thyagaraja's kirtanas except *Rara sita*. I do not know why Athai did not...I think she felt there is only *bhakti* in them, but I have shown that even in *bhakti* there is so much variety.

'I also did the *ashtapadis* where Krishna's feelings are explored. Men also can express their feelings, not women alone! I chose lyrics that lent themselves to being portrayed by a man and it worked! People paid me all sorts of compliments, "When you do it, you do it as a man should..." "Your items are so manly, we appreciate it..."'

In an interview[20] he explained, 'I avoid seductive *sringara* which the critics talk about as being synonymous with Bharata Natyam. Mine is an approach in which *bhakti* is the dominant force. I consider *sringara* itself to be an aspect of the all-embracing *bhakti*.'

He did choose select Kshetrayya *padams* to teach his students, but only when they reached a certain maturity.

Ironically, as the times get more permissive, it is possible for dancers today to present some of the more explicit *padams* without facing the kind of approbation they might have in the thirties. Presented as human-interest situations that reveal the various shades of intimacy between men and women, they do not attract the judgement that the dancer has an immoral or sexually promiscuous world-view.

Finally, 'For the *tillana*, we chose the first *tillana* Balamuralikrishna composed. He is a true *vaggeyakara*, a fabulous composer. I have great respect for his compositions. His *tillana* in Kuntalavarali, nothing equals it...Pandit Ravi Shankar was a *tot-al* fan of it. He *loved* it; "So many I have heard, but nothing like this," he said. Whenever we met Panditji, Shanta *had* to sing it for him. That *tillana* became a hit.'

A fresh repertoire in place, the next problem was that of income. There just weren't that many paying opportunities in classical Bharata Natyam to support a family. When he approached the sabhas in the late 60s, he was told that his 'rate' was six hundred rupees for a show.

Shocked, Dhananjayan wondered how they could decide what his renumeration was.

At the time, the other dancers on the scene, female solo artists, came from well-to-do families. They were not dependent on their income from dance to make ends meet, nor were they expected to place food on the table. They could accept a lower fee from a sabha while charging higher elsewhere, something Dhananjayan, supporting a large extended family, could not do. He refused to perform for such a ridiculously low amount.

It resulted in his getting a reputation for being money minded. 'People used to call me Maha Money. Many people thought we…no *I*…am money minded. That is why we never got sabha shows. They thought we would be like the affluent dancers, performing for free, but we could not. Only Sri Narada Gana Sabha gave us support, for which we are grateful to them always.'

Dhananjayan is unequivocal on the subject of fees. 'Generally when people ask for programmes, I fix my payment. I do *not* do it free. I always charged a fee, even though I may have wanted to do the show for its prestige factor. Especially at the sabhas.'

As their fame spread, 'One by one the sabhas started inviting us with proper payment. I chose carefully the ones to accept…Wherever we got our fees, we danced. When sabhas in the mofussil areas such Sarangapani Sangeeta Sabha invited us, I did not charge as much because I wanted to take my art there. They had a very appreciative audience.'

Ironically, it was the folk dance 'variety show' that brought in money.

'*Aikya Bharatham* was a big hit. It clicked very well. At every wedding, conference or tourist show, we presented it! In one particular Gujarati family, there would be a wedding every six months! And they would invite us to perform. We did about fifty to sixty shows a year and it gave us a good income.'

Teaching, though the fees were low, did bring in a steady monthly income. Even there, 'We had a lot of foreign students, the people thought they are charged differently and that we earn a lot from them. What no one knew was that we train a lot of the students for free. Especially the boys, mostly taught free.'

Unlike other gurus known for making demands from students, Dhananjayan did not charge high rates for teaching. 'In those days,' he referred to the 70s, 'coming from Kalakshetra, we concentrated on the performance side, not the commercial side. In our early years we did not charge for *arangetrams*, some we did free, did not even get the customary *dakshina*.'

As to the prejudice against male dancers, well that would take many decades to overcome. It still cannot be said to be non-existent.

28

Recently, I watched a new student sashay past the gates of BK wearing tight jeans and a skimpy top, her hair cut very short. I tensed on her behalf: if Sir saw her she was in for it. Minutes later, she emerged from the changing room, demure in a dance practice sari, hair slicked back and I sighed in relief.

At BK, Sir frowned on western clothes, whether jeans or skirts. While he really wanted all of us to be dressed in saris and bangles, wearing bindis, kajal and flowers in our hair, he grudgingly accepted the churidar kurta or salwar kameez. Through the 70s, the 80s and even the 90s, Madras was conservative, especially when it came to clothes. Sleeveless and low necked blouses were considered most risque. Those who wanted to be daring, stopped with that. Generally there wasn't much of a discrepancy between what girls wore 'outside' and to BK.

Regardless, he was particular on many points.

So often, to our sly delight, someone would get hauled up for wearing puff sleeves – 'I can't see the line of your arms when you dance', too small a bindi – 'If you looked I don't think you could have found a smaller bindi. It's a dot! Why bother to wear it if it can't be seen?', or no jewellery – 'When you dance, shouldn't you look nice?' Among the boys and musicians, pant-shirt – 'Go change right now into a veshti'. Or, 'Why is your forehead bare? Wear a nice sandalwood tilak.'

Once, pulling up a boy who had just joined for a minor sartorial infringement, he said, 'Do you know Akka and I were applauded in New York, just for wearing our national dress?'

'No Sir! Tell us Sir, what happened?'

Class had finished. Sweaty and tired, we gathered around him on the steps outside his home.

'In 1976, a big break came out of the blue. We were invited to tour New York state introducing dance education in schools, just the two of us, and two musicians. Within hours of landing, it was the next day, and jet lag or not, we were expected to start work.

'We started at Long Island, visiting schools there. They were so badly disciplined, my whole idea of America was shattered. Those children were totally clueless, they didn't know where India is, nothing. As to understanding our art, that was another thing altogether. I realized it was going to be a real challenge.'

'What did you do?' asked one of the boys.

'Well, to make them sit through the class itself was tough. We visited many low-income districts...we could see their upbringing is different. Shabby clothes, the kids smoking. I was shocked at the way the girls and boys behaved...hugging and kissing in class, girls entering the men's bathroom...And we were warned by the teachers, "We don't know how you will handle them."

'Gradually, we got their attention. 'They liked the expressions more so I showed them the movements of animals, how a deer leaps or a tiger prowls. We had to visit five schools a day, five days a week, two days rest. Supposed to be 5 hours of work a day but it was a lot more because we had to travel very long distances between each school.'

Sir chuckled in amusement. 'When we said we are a couple, they would ask us if we were married! When I replied that I had been married for ten years, they would ask, "To the same wife?"'

Three youngsters broke into giggles.

'At one particular school, we were warned that the children were particularly unruly. I went in smiling and greeted them confidently. One group at the back was making fun of us. I ignored them. But when I performed, my attention was focused on them. I began with *navarasa*. I looked at them with anger in a very powerful way. When they saw my facial expression and heard the fury of the *chenda*, they really got frightened. They thought I was angry with them, and they subsided. Afterwards, they came and apologized. All five of them. The teachers were taken aback. I told them it is the power of our art.'

One of us remembered that this was supposed to be a chastising. 'Sir, clothes, Sir,' she prompted mischievously.

'Yes, yes, I am coming to it. At the end of our tour, there was a conference on Art in Education. Almost 3000 delegates from all over the world! For the first time we enjoyed some luxury. The hotel was very plush. Breakfast was sumptuous. Honey dew melons, cereals, bacon…all new things for us. I started enjoying western food…

'At our session, we were invited on the stage and we went dressed the way we are, Shanta in a sari and me, VPD, in dhoti and kurta. Everyone stood up and clapped for us.'

We beamed, thrilled vicariously.

'It was very exciting for us of course, but we were wondering why so much honour for us, dancers. Then they explained, "People liked you for appearing as you did, keeping your national identity."'

Sir turned his gaze on the errant junior, 'So you see, just because everyone is wearing pant-shirt does not mean you should stop wearing kurtas.'

The boy stuck his tongue out, and hung his head.

All of us grinned.

What Dhananjayan did not narrate, because it would have undermined the point he was trying to make, was the infuriating time when the same national dress came up against the remnants of our colonial past.

Sometime in the mid-80s, Dhananjayan and Shanta were invited by the eminent Dr. Srinivas and the Medical Council to attend a reception at the Madras Gymkhana for a famous European neurosurgeon. Both wore silks, Dhananjayan a silk jubba over a gold bordered veshti and Shanta in a sari.

Shanta sailed in while the doorman stopped Dhananjayan. In a veshti and smart chappals, he did not conform to the dress code. Dhananjayan argued with him to no avail. 'The Manager came. He said,

"These are the rules, I can't do anything. I will lose my job." Dr. Srinivas tried to persuade him but they were all adamant!'

Smarting, and not one to take it lying down, Dhananjayan returned home and called the press. 'The next day it came in the papers. "Famous artiste not allowed into Gymkhana in national dress."'

That was about twenty-five years ago. Recently the Dignity Foundation had booked a room at the Madras Boat Club for the jury to meet to discuss the Dignity Foundation's film awards. The Dhananjayans were part of the jury along with Vyjayanthimala Bali and film critic Malathi Rangarajan. Fumed Dhananjayan, 'At the reception they stopped me saying, "You can't go in wearing a dhoti." We had no option but to change the venue. The dress code is absurd...it affects only the men. Women get away with any odd dress. We have no pride in our Indian attire which is more suited to the tropical climate.'

29

Largely due to Rukmini Devi's foresight in training young male dancers as well, the male roles in her dance dramas were played by men. Elsewhere, Bharata Natyam dance-dramas were staged with females playing men, their breasts flattened or camouflaged.

That situation had not changed even when Dhananjayan left Kalakshetra. When he wanted to present dance-dramas, in the early years, before he trained enough boys, he was constrained by the lack of male dancers who could partner him.

When the Tamil Isai Sangam asked him, in 1976, to create a dance-drama with lyrics drawn from *Rama Natakam*, written by Arunachala Kavirayar, Dhananjayan accepted. *Rama Natakam* as he conceived it was unusual in many ways, chiefly in how it worked around these constraints of a low budget for costumes and a lack of other trained men.

Dhananjayan seized upon the concept of *ekaharya lasyangam*, where the dancer portrays many characters, as in the course of a Bharata Natyam performance, without wearing a costume that identifies him as specifically Shiva or a king or a bird. He decided that the dancers would wear throughout a standard Bharata Natyam costume, the girls a basic sari-costume with minimal temple jewellery and the boys, dhotis. In one scene a girl might be Sita, in another a monkey but this would be communicated with body language and *abhinaya*.

The dance-drama itself was made up of a few important link scenes, and the audience who knew the entire Ramayana imagined the rest. This reduced the need for a large cast; the entire war was depicted by just two dancers. For the fight scene, Dhananjayan managed with just another male dancer, Kathakali-trained N.V. Krishnan. 'That is how we did Rama Natakam with one male doing all the roles... *ekaharya lasyangam*. I did all the roles!'

In the early years, Dhananjayan played Dasharatha to dramatic hilt, falling insensate with a thud on hearing Kaikeyi's terrible demands; crafty Ravana who chopped off Jatayu's wings and left him bleeding; anxious Rama supervising the construction of the bridge; devoted Hanuman finding Sita in the Ashokavan; and, if necessary, young Rama stealing his first glance at Sita. He was supremely confident of his ability to play each of those characters differently, but it did make the production overly dependent on him.

The Times of India commented, 'Dhananjayan has to portray Rama, Dasaratha, Ravana and Vali...[as] eventually...such attempts [to stage dance-dramas] centre on an individual, and, at best, a partner.' And 'Rama disappears after his "hurried" wedding only to appear later as a bridge-construction supervisor. Why? Dhananjayan cannot take up a face-to-face double role...as in the films.'[21] The *Midday* observed that 'The troupe itself consists of several gifted dancers, unfortunately, most of them are women. Men have yet to see the splendid scope that Bharata Natyam offers them it seems.'[22]

Taking the idea of *ekaharya lasyangam* further, the versatile Dhananjayan once played the part of the female hunchback Manthara craftily persuading Kaikeyi to ask for Rama to be banished. Shortly after that, he played Dasharatha, evoking the king's tremendous anguish on hearing Kaikeyi's two heartless requests.

The audience willingly suspended disbelief and was drawn into the drama and emotional power of that scene but the critic Subbudu disapproved.

'He said that a robust male dancer imitating an old lady like Manthara was absolutely gross. When I met him, I said, "Maama, you were a stage actor. If, as the old, crooked Manthara, a man can evoke *rasa* in you that itself is a compliment." He thought about it and agreed with my reasoning.'

It is a testimony to the growing number of male dancers who took to Bharata Natyam as a profession that just ten years later, when Dhananjayan presented the same dance-drama across the USA, he had three highly trained men in his troupe and was able to relinquish some of those roles to them.

One of them was good-looking Satyajit, his son, groomed from the age of six to become a star dancer. 'I enjoyed being the centre of attention. I was not technically a student so I could fool around. It was home!'

At BK, we students were happy that Satyajit was learning Bharata Natyam. It proved that Sir believed in his art, and if his child had the talent, he would push him in this direction.

On May 1, 1983, when he was nine years old, a photograph appeared in the *Trident*, marking Satyajit's stage debut as a squirrel bounding across the bridge in *Rama Natakam*. He continued to be cast in his parents' productions as a goat, a squirrel, cow, monkey or child, anything that was suitable to his size and tender age. A year later, in 1984, he played the young Mowgli in the *Jungle Book* production done in the UK, alternating with the then unknown Akram Khan.

Satyajit had his *arangetram* in 1988, when he was only fourteen. It was a hit and set him on the dancer's path. Music had claimed Sanjay, the elder son, dance claimed Satyajit and his parents had an heir, or so we thought.

'They never said you are the next in line, you *have* to do this. Everyone assumed that. My parents only wanted me to dance well. *That* they wanted from any student, and maybe a little more because I was their son.'

Some might even have secretly envied Satyajit. He would not have to struggle to earn a living, nail slippery sabha secretaries, or even battle his family in order to dance. It was all handed to him on a platter; the lineage, the training, the contacts, the BK establishment and the immersion in music and dance.

His personal view of it: 'Of course, I took it for granted. It was just another thing that I was doing. It came naturally.'

Satyajit was the prince in a small vibrant kingdom whose student population adored his parents and by extension, him. In 1997, to his father's great shock and his mother's distress, Satyajit would renounce all of that and change the course of his life.

30

Debut done and praise won, I could now perform solo. I had found something that was bigger and beyond me, that *was* me, that I loved with all my heart. That love stemmed really from *who* I was while performing.

She gathered herself about three hours before the show was due to start, as I began to dress. There was an order to be followed, and in the course of adhering to that calming order, I let go of my everyday self and the dancer emerged.

My temple jewellery, studded with cabochon rubies and lined with pearls, my makeup box, my *ghungroos* with their melodic sussurus, just the act of unpacking them brought a deep thrill.

A central parting, and at the crown, hair threaded through the big circular *rakkodi* keeping it in place. Tightly plaiting my own hair, thick and long enough to not require a switch, attaching a jaunty *kunjalam* at the end, made it ready for the distinctive hair adornments. Two layers of pancake later, my eyes enlarged with kohl, I was ready to bear the sun and the moon on my head, drape the vivid costume, accept the cruel tightness of the golden belt around my waist.

Like a talisman, I bore a nose-ring to Akka, wincing as she pressed it forcefully in place. Presenting myself to her, accepting gratefully her pinning in place a necklace or blotting excess lipstick, I waited to be pronounced ready. My feet and hands were stained red with *alta* transported in opaque glass bottles from Calcutta. Already I could hear preparatory taps on the mridangam and knew that the many

Author Tulsi Badrinath in performance

musical instruments were all cradled in their master's hands, ready to swell into notes at a single touch.

The sacred ritual when Sir held my *ghungroos* and I bent double at his feet; the transfer of energy as he handed the bells to me, blessed.

And then, that dreaded, much anticipated moment: finding myself alone in the wings as the music began, signalling my entry on the stage. By now, I held no memory of the world outside. An inchoate bunch of thoughts crowded my head, chiefly a sudden terror of having forgotten set steps, the excitement of heading into the moment and the joy of looking down at my silken self, *dancer*.

Dancing solo under the hot blinding lights, I learnt many things about myself. If the performance radiated outwards towards the audience, it also drew from something within. And that discovery, of what lay within, could only be made *while* performing.

Supreme self confidence, a lack of stage fright, a will to give of myself in dance *through* dance, to take the audience with me on a journey, I discovered all these things about myself on stage. Gone the diffidence that sometimes overcame me in class, gone the self-imposed shackles. All that training had led to this flowering.

Music sung live, notes spilling out of a simple bamboo reed, violin strings vibrating to the bow, the rich pleasure provided by the veena, the stirring echo of the cymbals, all combining to create a mood, support emotion – my *abhinaya* both harnessed and rode on it.

There was my heartbeat, and the sound of percussion, fingers striking taut leather. There was my racing pulse, a smile masking my panting breath and a festive tempo. There were my dancing feet and a flurry of leading syllables. The mridangam was struck, struck repeatedly and my ankle-bells responded, a unity of sound that had to be called into being at all times.

If the writer in me was condemned always to stand outside of myself and watch the world, dancing was the only time when the self that stood apart was put to good use. It was the self that conducted my performance, holding on to that last bit of awareness necessary to judge space and movement and position. It freed me of Time, freed me to *be* my passion.

Gifted this space and attention for the length of the performance, as my body leapt and walked and swayed, now unabashed Radha, now sandal-fragrant Krishna, now austere Shiva, now a human soul seeking its own divinity, there was a making throughout, a creating of beauty, of flavour, of feeling, of transcendence.

31

As Dhananjayan's fame grew, boys and men who wanted to learn Bharata Natyam made a beeline to BK in the mid-80s. While their numbers were certainly fewer than the girls, that they were there at all was the important fact. Other than Kalakshetra, no other school of dance had so many male students, around thirty at one time, as did BK.

The colour white, off-white really, symbolizes for me the male dancer's presence in class. His cotton dhoti was tucked between the legs, waist braced with a red or green sash and upper body left bare, as it would be on stage. The boys practised in simple dhotis – in the freshers' batch, one might chance upon an adorable little dhoti-clad brat – until they performed on stage when they burst into all colours of the rainbow. I soon discovered that a male dancer will spend as much time and express as much delight over the precise colours of his silk costume as his female counterpart.

Learning side by side with them, my own understanding of dance was enriched by their presence.

Peering out from my female body, I envied the male dancing body for its elegance, finding in it a certain spare quality that the female body, wrapped in yards of cloth and given to curves, did not. But I could also see that the bare torso rendered a male dancer vulnerable. All the drawbacks of his physique and the flaws in his technique were magnified. There was no hiding a paunch or an undernourished, scrawny body. Equally, when the body was taut and right in its contours for dance, nothing equalled it in sheer beauty of line. Those bodies were rare.

Dhananjayan's own body was of the right proportions for dance. Slightly taller than his dancing partner Shanta, he was not so tall as to look gangly. Skin and bone in his younger days, he acquired bulk as he grew into middle-age but was never fat or overweight. Although handsome, with a full head of hair, what counted most was that he had a wonderfully mobile face that could express just about any shade of emotion he wished.

The Indian Express once captioned Dhananjayan's rare solo at the Museum Theatre as 'An Occasion for Rejoicing'[23]: 'Few male dancers in recent memory have given solo Bharata Natyam items so full of vigour grace and and carefully leashed power. He demonstrated how movements that are usually thought to require feminine pliancy to acquire their fullest bloom, can be even more beautiful done with the cleaner lines of a male body. Lean and live like a whip, he flashed life...'

Aspi Mullah was Dhananjayan's first male student. A Parsi by birth, he was a well-known hairdresser in the sleepy Madras of the late 60s. He arrived at the nascent BK one day, wanting to learn dance. During the day Aspi was busy styling the hair of film actresses, so Dhananjayan accomodated him by giving him one-on-one classes early in the morning or late in the evenings.

Dhananjayan spoke affectionately of him. 'He was one of the few Parsi boys who took up Bharata Natyam. He had long limbs and crooked fingers, so it was a challenge to correct his postures and positions and work around the crookedness in *mudras*. He was a bit effeminate when he joined our class, but I gave him special exercises to do...with a lot of hard work he overcame this deficiency while dancing.'

Though he had begun learning as an adult, Aspi was so committed he was able to complete his debut performance in 1974. Unlike later, where Dhananjayan would choreograph a singular 'special' item for a student's *arangetram*, Aspi performed standard items, the only one with a male character being *Nee Uraippai*, where Rama pleads with

Hanuman to find Sita. 'After that Aspi emigrated to London, took up flamenco and became famous. He was a very sought after male partner to several mainstream female flamenco dancers.'

Like Aspi Mullah, the men who came to learn at BK later were there of their own choice and volition; their parents had not enrolled them. Some had seen Dhananjayan dance and wanted to dance like him. Others wanted to learn in the hope that they would become dance directors in films. Still others, aiming for cine stardom, wanted to acquire dancing skills. A few, very few, were there committed to making it their profession. And then there were the unusual, like V.A.K. Ranga Rao, scion of the zamindar of Chikkavaram, variously an art-critic, scholar and collector of 78 rpm records, who learnt for the sheer love of learning. In his forties then, he was proud of the fact that he was Dhananjayan's oldest student.

Out of a hundred dancers trained, only one or two would make it as a solo artist and take up dance as a full-time career. To Dhananjayan's dismay, the ratio was even lower when it came to the boys. He understood the reasons, after all he had suffered to get where he was, but it was disheartening all the same.

'People still think Bharata Natyam is a female dance, not male oriented.'

Many of the boys who knocked at Dhananjayan's doors were impoverished, or in no position to pay fees. He taught them for free. In return, as is traditionally the case in a guru-sishya relationship, they ran errands for him and helped out with chores at BK. Many of the boys I danced alongside in class had been helped by him, I discovered, not only in terms of a fee-waiver but also being placed as a dance teacher in a well paying school, or finding a position in another dancer's troupe.

One such boy was Narendra Kumar.

Sometime in the early 90s, a sixteen-year-old named Narendra Kumar happened to watch Dhananjayan dance on television. 'He was doing Ganesha *shabdam*, and I loved his *abhinaya* depicting the competition between Murugan and Ganesha to win the mango fruit from their father Shiva.' A tiny seed of hope planted itself in his heart: that he might one day learn from him.

At the time Narendra learnt dance from a teacher called Shanta Madhusudan. His home was in Villivakkam and his teacher lived in Triplicane, thirteen kilometres away. 'I had a free government bus pass. I would go to dance class before school, and then return there in the evening, hanging around in the hope that she would be free to take class again.'

His formal studies did not interest him. 'I got very low marks, a fail in all subjects.' It was in school that, moping about having a dark complexion and worried he would never succeed on stage, Narendra unburdened himself to a friend. The friend retorted, 'Look at Rajinikanth. Has he not achieved so much despite being dark?' Then onwards, 'Rajini was my hero. Kamal Sir is a fantastic dancer of course, but there is some magnet to Rajini.'

One day while cleaning his guru's home, he was about nineteen then, Narendra chanced upon an invitation to one of Dhananjayan's performances. 'I got his address from it, and discovered that there is such a place as Adyar.'

When Narendra reached Bharata Kalanjali, 'Sir was sitting outside on the verandah. I saw the face I had seen on TV; it was divine. I did not know what to say. Only two sentences occurred to me. "I like dance. I want to learn from you." He made me do *alarippu*, said I would have to correct some positions, and agreed to teach me.'

At the time, 1995, his father was unemployed, and Narendra's sister's wedding had emptied the family's meagre coffers. 'My family's financial condition was so bad we could not even afford a tubelight.'

Narendra no longer had the comfort of the bus-pass. Undettered, he walked twenty kilometres each morning from Villivakkam to Jeevaratnam Nagar in Adyar. 'I was very scared of Sir, even more scared of Shanta Akka! I would hide from her. Arriving early at BK at 6 a.m., I'd peek through the window to catch a glimpse of him. On some days he would look up and smile.' In an otherwise bleak situation – 'I had only dance' – it made his day.

His love for dance fuelled him through the day, because very often he did not have a proper meal. 'I'd pack plain cooked rice from home. There'd be nothing else in the tiffin box. Shanta Akka would enquire, "Have you brought lunch?" I'd lie saying I had. Once I forgot to bring salt and had to ask her for some. She said gently, "If you need some vegetables, do not hesitate to tell me."'

Touched though he was, Narendra never asked. Alone in a classroom expanded by silence and stillness, swallowing the dry rice, Narendra would console himself with the memory of a blessing his father and he had just received. One dawn, worrying about their finances, they had been standing near a Hanuman temple on their street. A well-built man with a radiant face beckoned to them. Narendra had been struck by the 'weird' garland he wore, 'To this day, I don't know what it was made of, but it was striking.' He gave Narendra's father a twenty-five paise coin and asked him to keep it in their almost empty rice bin. Saying, 'You will never want for food' the man had vanished. Their stores did improve gradually and the coin still remains enshrined in the rice bin.

L. Narendra Kumar

In the way that one can work with someone in an office and not know very much about them, I did not know this about Narendra at the time. In 1995 I had a baby,[24] and when I returned to dancing a year later I was too preoccupied with the changes in my life to notice all the new entrants at BK. I may have glanced at Narendra's acne-marked face, lingered at the single rudraksha bobbing around his throat, registered his physique – medium height, skin the colour of bitter chocolate, sturdy body and hurried back to my baby. Of his privation and suffering, I had no idea.

Narendra kept up this punishing exertion for five years, 'When I look back, I don't know if I could do it again,' which resulted in a perfected technique. 'In six months, I had corrected my style. I was dancing the whole day so the progress was quick. I did not find it hard because this was all I wanted to do. Sir was touring a lot, so I learnt more from watching him perform than at the classes. My eyes drank it all in.'

One particular day in 1999, when Sir summoned him to our senior class to demonstrate the fast whirling movement done on the knees by Russian folk dancers, Narendra swam into focus. I was impressed by his lack of self-consciousness as he obeyed our guru, doing something he was not trained in.

Soon afterwards, Narendra left BK to become a freelance dancer. He started working in dancer Anita Ratnam's productions.

32

Having gained a lot of stage experience thanks to the variety shows and our own solo performances, we were included in the Bharata Kalanjali dance dramas. Whenever they were to be staged, at various places across the country or say at the Festival of India USSR in 1988, we were on call for rehearsals.

At the time, the three main accompanists – vocal, mridangam and violin, spent long hours uncomplainingly at BK. Sir was particular about choosing the right variation, or *sangati*, in a particular raga. Variations that might showcase a singer's talents were not necessarily suitable for Bharata Natyam. Plump cheeked singer Aravindakshan, blind, square-set T.K. Padmanabhan whose sharp mind could recall set patterns of choreography complete with the flow of music, and Nellai D. Kannan whose hands, calloused from years of playing, teased sparkling rhythm from his mridangam, patiently repeated passages when we dancers blundered. That sense of collective effort, both musical and rhythmic, colours my early memories as a dancer.

Held mostly in the evenings, after school and college, rehearsals stretched for hours. As Kannan adjusting the pitch of his mridangam with a series of sharp taps, and Padmanabhan waxed his bow, Sir wore an abstracted expression on his face as he essayed various positions of the body before chosing what seemed instinctively right to him. That then had to fold into the rhythm cycle seamlessly.

At some point, steaming tea would arrive for the musicians alone and for the longest time I thought it was theirs by virtue of being adults.

In an era of few distractions – no television, computer, iPad, Facebook nor Twitter, I was happiest spending time at BK, watching Sir and Akka rehearse when not dancing my bit roles. Sir believed that one learnt as much from watching as from practising.

Once, in 1976 when Sir was choreographing the scenes in *Rama Natakam*, a baby squirrel fell from the thatched roof. Promptly adopted by his elder son Sanjay and called Ram, it inspired Sir to add a part where a little squirrel bounds across the just-completed bridge to Lanka, providing selfless service to Rama by testing it. Rama strokes its back gently, and the imprint of his grateful fingers mark it forever with three stripes. That scene won the most applause, especially when little Satyajit played the squirrel. Sadly, when the family returned home after the premier of *Rama Natakam* they discovered the squirrel dead in its tiny bed.

Sir talked about his many dance dramas, how they were conceived and executed with a small budget. 'We composed according to the practicality of the situation. In *Rama Natakam*, the concept of *ekaharya lasyangam* allowed me to stick to one costume throughout. In Sri Valli[25] I could blend the folk element with the classical medium. It was the first full scale production with my own troupe. I took my students everywhere by van all across Tamil Nadu. By paying only the musicians, I managed to keep afloat with the performance fees received.'

It was in the Buddhist themed *Sanghamitra*[26] that Dhananjayan attempted a full 'costume drama'. In *Magdalana Mariam* and *Stree*,[27] he explored Christian themes with novel ideas of presentation. 'In Kalakshetra, the same type of presentation was used for all of Athai's dance-dramas. I did each of my dance dramas differently.'

Watching him choreograph offered priceless insights not only into the creative process but also the creative circumventing of practical difficulties. Both *Rama Natakam* and *Mahabharata*[28] involved scenes of war. How to create the large scale impact of a war with just a few dancers? In *Rama Natakam* Dhananjayan did it with two dancers describing the war but that would not work in the Mahabharata.

Shanta, normally the rock of calm, was very worried. 'I kept pestering him "What are you going to do?" He said, "Don't bug, *summa irru*, when the time comes I will figure it out." That was the only production where I was so scared.'

He managed 'with eight dancers, that's all. Finally, with lighting and shadows it looked like a big war!' He chuckled, 'Kathakali is the art of storytelling, that foundation stood me in good stead.' The dancers would march ahead as though at the head of a phlanx of soldiers, and then vanish sideways into the darkness only to quickly rejoin, at the back, the line of dancers marching forward. This created the illusion of a mighty army of soldiers on the move.

Sometimes the flow of creativity stalled. 'When trying to visualize a *shabdam* on Murugan, I did not get any ideas. I tried a lot of things, nothing clicked. I was disheartened. Then a big storm blew and I wrapped up the class. Suddenly, a calendar with a picture of Murugan flew to the ground, as though cautioning me from leaving the room. I was inspired. For the next thirty minutes, I asked my student Sumathi to dance as I choreographed. Shanta was busy in the kitchen. By the time she finished cooking, I had completed the item! The ideas I used are still fresh. When you do something with inspiration, it lasts.'

Because Sir and Akka were professional performing artistes, while learning items from them one engaged with two worlds at once – the practice studio and the imaginary stage. One danced in class facing an invisible audience. One was corrected anticipating the day that item would be performed in costume with a live orchestra. One practised it over and over again, so that when the golden chance came, it would be a polished solo presentation.

When we rehearsed dance dramas however, their performance on a certain date was a given. Sir would brief us about which city we were travelling to, assign us our roles and voila, we began counting down to the show. Excited and nervous in equal measure, our chief but covert imperative was to get a brusque nod from Sir after the show which meant we had done well. Overtly of course we danced to please the audience.

No role was insignificant. Any appearance on stage, however brief demanded one's best effort. Fly-whisk bearer, apsara, village belle, friend, attendant, court dancer, I have done it all.

Above all, one thing was certain: on the dance floor and on the stage, differences in wealth and education and privilege, caste, creed or religion simply fell away. The minute the first beat struck on the drum and the cymbals provided us an aural tightrope, the rhythm held us safe within it. Then on, the single high purpose was that of the immediate art spun by a joyous spirit in a dancing body.

33

In BK, the space in the studio was sacred for dance, but within it students of many religions, including an American Jew, and castes had come to learn. On entering class, all distinctions, so marked otherwise in our daily lives, fell away. Here, what mattered was whether you danced well or not. Stocky, good looking Shafeek had the cleanest, deep *araimandi* possible and that was what defined him in class.

However, outside it is otherwise. 'When I perform, the headlines say "Muslim Dancer" and no one comments on my dance. So now when journalists interview me I tell them to write about my art first!' says Shafeek flatly.

Shafeek came to Chennai in 2004 to do an MA in Bharata Natyam at Madras University. A college degree in Indian classical dance is somewhat of a contradiction in terms. So much of the instruction is oral and one-on-one, so much depends on the guru-sishya rapport, so much of the training unfolds over infinite time...Shafeek explained, 'Having decided that this is my field, I needed a certificate of some sort. I wanted a degree. Sir says "We never needed certificates." Nowadays they need first to see the paper and then if you can dance.'

Having watched Shafeek dance energetically a *varnam* on Shiva, *Parama Shiva*, packed with many mythological stories, in the Ganesha temple at Besant Nagar in Chennai, in 2009, I had given only a passing thought to the fact of his being Muslim. His lines were clean, and a pleasing sincerity permeated his *adavu*-technique.

B.K. Shafeekuddin

When he could not join the BK troupe invited to dance at a temple in Kerala in 2012, it did bring his identity into focus. He could not go *because* he was Muslim. There was a strong possibility that he would not be allowed to dance inside.

For any dancer, missing a 'chance' to dance is an occasion to mope. So also with Shafeek. 'They should allow…I am not going there as a normal Muslim. I am going there as a dancer, and in costume I am doing as Shiva or Krishna, so they should not be such a feeling. There were two or three such places where I could not dance because of being a Muslim.'

Growing up in Mahe, Kerala, the son of a textile shop-owner, Shafeek had never watched Kathakali nor any Bharata Natyam in his childhood. He had no interest in it either. Until 1993. It was in his first year as a Commerce student at junior college that he was to discover a latent talent. Grooving to the then popular song *Di di* by the Algerian

Khaled, Shafeek made up his own steps. His friends who watched declared it a hit.

'The next year, a lot of people came and asked me to teach them. I did a lot of this in college. In the films, there were a lot of songs with a classical touch. So I would learn a little Bharata Natyam by watching to mix into my songs.'

His interest piqued by the positive response he got, Shafeek went to many places where versions of Bharata Natyam were taught. 'In Mahe, I saw a man dance very effeminately and did not like it. Then right in my own village, I discovered there was a good school! It was luck! I liked the style a lot.'

Shafeek did not know that the style taught there was that of Kalakshetra. He had seen so much dance by then, bad, indifferent, that 'I could tell that this was good. There was a boy there who danced like a man. I decided to learn.'

Without telling anyone at home, Shafeek began lessons with Kamala Devi at Kalagramam in 1995. The pace of training in the classical arts was frustratingly slow. 'I was nineteen years old. One month passed, two months, I was doing only the first steps.' He could not understand why his teacher kept asking him 'Have you learnt elsewhere?' 'Only later I realized it was because I was neat in my positions and my *araimandi* was good. I did not know that it was such a difficult thing. I just followed what they asked me to do.'

A year later, Shafeek had progressed enough to be included in his seniors' class. His parents still did not know; he changed into his practice veshti at Kalagramam and before leaving, washed and left it there to dry. To his dismay, he ran into a big problem.

'The fees were hundred rupees a month. But I could not pay even that. I lagged behind, and when I had arrears of eight months fees I was asked to leave.' His family unwittingly provided the solution. 'When Bakri-Eid came, I got a lot of Eidi for new clothes and things. I saved all that money, did not dance for two months, and so was able to catch up on the fees.' By now, he had grown out of his 'cinema type dancing' and was fully committed to the classical.

Three years later, his photograph appeared in the paper, with that of a girl, both of them in Bharata Natyam costume. 'My father asked me "Who is this boy? Looks like you." He showed it to my mother.' With complete sang froid, Shafeek squinted at the photo and said 'Yes it looks like me.' It was so beyond the realm of possibility and imagination, his parents did not catch on.

One day, a dance classmate of his met Shafeek's mother at a wedding and exclaimed excitedly, 'Oh, you are Shafeek's mother! We learn dance together.' On her return, trouble erupted at home.

'My parents could not understand. "Why do you want to learn dance?" they kept asking. They were upset because they felt it is not for boys, and in our community, Muslims don't dance. "You learn along with girls there," they objected. My brother had gone to the Gulf. They wanted me to go too. I bought time by saying "Now I have stopped." But my brother would come to the classroom and interrupt rehearsals.'

Time passed. In 2002, Kalagramam was invited to the Hermann Hesse Festival in Germany and of course, Shafeek was part of the troupe. Earlier, when his parents had begged him to get a passport so that they could try sending him to the Gulf, he had put it off. Now, galvanized by the possibility of going to Germany, he applied for one.

On the eve of his departure, he told his father, "I am going to Germany tomorrow." "Germany...What Germany?" countered his father. "You're joking!" "I had to pay to go to the Gulf and you are going for free?" scoffed his brother. Shafeek explained the circumstances. It marked a turn for the better. 'They understood that was not some local timepass thing. There was a certain standard and future possibilities. They had told me so often not to dance and I did not listen, now they gave up.'

Even then Shafeek was careful. 'I would never dance at home or practise the steps. Did not provoke them that way. A lot of people in the village still don't know I am a dancer.'

The news spread. 'The local Muslims asked me, "Why do you want to dance, mix with Hindus this way?" I replied, "I have not done anything wrong. I have learnt an art, that's all. I do namaz five times."

Earlier I would skip sometimes. Now I feel I must first respect the faith I was born into and then I can dive into a Hindu culture. I was always seen in the mosque, they knew that. Whereas other boys were getting into trouble. So I said, "I am not roaming behind girls or drinking. Set those types right first." They could not say anything.'

Having triumphed over such opposition, Shafeek faced other challenges at Kalagramam. 'It is difficult for boys to dance. Not everyone has the ability, and some struggled with rhythm or keeping time. One was a tailor, another had family problems. One by one, they dropped out.' He ended up being the only boy in the class.

While the pure dance or *nritta* sequences and items posed Shafeek no problem, *bhava* and the items that emphasized facial communication did. Shafeek became self-conscious among all the girls. 'I was the *only* boy, so when it came to the *shabdam*, I would not do *bhava*.'

Did not the characters of Shiva or Rama or Krishna pose a problem? I asked him. 'My teacher would explain to all of us why Shiva is like this, or Krishna like that, in the particular dance. I used to read a lot of mythological stories. So when I danced, I did it with understanding.'

Shafeek was encouraged by the fact that whenever he performed items on Shiva he was praised. 'People liked them, I don't know why. Now I am doing more of Krishna, slowly.'

Meanwhile destiny was arranging something special for Shafeek. All the way from Chennai, it would bring him a guru who would take his training to a level Shafeek had never thought possible.

First, Dhananjayan would be gripped by the idea of creating an institution similiar to Kalakshetra in Kaithapram near his home town in Kerala. Then in 1999 he would amass donations from students and admirers across the globe, construct a brick and mortar building in a remote place and finally in 2000, where once there was only thorn and scrub on a desolate hilltop, Shafeek would think himself lucky participating in a residential camp at the newly inaugurated Bhaskara.

We returned to the problem at hand, the loss of a 'chance' to dance in a temple, and the solution.

'I was invited to teach in Singapore, but they wanted me to change my name. I said I will not change my name. I am the same man regardless of the name.'

Dhananjayan wanted to take him to America. 'Sir said, "Perhaps if you change your name, it will be easier on you."'

Shafeek refused: 'I didn't want a stage name just for money. There would be no satisfaction there. I would be going only to earn money. Now at least a few people know me as Shafeekudeen.'

Bhattakari Kayanadath Shafeekudeen.

34

Having grown up listening to the best of Carnatic musicians at Kalakshetra, both Shanta and Dhananjayan placed a great value on finding the right musicians and training them to meet their requirements. Shanta herself could sing with feeling. This gave them the confidence that they could guide any musician who played for them in the finer aspects, rather than being dependent on them.

Dhananjayan, in his one-man dance-dramas like *Nandanar Charitram* or the one on Sage Vyasa, could completely give himself over to his art, because Shanta, seated to his right on the stage, diamond nose-pin flashing errantly, anticipated every move of his with her cymbals. She has the remarkable ability to steer the many musicians on one common path, like a charioteer holding the reins of five different horses. In this area as well, their personal rapport became a professional asset.

When both danced on stage however, they perforce had to trust their team of idiosyncratic musicians.

Early on, Rajasekharan provided the male vocals for Dhananjayan. 'In 1976, when we went on a long American tour, he became a little restless and homesick. Otherwise a good person, when he was moody it was difficult for Shanta to manage. After that, I cut him off. Much later, when he wanted to buy a house, I helped.'

It was with Aravindakshan the singer ('We taught him *nattuvangam*. That was a great advantage.'). Nellai Kannan the mridangam player; and T. K. Padmanabhan ('It's not easy travelling with a blind person but we took him all over the world, Shanta would even wash his clothes for him.) – that the Dhananjayans were to have a long fruitful relationship. The flautist Raja and Veena player Kannan completed this ensemble.

'They were a good set of musicians who worked with us and stayed here almost the whole day. We were able to do a lot because they were available full-time, were dedicated in their approach and needed the work,' mused Dhananjayan.

There were some rogues in the gallery as well. Once, another flautist joined the ensemble. 'He was a vagabond but he played well. As long as he behaved himself on stage we let him play. But once, we made the mistake of taking him to Germany, and he behaved very badly. He would drink, borrow money and worst of all had a bad character. He made very lewd comments about women. Slowly, everyone stopped hiring him.'

Dhananjayan felt that in general, especially in those early days of restricted foreign exchange and tight visa requirements, when musicians were taken on trips abroad, it went to their head. 'The atmosphere is spoilt when musicians behave badly. I don't like them drinking, and asking for favours from the host. If we are taken to museums or performances, they are not interested; they only come if it's to a movie or a mall. Sometimes, we have to leave them behind and I always worry that they might take off on their own and get lost or injured.'

It was a valid concern.

In 2003, dancer Mallika Sarabhai was accused of helping people emigrate illegally to America under the guise of being members of her troupe. It highlighted the dangers any organizer of large productions faces when taking a troupe abroad. Dhananjayan forestalled any attempt by a troupe member to stay back in a particular country. 'I am very strict with them. I keep their tickets and passports with me. They think I am curbing their independence but it's the only way.'

One day, a singer, Reji, who had trained at the Music College, Chennai, but unable to find work had ended up painting cars and posters in a garage, arrived at BK. Dhananjayan gave him a place to stay in his home, and while he assessed Reji's calibre, made him play the tambura as Aravindakshan sang. Soon, Reji was composing music for them, notably for the dance-drama *Karuna*.

'While essentially a nice man, Reji had some ego problems. He did not like Shanta singing with him. At times, he was very rude to her. He had a big problem with me because I would not allow him to drink on out-station tours. "I am a Christian, I can drink." I used to reply, "I do not care what your religion is. Drink is bad."'

While we students obeyed Dhananjayan's strictures both out of respect and fearful love, *bhaya bhakti*, the musicians were grown men who resented being given a list of dos and don'ts. Reji was perpetually late, once missing a train which resulted in Dhananjayan having to shell out hard-earned money for a plane ticket for Reji though he himself had travelled by train, hated being told to arrive on time for rehearsals, and disliked Dhananjayan's insistence on his wearing a jubba-veshti or kurta-pyjama especially when abroad.

Reji proved to be a divisive presence. 'After a major tour of America in 1993, he rebelled, "Oh, I have been going through this for the past 8 years. Shanta Akka keeps correcting my singing." Shanta was very hurt. When Reji's leg was broken, she had taken care of him and Amamma, her mother treated him like a son. Shanta said, "Enough is enough, I don't want him to sing for us anymore."'

Reji, Padmanabhan and Kannan, who were the face of the BK orchestra, felt that Dhananjayan was not paying them well. In the old world way that things were done, money was not discussed but placed in an envelope and handed to the musician after a show or tour. 'Reji was at the front, the rest kept mum. They were not happy with what I gave. I told them whatever we get, we share. They do not know how much money is invested in taking a group abroad, in all our overheads.'

After the falling out, they ceased to play for BK. 'People used to say the BK orchestra was the best in town, and wanted to use them. There were now more dancers on the scene, offering more money so they started going to others.'

There was some black humour in all this. 'People took our musicians away from us thinking our orchestra is the best behaved. They soon learnt the truth!' It was only many years later that a rapprochement was possible with Padmanabhan and Kannan. Reji died of liver failure.

It marked the passing of an era in a way. After that, many new and young musicians, were trained by Shanta and Dhananjayan. Vanathy, their female vocalist, daughter of Sangeeta Kalanidhi S. Ramanathan, was at first a student of dance. 'She left and years later, I heard her singing for the KFI Annual Day production and invited her sing for us. She is very disciplined, sings excellently and you can depend on her. Again, after we found her, she started singing for Vyjayanthimala Bali and Kalanidhi Narayanan!'

With changing times, musicians were hired increasingly on an ad-hoc basis, when there were dance-dramas or performances by the Dhananjayans. 'Our strength is that we can train anyone. In fact, if they wanted to play for our students as well, we agreed. All of them got new vehicles after joining us, from a cycle to a bike to a car; that was the BK luck!'

One musician kept Shanta on her toes. She recounted the many testing times she had with him. 'We took him to America, and there he started saying "I want to go back. Something terrible is going to happen to me." One evening, we looked for him and he was nowhere to be found. We had a show starting in minutes, so we were searching searching searching and getting very worried. We learnt that he had woken up saying he could not see properly and had asked his host to take him to the hospital. It was some sort of pollen allergy. Later, he insisted on returning to India saying, "What if I die halfway? I need someone to travel with me." Can you imagine, in the middle of a tour!'

Dhananjayan assessed the many changes. 'At one time, other dancers complained that I was pampering the musicians too much. Others would not even introduce them on stage but I used to honour them. "It will inflate their already big egos," my fellow artistes told me. But I felt they are all good musicians, so we should recognize their merit and talent. I used to give them loans. I wanted them to come up and their children to do well. Sometimes they would acknowledge, "We have prospered because of you." In the end, it boomeranged on me.

'Now, they are so busy, they are not available for rehearsals. They want more and more money, so even *I* am not able to keep a permanent musician, which is how things are currently. Their attitude has changed, they are very commercial now. Earlier, they would accept what I gave them, now they state upfront the fees expected. They earn plenty in their profession as accompanying musicians because they get paid for every show and very often it is the dancer who pays from his own pocket.'

From my own experience, I can say it is the quality of musicians, the fees, the time they are able to spare and, the low ratio of good musicians to dancers and indeed their attitude regarding rehearsals that marks a qualitative shift in perhaps the last twenty-five years of the history of Bharata Natyam.

35

A time came when there were enough male dancers, all in their mid-twenties or older, for Dhananjayan to hold a separate class for them. He concentrated a lot on his male students. Mainly, it stemmed from a genuine interest in mentoring them and wanting to give back; who better a teacher for a male dancer than himself? Partly, he required a trained team for his productions and also teachers for the junior classes.

Were they taught in a different manner, I wondered? Was there some secret Sir was sharing with them? On the occasions that our classes were combined with theirs, I could see that Sir's methods of teaching were the same, as were the items learnt.

However, the chief difference was with the basic position itself: arms akimbo, boys grasped their waist with four fingers visible on either side of their navel, whereas girls bent their hands backwards at the wrist. This gave the male dancers an air of perky showmanship.

There were certain positions or movements that were rendered by the girls in one way – say with a *kapitha* near the cheek which *a priori* was a feminine gesture – and by the boys in another – with their hands in an inverted *shikhara* near the shoulder denoting masculinity.

When it came to posture, the chief thing he insisted on for the boys was a chest held upright, an erect spine and no looseness or slack in the way the body was held. A man must radiate a certain dignity, an air of self-confidence and above all a manly quality. Just what was this manly quality is difficult to express in words but it had to do with carriage, gait and stance.

When any male dancer swung his hips loosely, exaggerated the swaying, bending of the limbs, or made facial expressions more suited to a woman, then one could instantly recognize this lack of manliness. It was in showing him how to dance like a man that Dhananjayan was the perfect guru for a male dancer.

Mainly, beyond the intricacies of technique, it was in *abhinaya* that Sir was to teach us a vital lesson. How was a male character to be portrayed in *abhinaya*? What made Shiva different from Krishna, or Muruga, or Rama, when depicted through dance? It was not just a simple matter of poses and *mudras*, but a vital inner essence that had to be communicated. Here, all the gods and heroes, as imagined in dance, were virile and full blooded.

Some of the top female solo artistes reduced Krishna-as-lover to a somewhat effete, prancing juvenile. In BK, regardless of whether it was a girl or a boy doing an *ashtapadi*, Krishna was first gifted his manhood and then his love for Radha was expressed frankly with intensity and ardour.

If they were performing Bharata Natyam, Sir insisted that the boys shaved their face and armpits, just before the show.

In class, when it came to actually grasping things, however, the girls seemed to have an edge. Many of the men had trouble with rhythm, maybe because they were learning at a later age. Just getting their feet to obey their mind was a problem. As they were made to do it over and over again, they floundered. Expressions, especially when it came to behaving as the female *nayika*, were beyond some.

Directions, angles and other geometric patterns were hugely problematic. A piece of choreography might require an *adavu* to be done on the diagonal, facing say north-east and north-west while the constant was north. It might involve moving towards the north-west while facing north-east. It might require tracing a circle with the moving body. All of these required spatial orientation, and some boys struggled with it.

Recently during a performance at a prestigious venue, eight BK dancers lined up one behind another to make an exit, save one boy. Losing his sense of direction he turned the wrong way, ending up face to face with the dancer behind him, blocking all movement!

So often in a master class, after she had tried repeatedly to make a boy understand that he was aligned improperly along the imaginary diagonal, Akka would say vexedly, 'All of you want to be MBAs, doctors, BA, MA, engineers, big big degrees and none of you can figure out which way a simple diagonal lies!'

Shanta herself had only studied until the tenth standard before quitting formal studies. She threw away her text-books, possibly the only area of her life in which she rebelled. Her more studious elder sister, who became a doctor, warned Shanta that she would live to regret it. 'That day has not yet come!' she confided delightedly to me. 'God was kind. I did what I loved. I've danced right from the age of six. I can write two or three sentences, add numbers, and speak. The calculations in dance and music I was very good at. What else does one need in life?'

36

It was a simple sequence of logic. I had the best of training, I was trained to perform solo, my solos were well received by critics and the audience alike. I *loved* who I was on stage, I had found my calling. Therefore the aim was to get *more* solos, and obviously through them, greater recognition.

While one solo was a miracle in itself, the real arrival was measured by how many solos one had during the Season, from December to January every year. I was not the only one enveloped by this fever; most of my classmates and seniors were all in the same ferment. We all competed for the same time slots, at the same sabhas.

BK was like a womb, incubating dancers. To acquire chances to perform meant breaching its safety to deal with the capricious, mystifying world of sabhas, government organizations supporting the arts, and temples that organized festivals of dance.

Outside BK, it was a melee. While just who one's guru was mattered as a stamp of quality, when it actually came to being invited for shows it was clear that influence counted. A 'professional' dancer was not so much one who depended for her livelihood on dance or had blazing talent, but one who had the right sort of influence to get the shows that would catapult her to the slot of 'professional'. For every dancer who made it, there were a dozen others who had flared briefly but languished for want of opportunity.

As for me, it seemed that I had the ace of spades in a winning hand: a father who was in the IAS. For the first three years after my debut, my parents did what any parents of a teenaged daughter would. If Sir indicated that a certain place offered a good opportunity to showcase talent, then they did approach the organizers. However given that they had no driving ambition for themselves, leave alone me; they had not used my father's position to their benefit; my father had taken on the Government of India in legal battle; *and* he was honest, therefore limited to his just-adequate salary, these occasions were few and far between.

Dancing was a costly affair, we discovered. Rather than *in*come, it demanded an *out*flow. While the jewellery and costumes were a one-time investment – and my mother generously gave me her silk sarees for costumes which lasted a very long time – each performance involved paying one's guru for *nattuvangam*, keeping time with the cymbals, and the various musicians. At the time, whether I was dancing for a sabha or a government organization, I don't recall ever having a surplus from a performance or breaking even.

Importantly, I remember being perplexed by the fact that no auditions were ever held, so how could they discern beforehand whether I was a good dancer or not?

The first time I actually earned money was when the Alliance Francaise of Madras, where I was a student, invited me to perform for the French Ambassador. The renumeration I asked for, to cover the cost of the musicians, was less than a thousand rupees but miraculously I ended up with some fifty rupees in hand! The year was 1988 and I had been a solo dancer for three years.

In 1989, my father took early retirement from the IAS and moved north. After that, the shows that came my way were due to my own efforts.

It was all about timing. No sooner had the Season ended, than I waited impatiently for March, the earliest I could apply for the next Season months away. In the days of landline and no email, it involved making repeated calls to the sabha office to find out just when the sabha secretary, or God, would be present. It was a strange fact but most of the sabha heads were advocates in their day jobs, but it was as the heads of sabhas that they presided on the fates of any artiste who wished to perform in their hall.

Then on the auspicious day, clutching my resume, photos, reviews, courage, I travelled some distance to the office. There, in a small ill-lit room festooned with portraits of famous musicians and posters of various gods, one would ask to be considered for a show.

The sabha secretary sat sphinx-like, implacable. A smile was greeted with a stare. 'Certainly, why not? The thing is...you have come too early. We have not made our lists as yet. Do come back in May. That's the time we will be deciding.'

In the voice there was infinite promise that he would really like to say yes right then, but his hands were tied until May.

March and April would go by in a daze, and then in May, another phone call to get an appointment. This time the great man would deign to speak on the phone, out of kindness.

'You are a bit too late this year. It is May and we have already decided, I had to accommodate so many people. I wish you had come a little earlier.'

The first time this happened, I believed him.

But when it happened at two different places the next year, and consecutively the third, then it was clear that some other factor was at play. In that sense, the rebuff was impersonal. It had to be; the man had never seen me dance.

The other factors at play, whispered about, were sexual favours by the dancer or her mother, or money. I remember an elderly gentleman who was quite familiar with the dance scene, telling me that he had observed the hand of a patron snaking around a dancer's supple waist and that the dancer herself had laughed it off as a minor accomodation for something as desired as the prime slot in a sabha. This truly was inconsequential when compared to the other arrangements one heard about, whether it was Delhi or Madras, involving patrons – variously industrialists, or politicians, or bureaucrats – and certain dancers.

Money could buy one anything at all. If it was needed to bridge the gap between what a sabha paid one and what the musicians charged, it was the clinching factor in getting a show.

Between 1991 and '95, I worked in a multinational bank. At the time, it paid the highest entry level salary for executives. I was overjoyed. The money I earned being bored to death every day would buy me all the books I wanted to read, and fund my shows, new costumes and additional pieces of jewellery. Strangely, the fact that I had a 'prestigious' job worked favourably when it came to applying for shows.

Once, a colleague helped out by speaking to one of the patrons of a sabha. It meant I had a foot in the door. But it was also accompanied by a request for a 3000 rupee advertisement - a euphemism - for their brochure. My heart sank. In 1997, 3000 rupees was a lot. It was unthinkable to just hand over my hard-earned money. Colleagues in the bank promised to get an ad out of one of their clients.

And so while for months I knew I would dance that Season, all the way until the evening of the show, the advertisement did not materialize.

I remember standing in the wings, all made up, fear in my heart that some sabha functionary would realize they had not got the advertisement and would either cancel the show or make me pay up in cash. No one did, but the fear gnawed huge chunks out of the joy of performing.

It was a big price to pay; it was the beginning of a breach.

37

An uneasy tension exists between films and classical dance. Most dance movements in films are far removed from the aesthetic demanded by the classical arts. While their aim of entertaining might be common, their way of achieving it is different. For a dancer who trains for years and years with strict discipline, it is demotivating to see the kind of cultural acceptance hip-thrusting and chest-jerking Bollywood moves have acquired, invading wedding sangeets and government sponsored presentations of Indian culture.

The attenuated treatment of time, and a marked interiority of the classical arts are at cross purposes with the quick pace required of celluloid. What might seem fleeting in a live performance, say three minutes of dancing, can seem excruciatingly slow on screen. Perforce, sequences of classical dance are shot at a fast pace.

If the dancing hero was a staple of Indian cinema, Kamal Haasan's arrival in Tamil cinema inspired countless young men to learn dance. Here was a hero who could dance Bharata Natyam, carrying an entire dance-based movie such as *Salangai Oli* on that strength. He inspired many boys to learn Bharata Natyam. Of those who found their way to BK, some wanted to become heroes, others settled for being choreographers. Actors just beginning to make their mark also came to polish their dancing skills.

Dhananjayan has a theory as to why actors are cult figures in our country, whereas a far more gifted dancer, relying solely on his face to emote, without the advantage of using his voice, can never aspire to reach those heights of popularity.

'Film projects the human figure as larger than life. It automatically makes a hero of a man. When we dance in a big auditorium, at a distance from the audience, we appear smaller! If we can project our performance simultaneously on huge screens, that would work very well. When the audience see the dancer's face in close-up, the eyes particularly, they understand and like it. Just last week, they broadcast a show of mine on TV, and strangers came across and told me, "When we saw you address Yasodha in *Yenna tavam*, we cried."'

Why not present classical dance as is, undiluted, in a film? It was perhaps with this thought in mind, that Dhananjayan accepted the few assignments that came his way, early in his career. With his looks, histrionic ability and well-proportioned body, Dhananjayan too might have achieved mega-star status dancing in films. After all, there were so many classical musicians such as G.N. Balasubramaniam and M.S.Subbulakshmi who achieved cult status after having sung in movies. Closer in time, Baby Kamala's quicksilver dancing had made countless girls aspire to learning Bharata Natyam.

Somehow though, when it came to films, Dhananjayan was jinxed.

Herbert Coleman, an associate of Alfred Hitchcock, was making a film *Holiday in India*. The dashing Shammi Kapoor played the lead with TV star Diane Baker. The plot line was simple. An American girl falls in love with an Indian boy and they decide to travel together through India. A collaboration with Air India, the film would highlight the special features of each place they travelled to.

Coleman was so impressed by the Dhananjayans, he decided to cast them in his movie. 'We were one of the couples the lead pair meet. Naturally in the film, we would be dancers. He wanted shots of the two of us performing, teaching students and also of the family. He left saying he would get back to us.'

After a year of silence, Coleman landed in Madras all of a sudden in 1974 with camera and crew ready to shoot. The Dhananjayans were taken unawares. Coleman was crestfallen when he saw Shanta. What was a happy reality for Shanta now created an unexpected problem. 'I said, "I can't dance, *I'm pregnant!*"' However the very next day he was back, having mulled over changes in the script. He said to Shanta, 'I want you in my movie. Can you appear as you are? Is it alright for me to ask you? Can you say you are pregnant? This is a wonderful message for us Americans that a professional dancer can have a family life and raise children while continuing to perform. This is the most touching thing!'

Shanta was overwhelmed by his interest. 'The script was now changed to the lady asking me, "Oh Shanta how nice to see you again. I thought you would dance for me." And I reply, "No, not this time, I am pregnant."'

Dhananjayan narrated the exciting experience of shooting a film: 'He wanted to shoot in a temple and I choreographed a ten minute sequence accordingly with the backdrop of the temple gopuram and gave him ideas for shots. Our girls had no experience at this, but once they explained how it would be done, we practised hard. Shanta made special costumes for the children doing a *tillana*.

'In three days we finished the whole sequence. They thought it would take ten days, so they were very pleased. We were to be paid 10,000 rupees which was a windfall for us in those days. Instead of 10,000 they gave us 20,000 because we saved them a lot of money!'

The Dhananjayans were beside themselves with anticipation. Appearing in a film made by Paramount Pictures and promoting Indian tourism would give an impetus to their career. Months passed, and then a year. 'We were waiting waiting waiting for the release of the picture. After a long time we found out that there was a fall out with Air India and the film was shelved. It was finished but not released. A friend of ours traced it in the archives of Paramount Pictures, the can is still there!'

One day, an unexpected guest came calling on the Dhananjayans. He was G.V. Iyer, the well known director of Sanskrit films, and period films with a strong spiritual component. 'He looked like a sage – long hair and beard.'

G. V. Iyer was making a movie in Kannada, *Hamsa Geethe*, about the journey of a musician in search of a guru and god. He wanted Dhananjayan to choreograph the dance sequences in the classical style for the *ashtapadis* of the *Geeta Govindam*. 'He left the choice of songs to me. Jayalakshmi Easwar would dance and Mani Krishnaswami was to sing. Since we were all from Kalakshetra, our preparation was meticulous.'

Dhananjayan got to work. Each afternoon, trusted taxi-driver Mohan Raj drove him and Mani Krishnaswamy to G. V. Iyer's house, where they worked with noted music director T.G. Lingappa as he set the music. 'We dug up an old *tillana* by Oothukadu Venkatasubbier, the *Kalinga Nartana tillana* in the Suruti raga and used it as a period piece. Everything came together beautifully.'

The recording was done, the music was ready but the shooting did not commence. Just as had happened with Coleman, there was a long passage of time when there was no news of the film and no contact made by G.V. Iyer.

One night, in 1975, Dhananjayan's neighbour frantically rang the door-bell and woke him up. 'We did not have a phone…we used to receive calls at our neighbour's house. Suddenly, we got this call from an unknown man. "Sir, you must come to Chitradurga Fort tomorrow."'

Disturbed from his sleep, Dhananjayan was puzzled. 'Where? For what?' he enquired.

'Shooting.'

'What shooting?'

'Iyer.' Another cryptic answer.

'Which Iyer?'

'*Hamsa Geethe.*'

The Dhananjayans were leaving the next day for the Sanskritik Festival in London. 'I can't come,' replied Dhananjayan.

'No, no you have to come. We will put case in court.'

'What case? There is no contract.'

'You are the dance director.'

Dhananjayan was hugely annoyed. 'I am sorry.'

With the set ready, and production costs mounting, the desperate crew turned to Adyar Lakshman. He travelled immediately to Chitradurga and contributed some fine choreography on the spot. But Dhananjayan was very disappointed that all his hard work had gone waste. 'They wanted big names and so finally M. Balamuralikrishna and M. L. Vasantakumari's voices were used.'

A fortuitous choice as it turned out, for M. Balamuralikrishna won the 1976 National Award for Best Male Playback Singer for his song '*Himadri Sute*' in *Hamsa Geethe*.

But there was a silver lining to the story. When Dhananjayan returned from the Sanskritik and Carthage Festivals, he got a call from Doordarshan. 'The Madras channel was being inaugurated and they wanted a dance drama overnight! With only two of us! I used Lingappa's music, and strung the *ashtapadis* together in *Radha Madhavam* and it became a hit! We did *Lalita Lavanga, Yahi Madhava, Vadasiyadi* and the *Suruti tillana*!'

Dhananjayan in performance

The Dhananjayans went on to perform *Radha Madhavam* innumerable times as part of their concert repertoire. Radha and Krishna's imagined love quarrels conveyed by dancers who were actually husband and wife tickled the audience's imagination.

The next interaction with the world of cinema, which confirmed the three-times-unlucky jinx, was the Tamil movie *Kann Sivandhaal Mann Sivakumm.*

Young director Sridhar Rajan had seen Dhananjayan dance. He wanted to incorporate the story of untouchable Nandan, one of the sixty-three Shaivite saints of Tamil Nadu, in a film. 'He talked to me about his ideas. There was a lot of labourer unrest in the Thanjavur area at the time in 1982. He wanted to explore revolutionary communism and link it with this story of Nandanar in the film.'

The actress Purnima Jayaram was cast as a student who comes all the way from America to research *therukoothu*, the regional theatre art. Dhananjayan would play himself, a dancer and guru to this young student. While travelling, she would remember in flashback her guru performing Nandanar's story,

Dhananjayan was vastly pleased. His artistry had been recognized by this mass medium, and he did not have to compromise with the classical boundaries of his art. He agreed to feature in the film and help with the music.

Maestro Ilayaraja was the music director and Carnatic musician T. V. Gopalakrishnan, versatile in both vocal Hindustani and vocal Carnatic *and* a mridangam expert, the playback singer. 'We selected the songs. Ilayaraja was just getting into the limelight then – he rearranged the tunes. We had the awesome experience of recording in a proper studio. It took almost a month.'

The shooting took place at the busiest time in a dancer's life, during the December season in Madras. The parts that showed Dhananjayan as a guru were shot in BK. I remember arriving one evening for class and finding the brick walls a brighter red, with kolam decorations drawn on them in white paint. Thinning thatch had been replaced and the place spruced up. The tension and excitement and a sense of big possibilities was palpable.

'Soumendu Roy, Satyajit Ray's assistant, and his camera unit came to BK, watched me dance and decided the shots. They saw it so often, the Bengalis started singing the Tamil songs!'

Then the shooting began. An open-air spot at the Cholamandalam Artists Village was chosen. 'I used up all our money for costumes. We went there every night! I danced for thirty minutes lit by giant flares. The idea was that it was a village scene, so no artificial light was used. For fifteen nights we worked very hard. I felt so good!

Mystifyingly, after finishing the shoot, there was a break in communication. Again the anticipation, again the frustration. 'For almost two years, no contact, no news. I was able to contact neither Sridhar Rajan nor the producer Venkatraman who was K. Balachander's assistant.'

Out of the blue, in 1983, the movie was released. To Dhananjayan's shock, and chagrin, his dance scene was down to three minutes! 'I was so upset, I refused to watch the film. It was the same old excuse...The director said he could not help it, they wanted more masala which he finally had to agree to.'

Some of Dhananjayan's acquaintances reported that there was a tremendous audience response to his fleeting presence in the film. Intrigued, Dhananjayan decided to attend a screening, temporarily putting aside his rage.

'We went to Midland theatre to see it. To my surprise the frontbenchers clapped when I danced to the song *kanakasabhai thirunatanam*. These were the uneducated masses...rickshaw pullers, auto drivers, labourers. It proved to me that even they could relate to the classical arts provided it was done with complete integrity. During the interval, some of them recognized me and I was mobbed! They shouted, "*Sar romba joraa irundudu*. You should have danced more."'

Dhananjayan identified so strongly with the character of Nandanar, he worked on the songs of *Nandanar Charitram* and strung them into a solo dance drama. His gut-wrenching portrayal of the longing of Nandanar to see Shiva just once at Chidambaram and the caste-arrogant Brahmin landlord's insults moved many an audience member to tears.

With all these rollercoaster experiences behind him, Dhananjayan was wary when some Malayalam producers approached him in the mid-eighties for a film on Swati Thirunal. They wanted him to choreograph the dance sequences. 'They were offering me a pittance. 7000 rupees for finishing 12 songs in a week, more than a song a day! To test them, I asked for a fantastic advance. About a lakh!' The producer snorted, "I can finish the film in that amount!"' The movie became the hit *Kamaladalam*. And with that ended Dhananjayan's foray into cinema.

38

Of the many unforeseen elements that can mar a performance, illness and injury are the worst. When a dancer commits to a performance months in advance, there is no way of knowing whether he will indeed be able to perform on that day. And yet all plans and rehearsals have to made on the assumption of good health.

It so happened that once Dhananjayan had a very high fever. It would not have mattered at any other time, but he was in Mysore to dance during the Dussehra festival. The show had received wide publicity, but hours before the show was to begin, Dhananjayan was in no state to perform. It was decided that Shanta would perform solo.

'I was so weak, I could not even get up from my bed. They did not want to leave me like that alone at the hotel, so they carried me into the greenroom.'

The place was packed. Shanta waited in the wings as the musicians sang an invocation to Ganesha.

Backstage, Dhananjayan lay still on a couch. 'An old man came into the room. He looked very disappointed. He said, "I have travelled forty kilometres to watch you dance but I heard you are not performing." He sighed and said, "What to do?" He had brought some prasadam from the famous Chamundeshwari temple and he gave it to me.

'I ate it. Suddenly, I don't know how, I stood up! I was touched by what he said. I just wore my dhoti, no makeup and went onto the stage. Shanta and the musicians, they all stared at me. I don't know where I got the energy from but I was in my element.'

Dhananjayan went on to do a *varnam* on Rama, an energy-intensive one on any given day, for an hour and 15 minutes. Stimulated by the sight of the large appreciative audience, he braved a *tillana* as well. When the curtain fell, he collapsed on the stage and had to be rushed to the hospital where he was hooked to a drip. There was a consolation though: 'Because I had sweated, my fever went!'

He went on to remember another distressing time. 'When you dance, you forget everything, pain, weakness. You're not thinking about it. Once I had a boil on my bottom. It was so painful, I could not sit down and suffered a lot, travelling to Boston. Still, I performed there. If you prepare the mind, it gives you the strength to endure. Later, while dancing at a house-concert, the boil burst and I was relieved of the pain!'

In 1977, the ICCR invited the Dhananjayans to go on a lec-dem tour to East European countries. 'Towards the end of our tour, it became very very cold. It was freezing in Czechkoslavakia and we had not taken enough warm clothes! We had to stay indoors, and in the hotel the heating was not so good, so we spent all the time under blankets. Soon, I caught cold, and Shanta too was feeling ill. We had to give a lec-dem the next morning, did not know what to do. Then our driver, he advised us to have *brandy*!

'He was a nutty character. The Kamasutra was banned there and he desperately wanted to read it. "Can you send it to me?" he pleaded. Anyway, he advised us to have brandy. He had to buy it for us. He brought it in a small bottle. "Just drink it and sleep," he said. "You won't get drunk or anything."

'We did not become tipsy. Instead we became hot. Hotter and hotter from inside, we were *burning*! Instead of sleeping, we spent the night wide awake, sweating away. Could not call a doctor so late at night. And we were worried how we would perform the next morning! There was no question of cancelling. We did the lec-dem! When you think of work, you forget about the body. But it was very difficult, and afterwards, we were knocked out and slept for hours!'

A performance is a sacred compact between the audience, that takes the trouble to come to watch a show, and the dancer, who spends all the hours of his life practising for it. Used to pushing the limits of stamina, a dancer will not think twice before taxing the body further during a show.

Dhananjayan's hero, the legendary Guru Gopinath left this world after a rousing performance as Dasharatha, on 9 October 1987, his *ghungroos* still on his ankles. That's the ideal way to go!

39

When Dhananjayan was given the coveted title 'Nritya Choodamani' by Sri Krishna Gana Sabha in 1983, 'They gave it to *me*, not us as a dancing couple. Said there was no precedence of giving it to two people together,' it was a stamp of approval by the establishment.

He courted controversy at the award ceremony. 'I made a very revolutionary speech. I accused the sabhas of not promoting the art. It was printed and distributed to the audience. I said that if the sabhas are not able to support dancers, then we have the present day maharajas in the form of corporate houses. They should help art and artistes.'

It caused an uproar. People thought he was all for selling out, commercializing the arts. 'What does that mean? An artist has to survive and needs money. When money enters the picture, it becomes commercial. I used the word marketing the way they do in the west. They misunderstood it as wanting to commercialize the practice of dance. But now, look, everyone is doing it. It has gone the other way. The corporate houses do sponsor shows, but instead of the money going to the artistes, it is going to the sabhas and secretaries who get richer. It was a good idea but it went wrong. Art management, a culture of professionalism, we need to have that.'

Dhananjayan did not stop with that. He went on to lambast the media and reviewers.

The reaction was instant. The *Indian Express* carried an article by Subbudu captioned 'An indecorous attack'.[29] Subbudu, P.V. Subramaniam, was a much-feared dance critic who was once taken to court by the dancer Yamini Krishnamurthy. She sued him and the *Statesman* for fifty lakhs, for having compared her gestures in the *alarippu* to morning ablutions![30] Scatology seems to have obsessed Subbudu, for he slathered it on one of Dhananjayan's best concert pieces thus: 'The artistes sitting posture and his fitful gestures reminded one more of acute constipation than delivery.'[31]

Sadanand Menon, journalist, captured it best in his article in *The Sunday Observer:*[32]

'Every December/January in Madras, a generally dyspeptic season of music and dance activises a brood of effete and senile venerables well into their dotage who pass off as "critics" and consume large chunks of column space in newspapers to foul the already turgid politics of the art world here with their own archaic and totally irrelevant personal prejudices and whims…These "critics" have become minor institutions [and have] managed to extend the suffocating mindlessness of the classical dance world, camouflaged with flamboyance and colour, into their own limp literary excursions.

'No wonder leading Bharata Natyam and Kathakali dancer Dhananjayan while…being honoured with the title of "Nritya Choodamani" recently, thought fit to say "Nowadays the reviews are not what they should be and constructive criticism is lacking in the Press. It is more often prejudiced, personal or parochial. The media are also afraid of criticizing or publishing adverse comments on a dancer or musician lest they lost their business…or (are afraid) that a particular industrialist or government department might withdraw its valuable advertisements."'

'Instead of reacting to this in the dignified spirit in which it was said and taking time off for some much needed self-reflection, we find *Express* critic Subbudu responding: "Having been groomed under the banyan tree at Kalakshetra, Dhananjayan appears to have imbibed the attitude of scant regard for the media of his mentor Smt. Rukmini Devi who gave vent to it in her speech two years ago. It has become the fashion for artists who have been built up by the press to cast aspersions on its bonafides...The sooner Dhananjayan mends his ways the better for him."'

Calling reviewers 'Dotards sitting and drooling over buxom lasses' Sadanand went on to rue, 'The role of the critic never fell lower than this...Writing on a male dancer, the well known C V Chandrashekharan [sic], Subuddu has no mention of eyes or beauty or any syrupy adjectives.'

Well, Subbudu did talk about Dhananjayan's beauty once. 'V.P. Dhananjayan gave one of the most spirited Bharata Natyam recitals that sent the audience into raptures. He is stunningly beautiful and is gifted with an admirable gait. And the *adavus*! How beautifully they were etched.'[33]

That was a rare instance of appreciation. For the most part, according to Dhananjayan, 'He hated the three K's, Kathakali, Kerala and Kalakshetra, so he never gave us a good review! He did not like men dancing.'

Dhananjayan remained unfazed by Subbudu's jibes and ill-chosen remarks, 'He once wrote a review of our performance in Delhi with the headline "*Dhananjayans, Dhananjayans, Dhananjayans*!"' Subbudu went on to complain that the ICCR was "hellbent on hastening the downfall of the dancing couple, the Dhananjayans, by presenting them too often."[34] Leela Venkataraman too echoed the sentiment with the caption, 'The Dhananjayan refrain' in her review of the same performance.[35]

Too often? These hardwon opportunities came to Dhananjayan courtesy his students Pushkala Gopal and Padmini Dorairajan who lived in Delhi at the time. 'When they were invited to perform, or when students from Madras danced in the Guru Sishya parampara series, then we would perform as well.' A remark like this, for artistes seeking the only too important recognition in Delhi, was like throwing a spanner in the works.

'Some of Subbudu's remarks, about mistakes made by a flautist or singer for example, were useful and I benefited from them. He was very knowledgeable. Later on, before he died, I received a handwritten letter from him where he called me a *sthithapragna*, one who remains unshakeably calm through life, despite any comments made about him.' That to Dhananjayan was the ultimate compliment from the most feared critic of his times.

40

The Sanskritik Festival in London, organized by Pandit Ravi Shankar's cousin Virendra Shankar with the help of the Indian Government, was a precursor to the Festivals of India held in the 80s.

Dhananjayan performed there in 1975. 'We danced with a lot of other artists from India, the Jhaveri sisters performed Manipuri, Indranil Bhattacharya played the sitar. There too I became the leader of the whole party, because I took the initiative. I don't sulk, I don't withdraw...that is my nature. There were some clashes, not all the artistes got along, especially those from Delhi. They had the usual demands, "I want to be first", "I want maximum time." We had to plan a programme without ego clashes. Virendra left everything to me, I had to convince them to think of the show as a collective effort. Since I say what is on my mind, not everyone took to me but everyone liked Shanta. We all had a per diem and lived in a flat, so we had to manage in that money.'

One evening, after a performance at Elizabeth Hall, to Dhananjayan's amazement, Pandit Ravi Shankar came backstage accompanied by Lakshmi Shankar and her sister Kamala. 'You look like my brother Uday,' he complimented him. 'I would like to work with you some day.' For Dhananjayan, his saying this was an honour in itself. To his joy, Ravi Shankar did visit BK when he next visited Madras.

In London, one of the Dhananjayan's students, Pushkala Gopal was the director of the Academy of Indian Dance. It was important to her to challenge the prevailing notion, in the early 80s, that Indian dances were only solo presentations, mostly worshipful in nature. A group production with a secular theme was possible. What was the best way to present it? She mulled over many ideas with Dhananjayan and they decided to do *Jungle Book*. *Jungle Book* the movie had just been released. In Mowgli, it had a loveable character who was different from the usual heroes Rama, Krishna.

Dhananjayan was excited about the project. 'The Arts Council liked the idea and were willing to fund it. They wanted Raviji to do the music. He was very open to the idea and said he would like to work with us.'

The idea was to use four of the main classical dances of India, Odissi, Bharata Natyam, Kathak and Kathakali in telling the story of Mowgli. 'I had to plan the script. My story is not the same as the one in the book, we had to adapt it for theatre.'

Other than the three human characters, the rest of the cast were animals. The wolf as such did not belong in the pantheon of animals that were usually depicted through Indian *mudras* and movements. Neither was the panther. Dhananjayan had to create the loping movements and animal-character of both.

'I met Kathak dancer Pratap Pawar, and discussed how to bring Kathak into it using *bols*. We thought of introducing the four styles by having a group of dancers in a village. One of the girls being the heroine Sita. It was a chance for people to see styles coming together.'

While the classical element was maintained, their rigid boundaries were softened and an element of contemporary dance brought in. Many of the movements were novel and the theme itself unusual.

Several boundaries were being breached at once. Dhananjayan wanted to expand the way Bharata Natyam was perceived and prove that it was not just based on mythology or tied to legends and history. It had enough power in its movement vocabulary to convey ideas free of religious symbolism or laden with spirituality. *Jungle Book* proved to be the perfect vehicle. He had always loved depicting animals on stage anyway.

The other difference was that the music would be scored to convey the storyline, unlike conventional Bharata Natyam, where the song came first. In a reversal of the usual order, the dance would be choreographed first, by Dhananjayan. It required great self assurance and vison to do that. The music would then be scored based on these movements, and it would be so evocative, words would not be required.

'To my great disappointment, Pandit Ravi Shankar said he could not do the music but one of his senior disciples would. That is how Pandit Vijay Raghava Rao came to score the music. It took about a month to record the music in Chennai. It came out so well!'

Since the Arts Council was funding it, the selection process had to be transparent. 'We had an audition to select the artists. We were looking for a child Mowgli. Some of the girls in Pawar's class auditioned, along with a girl whose parents were from Bangladesh. She was 8 or 9 years old and her brother came with her. At the time, he was not a student of dance. I noticed this boy running around, being naughty and making monkey faces. I asked his parents if we could use him, "He has a natural talent. It's a small part. I will be the grown up Mowgli." Finally, they agreed. I taught him some movements, and he had a good sense of rhythm and could follow me instantly. Today he is one of the leading exponents of contemporary dance. Akram Khan!' Dhananjayan beamed with the satisfaction of having spotted natural talent.

However, there was another problem. 'According to the rules for child artistes, Akram could not perform every day. We were travelling and had back to back shows. So we decided to take our son Satyajit. He was the right age! He and Akram danced as Mowgli alternately.'

Aspi Mullah, Dhananjayan's first male student, lived in London. He was cast as Akhela the wolf in the production. Unfortunately, Aspi broke his leg in an accident and a substitute had to be found quickly. Dhananjayan had used Unnikrishnan as his understudy in Madras while choreographing the role of Akhela. So, Unnikrishnan set off, as a last minute replacement, for London. Later, Pushkala Gopal was to invite him to stay there, teaching dance at the institute Mudralaya.

For the Dhananjayans it was the first taste of how far they could stretch their creative horizons given the right support and funding. Until then they had worked with small budgets and their costumes and set design were limited by that constraint. Here, for *Jungle Book*, the set was dominated by a single tree that kept changing from scene to scene depending on what was happening beneath it. The clever use of lights could make a forest or a village instantly.

The show premiered in London on March 17, 1984. It was a great success, in large part due to the music. This time as well Pandit Ravi Shankar was in the audience.

'Panditji was very happy with the music and dance. Once again, he said he wanted to do a production with us!'

41

From an African tribal princess to a sixty-three-year-old Norwegian, to Angelika Sriram, a German, Dhananjayan has had students from a wide variety of races bending their limbs to Bharata Natyam.

In the seventies, a lot of foreign students, having finished the course at Kalakshetra, came to Dhananjayan because they wanted to learn more. That attracted criticism in the small world of dance in Madras.

'People thought we were making a lot of money from foreigners. Because I insisted on proper payment of fees, there was a feeling that the Dhananjayans are very expensive, but finally people understood that was not so. We were "cheap and best" as our Japanese student Erina Kasai put it!'

Of the earliest group of foreigners who came to learn, 'the only exceptional one was the American, Sheila Christian. She had a good figure and the costume suited her. She had stayed in India for a long time and understood the culture...was interested in yoga, could play the veena. When she married into a Muslim family she could not continue. It was so sad. Later, she moved to America and set up a school of dance there.'

Paradoxically, as Dhananjayan became more successful and spent many days spent travelling across the country and globe, he was not free to spend the kind of time he had in drilling the basics into us. I was part of the only two privileged 'batches' that had their *adavu*-foundation directly laid by him. As more and more students joined every year, 'seniors' taught the 'juniors' under his general supervison. Of course, this attracted criticism and the disappointment of parents as well. However, when these freshers reached the stage of graduating, or performing their debut, or went on to perform solo, they received direct training from him.

One of the benefits of learning at BK has been the chance to interact with students from across the world. A steady stream of students has come from Sri Lanka, among whom there were 'lots of Christians. Wilma from Sri Lanka. Nirmala Benedict, for them it was not too difficult even though the themes and items revolve around Hindu deities.' Shanta, known to be a wicked mimic, would send us into gales of laughter by speaking the curious Tamil spoken by Sri Lankans. Needless to say, when it was used to hilarious effect by Kamal Haasan in the film *Thenali*, Shanta loved it.

There have been many students from Japan. 'One has to appreciate their involvement. They come all the way here to learn. Even if not all our foreign students are creative, you do communicate something to them, a love for the art. When you connect with a student, it makes you feel good.'

The oldest and most dedicated was the evergreen Daya Tomiko of Kyoto. Every second or third year, when she had saved enough for her ticket and fees and stay in Madras, she would join our classes. Recently, she gave a full length performance and was so agile, no one could tell she was sixty plus. I was curious about what drew her to Bharata Natyam.

Tomiko had successfully staged a dance drama on the passionate love story of Muruga with the tribal lass Valli, choreographed by Dhananjayan, in Kyoto in 2005. What did the Japanese mind make of this legend? Why this fascination for Murugan out of the entire pantheon of Hindu gods and goddesses?

Tomiko spoke slowly as she wrapped her thoughts in English. 'He is a god but as a lover, he sees no difference between Devayanai, who is Indra's daughter and Valli, a hunter-chief's daughter. High and low do not matter to him.'

As always, travelling to another county brought its own excitements. In Kyoto, Shanta had the unforgettable experience of bathing in the common sento-style bathroom at the inn. 'You can't wear clothes inside. All the women were naked! I soon learnt to creep in when it was the most empty!'

When students began to arrive from America, and the Dhananjayans themselves were travelling there frequently to perform, it was only a matter of time before Yogaville happened. Yogaville, home to the ashram run by Swami Satchidananda who had Woodstock chanting Hari Om in 1969, is set in the lush green Virginian countryside. In 1988, Dhananjayan held the first summer dance camp there.

'It started as an experiment. I did not like the idea of of doing one-day workshops. Here, students stay with us and learn from morning to night in a very intense way over two weeks. We focus on Swamiji's Three D's – Discipline, Dedication and Devotion. I can insist on their wearing a bindi, and proper clothes here which I can't do elsewhere. They were called ABCDs, but I have seen them show a lot of interest and commitment. Some turn out to be really good performers too. So now I call them American Born Confirmed Desis!'

At BK, we soon got used to the fact that come July Dhananjayan and Shanta would head to Yogaville. The Natya Adhyayana camp has now completed its twenty-fourth year. 'Under the able stewardship of Rukmini Rasiah, one of Swamiji's disciples, and Padmarani Rasiah Cantu, it became a trendsetter. After its success, people in different cities of America all wanted us to come and hold a camp. While we have done short stints of teaching elsewhere, nothing compares to Yogaville. There the atmosphere is different.'

The unique fact about the camp was that dancers from any style of Bharata Natyam were welcome. This only made it more difficult for Dhananjayan. 'When there are newcomers who have been taught the basics badly, or a terrible style, in three weeks we have to make them see it, correct what we can. Have to deal with them nicely and not make them feel that what they learnt is a waste, because they have to go back to their teachers. Shanta is more diplomatic than me. We cannot tell them, *Oh what you have been taught so far is very bad.*'

Doesn't he feel an ennui, to still have to instil the basics at age 73? I was playing with fire asking this question because Dhananjayan feels we 'seniors' are not teaching as much as he would like us to, to transmit the basics as precisely as we learnt it. I thought I would get a hollering. Instead, he replied, 'Of course! At this age, still going through the *adavus* and fundamentals, it is a little difficult. I want to go beyond that, to teach at the creative level.'

Of the many students at Yogaville, perhaps the most interesting one was the Nigerian tribal princess. 'Her father was a follower of Swamiji so when there was political upheaval in Nigeria, he flew with her to Yogaville. He had to return to Nigeria but he left her safe in Swamiji's care. She looked like an Indian girl, very nice features. She had an innate talent and a very good sense of rhythm. She trained in acrobatics at school, so some of her *dhalaanku*-leaps she did very well. She just learnt Bharata Natyam because she loved it. Before a show she straightened her hair out, and was able to wear the *thalai saaman*, hair ornaments. We heard that she has become a fashion model in New York.'

Far away from New York, a young NRI boy named Anand Satchidanandan had been learning Bharata Natyam in Jakarta, stepping up his training during summer vacations in India.

A comic mix-up at the Hong Kong airport over their identical names, led Anand's father to meet Swami Satchidananda in 1999. 'Out of the blue, Swamiji asked my father, "Do you have a son who dances? Tell him to come to Yogaville. The Dhananjayans are teaching there."'

At the time Anand was thirteen. But even before he was born in 1986, Anand's family was prepared to welcome the artist in him. 'My grandfather, a well-known astrologer in Chembur, predicted that the baby would be art-inclined and he made my mother promise that she would nurture whatever art it was.'

There being no proper teachers in Kuwait where they lived, his parents took him to Bombay during the summers, where he learnt from Nagarajan Pillai, Mahalingam Pillai's son-in-law. 'I started with a traditional *nattuvanar*-teacher. You could smell the paan juice in his mouth even before he rang the bell, yet when he enunciated a *jati* it was so clear.'

The sound of the doorbell however sent shivers down his spine. Coaxed out of his hiding place, the four-year-old would practise his *adavus* with his teacher, dreading what was to come. 'He was a very two-sided man. Until my mother left the room he would be solicitous. "How are you, dear? Here, let me rub your aching limbs with this special oil." When she left, he would be a demon. Beat me, throw things at me, hit me on the shins. All behind doors.'

Nobody believed Anand when he complained until the day his grandmother chanced upon the teacher hitting him. Nothing changed though. 'Mom thought it was needed. I didn't have a choice. To this day, she is proud of her strictness.'

Two summers later, Anand had a mini-debut in a Murugan temple. 'The chief priest was so moved, he carried me on his shoulders into the sanctum, took a garland off the deity and put it on me.'

It had a powerful impact on the young child. 'It showed me the benevolence and power of art, and a very real, almost tangible, divine connection we have with our arts and religion and spirituality. There is a connection between what we do on stage and everyone's spiritual consciousness.'

The family then moved to Indonesia, but Anand continued his dance classes, now with Usha Srinivasan in Madras. 'She was amazing. Having learnt from Dandayudhapani Pillai, she had a very subtle, gentle approach to dancing.'

Simultaneously, he found a teacher in Jakarta. 'Rekha Subbarao of the Mysore style. Both Usha Srinivasan and she were amazing in their give and take.'

Anand Satchidanandan

In 1997, when he was eleven, Anand did his *arangetram* with the involvement of both gurus. 'My parents did the whole jingbangboom NRI thing. I had two costumes. Orange with a black border, and green with a red border. I felt wonderful. I was not scared at all. I remember being a little nervous about how I looked. The makeup artist dunked me in a vat of foundation. My eyes were done in a super girly way. Ruby red lips...I hate lipstick!'

Until now, there was no self-consciousness in Anand about being a boy who danced, even if he was the only boy in class. Neither teacher emphasized his gender and, 'I was not effeminate as a dancer, or my family would have told me.' Even now, 'The way I think about my Bharata Natyam, is that it is genderless. Each *adavu* has a personality and you can attribute it to a certain gender in the way you do it but that is subsequent.'

Growing up in Jakarta, as a 'good Brahmin Iyer boy who does sandhya three times a day,' Anand did battle with the general prejudice, 'that if you are a dancer you must be gay'. It did not help that he was 'not into sports, the "guy" thing'. Was that a marker that he might be gay, he worried. 'As a young boy it's a ghost that follows you.' There was always the 'tension between *Don't break your legs or twist your ankle because you need to dance* and *You need to be in sports to be manly*. When I meet a male dancer who is also into sports, I am like *Wow you got both deals!*'

Another issue that ran parallel, was the extended family's curiosity about what he would grow up to be. A cousin of his recently told him, 'I'm happy you turned out normal. You were always dancing and I was worried you would turn into an effeminate guy.' Here Anand credits his father for stoicly bearing his family's taunts and being very supportive. 'The boys I've met who dance well say their fathers were very co-operative.'

All this time, 'While I was dancing it was on automatic mode, if you asked me about my shows I would not be able to tell you. I would blackout and my mind was left aside. I can only remember the lights in the front and on the edges of my eyelashes and hear the music. I was in my own bubble.'

And now he was headed to Yogaville.

Thirteen years old, away from his mother for the first time, 'in the middle of nowhere, guided by the fireflies at night back to the trailers,' Anand was to find his perspective on dance altered forever at Yogaville.

'Until then I never thought I was narrating something to connect to the audience. Their training gave me depth…every *mudra*, pose or movement was charged with the high energy of that purpose.'

After he met the Dhananjayans at Yogaville, Anand followed them to India. Attending classes at BK during school holidays meant a growing alienation from Usha Srinivasan, who did not believe that he especially needed to change styles.

In 2004 Anand headed to the US to study International Affairs at Wesleyan University. Until then studies and dance had gone hand in hand. 'It never occurred to me that I needed to choose, because I had been told all along that I can do *this* and that. The question was staring me squarely in the face at Wesleyan.'

There, 'The things that should interest me were not, while music classes were alluring. The music spoke to my soul, kept ringing in my head the entire day. I felt wonderful. On the other hand, studies bored me to tears, literally. If I find a book boring, my eyes water...I have a physical reaction to it!'

Graduation and a fund-raising job later, Anand 'sensed that India was the place to be.' He made the decision in 2010 to 'go back and dedicate myself to dance. I wanted to study music.' Setting down roots in Chennai, with his parents and brother, 'I was so excited to dance. The sound of the *thattu kazhi* and learning new items! There wasn't enough time in the day, it seemed. I was dancing morning and evening.'

Anand was so happy, in a fit of exuberance he told his gurus Dhananjayan and Shanta, that 'I want to learnt two full *margams* in a year, and they laughed at me.' At BK the pace of learning and choice of items would always be solely the prerogative of the Guru.

Well educated, well off, highly talented Anand was to break the stereotype at BK. Here finally was a male dancer who had the skills, the financial muscle and family support to make it as a professional.

And yet...

42

Being a male dancer meant Dhananjayan once having to wait at the gate of a girls-only college when the very stern principal refused to allow him and his party of male musicians' entry. But then, it was a situation of his own making!

In 1988, post-operation Bluestar, when no one wanted to travel through a militant 'burning' Punjab, Dhananjayan had volunteered to undertake a tour of schools there for Spic Macay – the unique voluntary effort started by Dr. Kiran Seth to spread an interest and understanding in our classical and regional arts, our cultural heritage, among the youth.

Dhananjayan rallied his team of recalcitrant musicians – who feared for their lives – by buying them life insurance, and set off with his ever stoic Shanta all the way across the country by train.

And now here they were at the gates of the Khalsa Women's College, Ludhiana, at the invitation of Spic Macay, where the principal stoutly refused to allow '*naach-gaana*' into her campus. Why were they thrusting themselves on her?

The students of the local Spic Macay chapter begged her for fifteen minutes of 'talk' time. The watchman grudgingly opened the gates just wide enough to let them through single file. 'Any other artiste in my place would have walked out, unable to bear the humiliation,' commented Dhananjayan. 'In fact, my musicians were very upset and did not want to participate, since only I was going to talk to the students.'

'I began speaking. Very naturally, as though it was part of my speech, I used *mudras* and expressions. Fifteen minutes passed, and when I asked if I should stop, 2000 girls loudly cheered us to go on. The talk became a lec-dem and then seeing they were so attentive, we performed *Radha Madhavam* for them. Watching Krishna and Radha's love story, they understood this was not some cheap entertainment; that one can reach the divine through art.'

Mid-way through the session, the principal hurried out. Her assistants scurried after her. The dance ensemble wondered if she was upset. To their surprise, the principal returned with shawls and a huge brightly wrapped gift and proceeded to honour them. Almost in tears, she confessed her ignorance of the classical arts and promised to open a Spic Macay chapter in her college.

Two hours later when the show ended, the Dhananjayans received an emotional standing ovation. As they were proceeding to the feast hastily arranged for them, a nervous teacher crept up to them asking for the showy gift-box. It was empty, she confessed. After lunch, they were taken shopping and, the principal having written them a blank cheque with typical Punjabi large-heartedness, were told to choose whatever they liked. They returned not only with their shopping but also suitcases in which to pack it!

One of their most memorable experiences, Dhananjayan cites it often as an example of the 'ability of art to win over hearts'.

Firm supporters of its cause, the Dhananjayans travelled to many states of India for Spic Macay. Since students are responsible for every aspect of an artiste's stay, many a time they had to deal with lapses in organization. Dhananjayan, otherwise a stickler, overlooked times when they had to travel without reservations on trains or when the accommodation was barely up to the mark. 'I treat it as an adventure,' he remarked, 'and do not make a fuss. When we went to Rajasthan for example, we would drive long distances just to reach two or three schools, it was very tiring. But I enjoyed it!'

He remembered one particular surreal experience. 'It was a lo*o*ong drive to a remote place where there was a hostel.' Dhananjayan's expression showed just how tedious it was. 'The driver said there was a short cut. But that took us off the main road onto a mud road and then through a quarry. We drove over stones! If the vehicle had broken down we would have been finished!'

They reached very late at night, by which time the hostel was closed so they did not get any dinner. Not a happy situation when there were three grumpy musicians to be fed.

'Somehow we managed to sleep. Early next morning, I heard strange cries. I opened the door and saw hundreds of peacocks dancing! It was as if they wanted to dance for us dancers. It was so exciting!'

There were lots of feathers lying around, and Shanta brought back a bunch. They would find use in a crown worn by Dhananjayan as Krishna.

It was in Nagercoil that both Spic Macay's purpose and Dhananjayan's inherent joy in teaching youngsters came to fulfillment. A young boy, Karvanan, who had never been exposed to the classical arts, was deeply moved by Dhananjayan's lec-dem at his school. He grew up and made his way to Madras, to join Kalakshetra.

Later he met Dhananjayan, telling him with tears in his eyes that it was all due to him. 'It was very heartening,' said Dhananjayan, clearly pleased. On graduation, Karvanan joined the BK troupe and travelled to many places including the USA with his mentor.

43

Sometime in the early 70s, a student named Sukanya made her way to BK. Fresh out of college, she loved playing with the new-born Satyajit. To her, BK was a haven where she could forget her domestic troubles. Good in music, she had always wanted to learn dance as well but her father opposed it. In a while, she moved to London, where a grand romance awaited her.

When the City of Birmingham Touring Opera invited Pandit Ravi Shankar to work with them, he wanted to focus on musical theatre involving dance rather than opera. George Harrison wanted him to create something to mark his fiftieth year of concert-playing and his seventieth birthday. Ravi Shankar, the 'godfather of world music' as the former Beatle called him, had many ideas but decided on a story with a setting in rural India. He would weave into it the story of an ancestor of his who had been possessed by a spirit. Since he was strongly against drugs, and did not believe they enhanced creativity, it would carry that message as well.

By now, 1989, Ravi Shankar had married Sukanya. In fact, it was Sukanya who promised Ravi Shankar that 'she would endeavour to find a way to have it produced.'[36] For both of them, the choice was unanimous – the 'great dancers and choreographers'[37] the Dhananjayans.

Dhananjayan received a phone call one day. It was Pandit Ravi Shankar on the line. '"I have something to discuss, very important. Come to Delhi immediately! I have an idea for a production, guess what it is?" he said.' Dhananjayan smiled at the memory, 'How could we guess? We started thinking of mythological stories, but he said, "No, *No*. Two words, Anti-Drugs! It will be called *Ghanashyam* which is another name for Krishna, but it is not Krishna's story."'

In Delhi, Pandit Ravi Shankar introduced the Dhananjayans to Graham Vick, the young trail-blazing artistic director of the CBTO, who had flown in from London. Ravi Shankar explained what he wanted – a theatre production where both music and dance were in dialogue, where Kathak and Bharata Natyam combined visually to tell an operatic story.

Ravi Shankar had a storyline ready. There are two families of dancers, one south Indian and the other from the north, happily co-existing as neighbours and practising their art. The Kathak dancing family is ruined by fake sadhus who introduce the husband to ganja and charas and hashish and bhang. He starts stealing to pay for his drugs. Through dance, the terrible effects of the drug habit would be shown – hallucinations, withdrawal symptoms, alcohol-induced stupor – ending in the husband's death. The dead Kathak dancer now becomes a *pisacha*, an angry spirit. Infatuated by his neighbour, the female Bharata Natyam dancer Kanta, he possesses her. A witch doctor, or *ojha*, is summoned. Pujas are done, and when the *pisacha* comes out, the branch of a tree falls. The Kathak dancer's widow, Lalita, volunteers to accept his spirit in her body. She then dies.

Pandit Durga Lal and his student were to take the role of the North Indian couple and the Dhananjayans would be their neighbours. The other dancers would be chosen by audition. In just five years, the standard of those auditioning was better than when *Jungle Book: Adventures of Mowgli* was done. 'In the early 80s, there were not many Indian dancers in London with a solid standard of performance in the classical arts. The better known among them had big egos and poor foundations. Now we were able to pick some very good dancers.'

The music would be live and the ensemble large. The Dhananjayans worked in Delhi with Panditji as he composed the music, choreographing along. Sometimes, he contributed with ideas for movements – he had been a dancer once – mentioning how his brother the great Uday Shankar used to do things. Dhananjayan was awe-struck. 'I had always thought of him as a musician, but watching him demonstrate his ideas, I realized he *is* a dancer too!'

Pandit Durga Lal (l) and Dhananjayan (r)

Ravi Shankar's beloved disciple Ashit Desai assisted him by marking all the notations, heading the orchestra and singing. Many of Panditji's other prominent disciples such as Ronu Majumdar and Vishwa Mohan Bhatt, famous in their own right, helped with the music. 'It was very inspiring to work with such top class musicians, at least 15 of them! One thing we realized is that if your calibre is high and you are confident of yourself, it is very easy to work with them. It is only when an artiste is not up to the mark that their ego shows.'

The music done, the entire company went to Birmingham. Pandit Ravi Shankar, Pandit Durga Lal and the Dhananjayans stayed in neighbouring service apartments. Every day there were rehearsals at the theatre from nine to five. The local artists chosen by audition were taught their parts, and the production slowly took shape.

'Panditji was very creative. In the evening he would take a walk, stop in front of our house and say "I have an idea, maybe we can do this today." Then he would call Ashit, "I have a tune, come write it down." He literally lived in the flow of music. He was the epitome of humility. Gave all the musicians respect even though they were his sishyas. They loved him, there was a lovely feeling around. No moody musicians!'

'Pandit Durga Lal too, such a big artiste, he gave us respect. Only once...he was a little upset because the BBC who covered the production chose me to be interviewed because I could speak English and he was not fluent. I had to convince him later on that it was not of my doing.'

'Then one day, we met George Harrison,' Dhananjayan said this casually, with no inflection.

'*George Harrison!*' A diehard Beatles fan, I felt a vicarious thrill and not a little envy.

'Yes. He would come and sit and watch the rehearsal, no airs. He recorded Sanskrit chants using Shanta's voice and our BK musicians. They were thrilled! They put it in their biodata...worked with George Harrison. He took us to his farmhouse.'

It is one of the ironies of the world; I'm sure none of those musicians had ever heard the Beatles before they met him.

Ghanashyam – The Broken Branch was on a scale even bigger than *Jungle Book*; the CBTO had a budget of 100,000 GBP.[38] The Dhananjayans experienced the positive side of the working life of a dancer in the West. Their sole job was to be creative and to dance. The rest, engineering their ideas to work on stage, would be done by others. How wonderful.

Shanta recalled the invigorating time she had working with the Artistic Director. 'Graham Vick wanted everything on stage to be realistic unlike our dance which is suggestive. There was a bathing scene where the Kathak dancer would peep at Kanta and her friends while they were bathing. I showed him the actions – undressing, dipping the clothes in water and then wringing them. Oh he loved it. "I want that!" he exclaimed. "We do not have that here, we have machines. I want people to see how it is done with hands. I want real water, real clothes, real dhobi wringing!" And I thought to myself, *Oh my god how will I do it with* real *clothes and* real *water and also dance*?'

'Paul Brown's team put it together. On the stage, they had a big platform with water underneath. When the platform moved, the water would surge and be visible. It was covered with a plank. For the bathing scene we would adroitly remove it and put it back. Like a sump cover. When Kanta is bathing, the Kathak dancer comes to the tree there, a real tree, and climbs up the ladder. We visualized a long sari hanging in such a way that only Kanta's head and feet would be seen but people would think she is naked. And when he is looking from above, she will wrap this sari around herself and run. Vick wanted a tap with water coming out. Later, blood would flow from it. All that on stage!' Shanta shook her head in amazement as she recounted all the trouble the CBTO took. 'We travelled to many cities, and in each place, they made a tank. An *enormous* truck would go ahead and set up. The whole set was in the truck. Paul Brown made it in such a way that it could be used at all the different performance venues. The bough had to break and fall from the tree at a precise point...his timing and stagecraft were perfect!'

'We had to show the passing of time. We did the six seasons with shadow play. Uday Shankar used to do shadow play, so Panditji wanted that. It was very interesting. The minute you heard his music, you knew this is rain and this is Summer. For Spring, we had everyone coming out and dancing. Winter he created the impression of cold, through sounds. Smoke over a kettle, warming hands over a fire.'

'Then when I get possessed I had to appear with my hair all dishevelled. Vick loved my hair coming loose. I had to figure out how to do that! I found if I did not pin my bun in place and flicked my head, my hair would fall wildly around my shoulders. Don't ask how I managed! For that alone, Vick would send me flying kisses. He wanted everything real, because their theatre is like that.'

'What a luxury it was when it came to costumes. I had a split second for costume change. The skirt was collapsed in a circle, I just had to step into it and someone would do everything for me. Just have to stand! And everything falls into place backstage. Then I understood how they do these big shows. With just twenty artists, it seemed like there were a hundred artists on stage!'

The world premiere on 3 October, 1989 at Birmingham was very well received. *The Independent* called it a rare hit with a very varied audience, 'The mime and dancing is throughout spectacular, a delight to the eye. The performance of Durga Lal is a masterpiece of versatility and concentration: his delirium...is nothing short of hair raising. Ravi Shankar's score...is both seductively lyrical and at times rhythmically complex'.[39] Tom Sutcliffe in the *Guardian* made a perceptive remark about Durga Lal and Dhananjayan, 'What is so exciting about this dance, is that it has little to do with a realized physique – unlike ballet and modern dance. Both these men, clearly great stars in India, are on the mature brink of middle age. But their virtuoso use of the tradition that lent them their art is stunningly ageless. The personality of the dancer is never overlaid with artifice.'[40]

The group, with its high profile orchestra, travelled across the UK to present more than 14 shows. After that success, Ravi Shankar wanted to bring it to India.

44

The difference between staging a production in the UK and in India was starkly evident from the beginning. It started with trying to get sponsors and funding. One might have thought that Pandit Ravi Shankar's name alone would have had people queueing to help, but it was not so. He was not able to raise the several lakhs required. Just when it seemed that *Ghanashyam* might not be presented in India, Sanjiv Goenka of RPG stepped in and the show was on.

Ravi Shankar wanted to begin the India tour in Madras, towards the end of 1990. It suited the Dhananjayans because they had all their resources there in terms of trained students, rehearsal space and tailors.

S. Krishnaswami, Secretary of the Narada Gana Sabha, who had always helped the Dhananjayans in their career, placed the stage at their disposal for rehearsals. *Ghanashyam* was to be a three day show, and he was proud to host Pandit Ravi Shankar.

Naturally, a different set had to be designed, keeping Indian theatre audiences in mind. Natesh was engaged to work on the sets and he came up with something that had more of the Indian element in it. For Madras, it was novel.

'We had a tap onstage but there was no water falling from it!' Dhananjayan's voice rose a bit in frustration. 'I remembered Vick saying "I want to see the water coming out. It must splash!" I had protested, "It will wet the stage." He replied, "That's okay, someone will wipe it. Don't worry about that." And we made a little dance around the tap! In the UK, we had live music, fourteen people, no restrictions, not bothered about money and costs, we had to only worry about the artistic part. That is how art should work. Unlike here, where every penny we have to think about it. We are not able to do things so elaborately in India. All our best productions we have done abroad.'

Not a costume designer, but an ace tailor nevertheless, Rajagopal brought his sewing machine to the auditorium. For days, he sat there making costumes.

The biggest difference however was caused by the sudden death of Pandit Durga Lal. Three months after the end of the UK tour of *Ghanashyam*, he had a heart attack while performing in Lucknow. He was only forty-two when he died, a great tragedy. He was incomparable, and yet a substitute had to be found. Not just for the role of the Kathak dancer but also that of the *ojha* which he performed with great flair.

'Pandit Ravi Shankar had auditioned some dancers but was not happy with what he saw. He was wondering whether to change the character's style of dancing. Then one day, I happened to be watching the National Programme of Dance on Doordarshan. There was a Kathak dancer called Maulik who was dancing well. I called Panditji and told him about this boy and asked him to find out who he was. It turned out he was from Kadamba Academy of Kathak, in Ahmedabad. He was newly married, to Ishira. Panditji auditioned him and decided to cast Maulik and Ishira as the Kathak dancing couple.

This resulted in an unintended disparity between the ages of the two couples, and Kavitha Shetty, reviewing it in the *India Today* commented caustically, 'Middle aged, with a thick waist and a broad face...one wonders why Ghanshyam [sic] would look at her when he has the softness and warmth of Lalitha. However...Kanta has all the sensual grace and tensile strength of an archetypal earth mother.'[41]

Kumudini Lakia chose the best of her students for the rest of the cast. They all travelled to Madras, stayed at Woodlands and rehearsed for a month. Venkatachalapati performed as the *ojha*.

The shows were ticketed, unusual for dance performances in Madras, and were sold out. Dhananjayan was frank, 'We had an overwhelming response, not all of it complimentary. Some people did not like the show. Maybe it was the subject. Maybe it was too contemporary and ahead of its time.

'I received a lot of threatening letters. People who believe in swamijis and sadhus felt we were going against Hinduism. I had to inform the police.'

Dhananjayan, ever the showman, invited the public to discuss the matter at Bharat Kalachar, a sabha run by the eminent educationist Mrs Y.G. Parthasarathy. There, young students came to his rescue, arguing that it was okay to portray fake sadhus on stage since they existed in real life as well – such as the ones who had attacked Sri Ramana Maharshi.

The stress of mounting such a huge production fell mainly on Dhananjayan's shoulders. He was in charge of ensuring that the sets and props, sent ahead by lorry, arrived at each of the major venues in time. 'I had to keep track of the lorry that was crossing India, from the west coast all the way to the east! So I instructed the drivers that wherever they stopped they had to call me. Nowadays, it's easier with mobiles.'

After three shows in Bombay, the cast travelled by ordinary second class to Calcutta. Generally blessed with good luck during their countless journeys across India, this particular one proved to be a nightmare for the Dhananjayans. There was no water on the train, and it was running late.

Sangeeta Vijeyasarathy, one of the cast, recalled, 'There was no food at several stations. As usual, Shanta Akka had saved some snacks like apples and biscuits and offered them to the ones who were most hungry. We put on a brave face and were singing to cheer ourselves. Akka had us in good spirits. We were so desperate for food, we could not wait to reach Calcutta. Ravi Shankar and Sukanya travelled by airplane. Sukanya cried so much when Akka told her about what we had gone through. I felt very bad for Sir and Akka, for not getting the same privilege as Ravi Shankar.'

In Calcutta, *Ghanashyam* was on for ten days at Birla Sabhaghar and two additional shows arranged on public demand. Because of Pandit Ravi Shankar's name, tickets were being sold at a premium. An audio recording of the music was made with HMV.

The cast then took a train to Delhi, braving the journey through Bihar, where hoards entered their compartment and occupied reserved seats.

Dhananjayan talked about the pre-performance frustrations in Delhi. 'I had a lot of problems there. We were dancing at Siri Fort which is a government-owned auditorium. The workers there were very un-cooperative. We ended up having to do a matinee and then another show in the evening. It was ennervating, dealing with them.'

Soon after the *Ghanashyam* India tour, Venkatachalapati died in an accident. He was 42 as well. Both the men who had played the *ojha*, Pandit Durga Lal and now Venkatachalapati had died tragically early. It made the entire cast of *Ghanashyam* wonder whether there was a jinx that came with the role: 'Later, whenever the question came up of doing another show, we would say, *Oh, but who will be the ojha?*'

45

Some dreams are born in a particular situation, and when that situation changes radically, it is not always easy to reconfigure one's dream.

The performances I had attended while growing up had always had a sizeable audience, and a palpable excitement in the air. By the year 2000, there were so many performances of dance being held through the year in Madras, good, bad, indifferent, that audiences had dwindled. A sense of ennui had set in.

It was inevitable.

While in the 70s and 80s there were a select group of gurus, who had accessed their learning directly from the great *nattuvanars* and whose teaching was of quality, by the 90s anyone in the city who had a smattering of training felt free to start teaching dance. If performing was fraught with difficulties, teaching was an area that had no barriers to entry. It resulted in large numbers of 'dancers' being taught, creating more supply than the already beleagured sabhas could absorb and promote.

In general, shows in the city were free, 'all are welcome' and really of a self-financing nature. Anyone who could get that coveted slot in the performance schedule, danced. Many girls danced until they got married, and if marriage took them out of the city, they rarely continued to perform. I, who had so assiduously prepared my folio every year, because that was the way things were done, began to see things a different way.

Life had been kind to me. I had never had to jostle for anything nor had found anything *worth* an aggressive jostling. Looking at my dancer friends who in their fifties still made the annual round of calls importuning sabha chiefs and bureaucrats, it was evident this jostling would be lifelong. A great review was no guarantee of a chance to perform coming one's way. A great performance at a particular sabha would still result in the sabha head developing amnesia the next Season. *And*, at the end of battering the sabha door, putting one's self respect on line, and paying for the musicians, there just might be no audience for a performance.

It was disheartening.

It called for deep introspection and an understanding of what dance really meant to me, its place in my life.

The more I thought about it, I realized that the training and as a consequence the performing were linked in my head. Naturally; to perform meant to reinforce the fact that one was a dancer. But, was one any less a dancer, any less an accomplished dancer, if one did not perform? The thought was so huge, so frighteningly radical, it took a long time for me to work with it.

And the answer, of course, was No!

If the true reason for my loving what I did was the way I *felt* while performing, then it was a falsity to believe that I could *only* feel that way in costume and in front of an audience.

I had to delink the two in my head. I would rehearse every day and know a performance was an imminent possibility, I would practise and not give up, I would dance in the moment, feeling the joy any time I danced, in cotton practice costume, in class. The fact that I continued to learn from my gurus, the only one left of my batch who came regularly to BK – that was something precious.

I stopped approaching the sabhas, knowing it meant a death of sorts. Every year, I would fight with my self and every year I would win against myself. It was like tearing my heart out, in order to live.

I also quarrelled with the gods. Many fine *ninda stutis* were hurled their way by me. They had given me great gurus, steeped me in a training that had lasted over thirty five years, endowed me with the will *and* stamina *and* talent to succeed but they had withheld something. I hoped to shame them into yielding.

So, I danced every day.

I continued to get fresh insights from my gurus.

I *lived* dance every day, my self respect intact.

46

Twenty-five years after they had set up Bharata Kalanjali, the Dhananjayans toured America in 1993 with their troupe, presenting the evergreen story of the Ramayana and that of King Ashoka turning Buddhist – *Sanghamitra* – in 42 cities. The audience, inured to solo performances of varying levels of skill, delighted in the group presentations.

'Uma Ganesan of the Cleveland Cultural Alliance had for long been wanting to present a professional dance company, as part of the mainstream American theatre experience. The success of these two dance-dramas in Cleveland convinced her that we ought to aim for something bigger. An East meets West sort of collaboration, with support from the Cuhayoga Community College.'

The *Adventures of Mowgli* production in London, based on *Jungle Book*, was a hit. Why not attempt something similar in Cleveland? The Ohio Ballet was known for its willingness to experiment, however founder and artistic director Heinz Poll had to be persuaded. A stern looking elderly man of German birth, he had never seen the Dhananjayans dance and was not taken by the concept.

'I thought it is impossible to choreograph such defined and different classical idioms into one thing and make it a coherent statement,' he explained in an interview with *The Plain Dealer*.[42] Would he at least meet with them to discuss possibilities?

'Poll was a conservative person. It was hard to convince him but after an hour, he was willing to explore ideas. So, we choreographed a piece with our group but he was not very convinced that Bharata Natyam and ballet together would work. Then we made him listen to the music of *Jungle Book.* He liked it very much. "This music is beautiful, we can do something with it."

'Now we had to come up with a storyline, change it for the American audience and to provide scope for ballet. Again, it was not the original *Jungle Book* story. Even then, Heinz wanted to see something choreographed. So with just our BK dancers, I worked on the movements and we went to Ohio.

'I did a jungle scene. The ballet dancers watched what we were doing. We told them it is not traditional Bharata Natyam, that we have created new movements to suit the needs of the production. Everyone there, including the press, liked the preview.'

Dhananjayan invited Pandit Vijay Raghava Rao to compose the music. He stayed with them in an apartment in Cleveland for two months and since he was much older than them, Shanta and Dhananjayan looked after his needs. 'After working the whole day, he would return to the apartment and compose into the night. He had a great memory. He would ask, "In this movement, there is a jump, can you do it again? What is the beat?" Accordingly he would notate the *swaras.*'

Work began with the ballet dancers, and the first task was to figure out how to allocate the scenes between ballet and Bharata Natyam. Working with the drummer, the pianist and Pandit Vijay Raghava Rao, Dhananjayan demonstrated to the ballet dancers a range of movements and expressions. 'They were amazed by our expressions. So I also taught them some. They were all trained dancers so they could pick it up easily. We used to start with a prayer. They liked that. Working with Poll was enjoyable. I would show him certain movements that I had in mind and he would reinterpret them to suit their bodylines and ballet.'

Since it was an Indian story, Dhananjayan blended movements from folk dances as well. Bharata Natyam is a very grounded dance form so the slower, heavier characters – ponderous elephants, the malevolent tiger Sher Khan and lurking panthers – were given to

Bharata Natyam whereas all the flying or leaping movements in ballet were used for soaring birds and leaping deer. 'The way Ka the snake slithered in ballet was outstanding.There was no clash of egos. We all worked very well together. People were surprised by our rapport-in-dance with Mr Heinz as he had set ways of thinking. We gave him a lot of respect because he was a lot older, nearly seventy. He was a very nice person, would bring food from home to share during lunch time. He wanted to come to India, to feel the pulse of life here. We said "Come!"

'In Madras, he watched our classes, and attended many performances. He liked Kalakshetra, got a feel for our art after watching their dance-drama. A typical German, he was a great animal lover.'

Chuckled Dhananjayan: 'He said the most beautiful thing about India was how we co-existed with animals. He loved the way cows dozed in the middle of the road, at an intersection! He said in America people would hit the animal, they would not bother, here the traffic flows around them. Cows, dogs, no problem!'

In an interview with *The Beacon Journal*, Poll said, 'I've never seen a dog walking across the street like this. They walk like people...It's wonderful; people really have respect for life.'[43]

The next stage involved the recording of music. Pandit Vijay Raghava Rao came to Madras. For an entire month, they worked on the recordings. 'Day and night. We were supposed to finish in 15 days but he was a perfectionist would not budge an inch if someone made a mistake. When he was working he was like a man possessed. No breaks for anything, no tea, no coffee, wanted everyone like that. Our musicians had a tough time working with him. I used to say, "Learn from him! He is working without sleeping..." He had trained earlier at Kalakshetra, so he had an idea of dance movements. He knew the characters, the themes. I still have his notation book, every pause is noted there! Pandit Ravi Shankar was also like that. Nothing can distract these great artists, their concentration and involvement is astounding.'

The entire production was to take two years to come together. Once the music was ready, the Dhananjayans flew to Ohio to practise with the entire cast.

'It was amazing! Every movement that we had choreographed, Panditji had notated in music. When the ballet dancers listened, they were able to sail through as if they had been practising forever with it. They saw how integral music is to our dance. We were also able to understand how *they* move.'

Satyajit as Mowgli

The cast comprised of twelve ballet dancers and ten dancers from BK. Of these, seven were male Bharata Natyam dancers, including Dhananjayan's son Satyajit. Satyajit danced as Mowgli and was charming in that role. 'His appealing innocence of expression perfectly characterized Mowgli, the young boy raised by wolves.'[44] It was one of the highlights of his fledgling career as a dancer.

Shanta had the time of her life collaborating with the costume designer Christina Giannini. 'She was acclaimed for her work in New York. She was like an eccentric, the way she looked and talked. They wanted the best for the show so they hired her but everyone was scared of her. She was very temperamental! And I had to work with her, because Indian dancers have certain requirements, our bodies are covered...I showed her how a veshti is draped. She loved it. "I want this, I want this!" she said and then the ice was broken. I had no problem with her after that. She stitched it in such a way that it looked like a veshti but was easy to change into.

'They wanted all the material from India. Instead of curtains in front, we had flags, like the *thirashila* in Kathakali. They used big flags, in silk, so it would billow across the front of the stage. Every bit of cloth was taken from here and we made most of the costumes there. In the theatre, they had a full tailoring unit! Christina would have trials for every costume she made. While we practised in the theatre, the stitching went on simultaneously. If she wanted a character to try on a costume, we would go between scenes.

'Some costumes took a long time to figure out. For example, Sher Khan had to look like a tiger, and yet be free to dance. We did not use masks, because the face had to show for the *abhinaya*. So he was made up Kathakali style with just a headgear to show that he is a lion and the coat and tail. The dancer who played Sher Khan complained for a whole month, "Akka it is high, Akka it is pinching, Akka it is loose!" until we got it right,' laughed Shanta.

For three continuous shows after it premiered, it was full house. The famous critic present, Wilma Salisbury of *The Plain Dealer*, was known for her caustic remarks. Dhananjayan immediately dubbed her 'Subbudi'. 'Subbudi' actually liked the production, captioning her review '*Timeless Jungle Book*, movingly choreographed, wonderfully performed'.[45] Declaring the $160,000 production 'a box-office hit' she said that, 'it drew a larger audience to its three performances in Akron than any other production in the Ohio Ballet's history.'[46]

'In the beginning, they saw Indian dancers and ballet dancers but when it ended they saw only Art being projected. The dancing styles had merged into one beautiful production. Heinz was very happy!' said Dhananjayan.

Then came exciting news! *Jungle Book* was nominated by the press as one of the best productions of the year. *The Northern Ohio Live Magazine* gave a yearly Award of Achievement for Dance in Cleveland. Calling *Jungle Book* 'a sheer joy to watch'[47] they sent plane tickets and an invitation to the Dhananjayans for the award ceremony on September 22, 1997.

'So we went to Cleveland. Everyone was there, the ballet stars, the press, the famous choreographers. It was a mega event and the suspense was unbearable! We never thought we had a chance. And then they announced that the best production of the year in dance was *Jungle Book*. The choreographers were introduced so the spotlight was on us! We were given the plaque and a prize of 25,000 dollars for the dance company. The governor gave us a community service award. That evening there was a huge party!

'The credit must be given to Uma Ganesan. She wanted it to be on par with the finest of western theatre in terms of presentation, and she achieved that aim.

'It was one of the best things in our career. After *Ghanashyam*, with Pandit Ravi Shankar, of course!'

47

In 1996, when Dhananjayan and Poll worked together on the US version of *Jungle Book*, it was a foregone conclusion that Satyajit, with his filmstar looks, would play the lead role of Mowgli and excel at it.

But the very next year, despite all the adulation, Satyajit refused to reprise his role. 'I didn't want the limelight. Dance and the limelight made you feel that you are somebody special.' He had doubts about wanting to continue as a dancer, and did not want to deprive someone whose profession it was of the chance of a lifetime. It created a throbbing rupture in his parents' life, but Satyajit stuck to his decision.

'There was no passion that was driving me towards it. As a dancer, when I performed, I loved the physicality of it. I don't think I could have conducted performances my whole life, or taught. At some point even before I left, I realized this is boring.'

Very often Satyajit danced with his parents in their demanding Bharata Natyam concerts. As he grew into a young man, 'The Dhananjayans' expanded from a duo to a trio.

Of the many components that a dancer needs to be skilled in, I asked Satyajit what he struggled with most. 'Physical ability, speed, *tala*, music...no problem,' he replied with the easy confidence of inborn talent. 'Had I continued, I would have problems with literature. I was never interested in Sanskrit literature, unlike my father. I would have been a good performer, and probably a good choreographer.'

'I personally never felt I was great at *bhava*. Keeping my father's histrionics in mind, I was nowhere near him. I knew I lacked the maturity to perform at a higher level at that time. There *were* times when I knew I had done a good show...there's a good vibration. Nellai Kannan, on the mridangam, and I had great times, challenging each other on stage.'

Within the dance, he was to find a different equation with his father, who was also his guru.

'I hated theory class. My dad used to drag me to Bharatiya Vidya Bhavan for class after class. But I loved doing impromptu variations with him. Like when we fought as Ravana and Jatayu. The moments that I related to were during the actual performance. I enjoyed the music, connecting with the audience. I liked the theatre of the dance dramas. I loved watching my parents dance.'

Given that he was working with his parents, could he not have demarcated his areas of interest? Told them that he would perform, but not take on all the roles that they juggled with such ease?

'The kind of person I was at the time, I would have found it difficult to say that I only want to be a star performer, I may not have had the clarity then. I would have felt it was a responsibility, part of the whole.'

Given his unique position as an insider, there were many issues related to the world of Bharata Natyam that troubled Satyajit. 'I was always an idealist. I still struggle with the way the world works.' He was disturbed by 'the whole sabha thing, their stranglehold. My concern was: How do the genuinely good dancers get a performing space?'

Though it was an issue that did not affect him directly, Satyajit and other dancers started Lakshya, an association for young artistes. 'Forty of us met at BK and we pledged that none of us will pay sabhas for a chance to dance. At the next meeting there were only five of us!'

Certainly, if all forty had taken a stand, it would have been very effective. Satyajit is disappointed with the thirty five dancers who did not feel they could survive without paying the sabhas.

'I found it shocking. Pay and dance. Still beats me. It's a mystery. It shouldn't be that people who can pay the most dance the most. Society creates its own small wells and there are frogs living in it and they are all happy. The dance world is like that. You walk into one place and you see the same people, you say the same things. This is your world, why would you change it? You *want* to complain about the sabhas.'

Is there no alternative to the sabhas?

'We have all accepted there is a norm, the sabhas, and we live within that. Let us say there is no sabha system, everyone will feel the world is ending. That's what people want. Somewhere everybody is resorting to it, they are accepting it. It's all what we have created. When you see it, you feel helpless.'

Satyajit's other concern was that 'most male dancers end up being teachers, because no one wants to watch a male dance.'

He understood the deep irony that while he had all the advantages, he was not really impelled to make it a career. 'I used to feel so privileged, I had the looks, the talent, I had the people. I was so comfortable...but concerned about the other males which is why we started Lakshya. There were a lot of good dancers like Rajesh, like Suryanarayana Murthy. The dance world ends up losing a lot of male dancers. Or maybe the good ones also decide not to dance.'

Satyajit also wondered about the nature of the items performed. 'It was what threw me off dance...the stagnation. The format of it is the same. The *intention* of dance has not changed. My problem is not so much the *margam*. My question was, "*Why* am I dancing?" I don't know the answer. When you see the really good dancers, they have thought about it. If you ask me to do certain items, I could have done them over and over again. I used to ponder, *What is it about this item that I did not find in the others*. So I needed to find more of those.'

The other issue was that 'I realized people are not taking it seriously as a profession. Especially the women, they have ample family and husband's support. It's about fame...of course some people are genuinely passionate...but female dancers have the comfort that if they want to do a show for free, they can cough up twenty thousand to the musicians. Not so with a male dancer, it's a huge struggle. It's the men who suffer.'

What draws the lower middle-class boys to dance? 'They idealize it when they see Kamal Haasan dance, or my father dance. Something is attracting them to it, some gratification or high. I don't know what it is. If it's a high, it is temporary, unfortunately. Equally, why is it that the rich boys are not getting in?'

The very boys who cannot afford *not* to earn seem drawn to dance. And yet, not everyone has the talent to make it. 'I don't think there is a money aspect to it. They do not come in thinking they will make money. Something is pulling them. It is a *nasha*. But there is a bottomline. How I look as a photographer does not matter; if you are a dancer it *matters*. There is a reality check. If you are average looking and you have average talent you are not going to make it.'

Many good dancers whine about the lack of performing opportunities. Satyajit is categorical that, 'Bottomline if you are not a great performer, the audience knows it. You're not star quality *yet*! It is a bitter pill to swallow. You cannot blame life. You are where you are.'

While Satyajit was questioning the dancer's situation, an absorbing passion had stolen him away from dance, and it was not a girl. 'When I discovered photography, I found what I was passionate about. Dance was readily accessible. For photography I had to search for everything that I wanted to learn. I never had doubts in dance because it did not interest me. I don't mind working in the darkroom till one or two but I definitely have a problem teaching forever or rehearsing forever, I would have found it stifling. Most of it was boring, it did not excite me.'

So in 1997, Satyajit decided to become an apprentice with ace-photographer Iqbal, spending a year and a half with him. 'I was lucky to meet Iqbal and work with him. He is an ultra perfectionist.'

And Satyajit bid adieu to a career as a dancer.

Shanta still rues the fact, 'I took it with a heavy heart. I said, "Do your photography, we will not stop you but do this also." Even today people ask us why he is not dancing. More than us they were disappointed. He had all the requirements, and our full support.'

Dhananjayan said, 'It was a big disappointment for me. Initially, I was *very* upset. He got a lot of invitations, which even I did not get. He would not accept the show or give it to other male dancers. He did not want to just practise for a few hours and give an odd show. One needs to keep practising. It is a terrible world, photography, it needs a lot of time. Afterwards we were able to digest this.'

It was not as though Satyajit said goodbye to dance without qualms. 'I loved planes. I thought, *I am travelling so comfortably as a dancer. I'm never going to go on foreign trips.* But now I am, as a photographer!'

With photography, there were additional benefits. 'When we travelled out of town on shows, we never saw the place fully. Theatre to hotel to railway station and back home. I wanted to stop and see the places. I can name a hundred places I have been to but not visited. Now as a photographer I make sure I spend time there when I shoot on location.'

A dancer who could still make it if he chose to, a photographer for the last fifteen years but still closely linked to the world of Bharata Natyam, what fresh insights does Satyajit have?

'What irritates me most *now* it is the lack of intention. Sabhas are external, no longer a reason. Once you have art in you, once you have the practice, once you are immersed in it, you will succeed. What is the *intention* with which you dance, why do you *need* to be on stage? Why can't you be happy with just a class or a rehersal? I don't find many people asking those questions.'

Satyajit's disenchantment lies with the fact that most dancers seem to set their sights very low. They tolerate shoddy auditoriums or cement platforms in thatched sheds for a 'stage', dubious entities masquerading as sabhas, pay money to dance and seem content to accept this as their lot. 'The problem is that we are we are not thinking anymore. Everything is set; this is "Culture." This big word means they don't need to think or move ahead. In this sort of set up there is no scope for deep introspection. "The Season"' – roughly the period between December 1 and January 15 when over 2000 performances of music and dance are held across the city – 'has become a big cultural thing. How did it begin? Why has it become commercial? Why are there no audiences? No one wants to know. Everyone feels there should be a Season or the world will end.'

He feels that dancers are not thinking out of the box, regarding the Season. 'This is the expected thing. Bagging so many shows in the Season. The more number of shows does not mean quality. Everything is washed away in one season; one performance. It's just a routine. You need to infuse something fresh. Something that involves the audience.'

Satyajit cites the performances by the Nrityagram ensemble as an example of what he appreciates. 'Nrityagram seems to have their intention right. They are not dancing for the sake of dancing. They've thought about the smaller aspects and that is communicating itself to me. The nuances they bring...is from their *reason* of why they are dancing. They are not doing anything different, they do the same *ashtapadis* but they have made an effort to package it. The whole package is a communication.'

His other peeve is that when people keep saying that Bharata Natyam 'is an ancient art, that pisses me off. I say "yes and no", what we are doing today is only 50, 60 years old. Some of the lyrics maybe centuries old but the technique is not what it was then.'

Maybe the spirit is the same? I ask him. After all, *rasa* must have been created then and *abhinaya* continues to communicate today.

'That is the *intent*, that's what I am talking about. Right now a lot of Bharata Natyam is stagnant, redundant.'

Satyajit talks about the collaboration of the Dhananjayans with Anil Srinivasan, the pianist, as 'something that pushed the boundaries. No mridangam, no *nattuvangam*, minimal makeup and costumes and yet people were transported. The artistes all had artistic bliss on stage! Sikkil Gurucharan experienced it that day, while singing he found his *bhava* being enhanced by watching my father's expressions. At that level, it has reached a perfection. There's a connect. My father was upset that a certain "set" of audience did not come there. But I said "You're reaching another crowd."'

Even though it was a success, disappointingly, 'No impresario asked them to do it again.'

Returning to his passion, he exclaims, 'Even in photography, I've done automobile photography for six years, and I want to grow. So now I've discovered where I want to be: Fine art photography. Until you find an art that you are true to yourself, you will never be happy. Dance did not do it, automotive photography did not do it, but *this* is where I want to be. There's a connect!'

48

In 2011, Anand and I found ourselves in the temple town of Thennangur, at a dance immersion camp held by Natyarangam, an association that promotes Bharata Natyam. Returning home, over five hours of a jolting bus ride, we found the time to talk about Anand's views about the world of Bharata Natyam and his place in it as an adult male dancer.

Having spent two years as a full-time dancer, pursuing his dream, Anand was to hit a wall when it came to the choice of songs available.

'That I should present things differently than a girl was not something I realized earlier. When we dance, we want to be seen as men and hence the machismo. But, not all men are macho and not all macho men are strong. It is difficult to find songs that express the strength and vulnerability in men's experience of love and god alike. Can't do one about the beauty of your biceps!'

Difficult but not impossible. 'There is a stereotype among male dancers, that there are very few songs we can do. That is not true. We haven't written songs. The male perspective is not being written, with a few exceptions like rare Telugu pieces or Madurai Muralidharan's compositions, in the classical arts. The male dancer in the traditional *margam* is like an illegal immigrant – always yearning for space that is his truly his own. We have lost out on translating our grief, our loves, our romance, our experience to our dance. Unless we do it, we are going to be a relic of the past, dancing sculptures.

'Let's develop and popularize a repertoire that conveys the male side. Wouldn't it be wonderful where the man says, "Why didn't I meet you two years ago, now I am married with two children?" Or, where the hero sends his friend to approach The Girl of his dreams and the friend advises him to stop drinking and dress nicely? Not all can or care to relate to *bhakti*. So describe those situations and then there will be an actual place for men to dance as men if they choose to.'

Anand feels that, 'The whole notion of dancing like a man has come about because of the popularity and financial necessity of dance dramas. More and more dancers are fit to do only a particular role. The ingenuity and freedom of expression, the individuality of the solo form has almost died out.'

In the future, 'You will see two categories, specialization in dance-dramas and specialization in solos. And this causes a lot of distress to male dancers, we feel like we have to choose between the two. It affected me as well in terms of how I should dance.'

Anand has spent a lot of time analyzing his appearance on stage. 'I'm not fair skinned. I am dusky and very conscious of what colours I wear.' Because the torso is most often left bare, 'To gym or not to gym is a huge question among male dancers. Dhananjayan says, "*Don't!*"' Ironically, 'the muscles that you attribute to masculinity are not what you train the most in Bharata Natyam. "Athletic" male dancers are toned; not muscular. The idea of male beauty is a solid chest, broad shoulders, nice biceps, flat stomach, sculpted back muscles, *not* the thighs, waist or the legs which a dancer trains the most.' Therefore, Anand reasons, 'Guys have to go to the gym if they want to be presentable on the stage.'

He worries over decisions that a female dancer would not think twice about. 'There's a fear in my head that I want to wear more jewellery but I shouldn't.' In an inspired moment he designed a snake-hood ornament clipped to his gold sacred thread. 'I studied the idols taken in procession, sculptures, the gods are all wearing a lot of jewellery!'

He dislikes wearing makeup. 'I will spend hours tying my veshti but will spare barely five minutes on makeup. I did not have a role model. I have never seen Dhananjayan in his youthful manly days. Makeup reminds me that I am putting on a show, merely entertaining and being false. It's not real. I am here to share *me*.'

Buying makeup is doubly painful. 'I remember how embarrassed I was buying foundation in America, telling the salesgirl it was for my mother. I'm sure she thought I was a drag queen.' Shopping on the internet has the great advantage of anonymity.

Anand has strong views on the content of the dance itself. 'When men do compete in Bharata Natyam, it is always in the physical ability. How high can you jump, how long can you do four speeds without giving up, that sort of thing.' Aren't they confusing our classical dance for gymnastics or exercise or an endurance test? 'Within the guys circle... very little appreciation for a boy who can do better *abhinaya* than a girl. If anything, it is how do I make my Rama more invincible than human.'

He critiques the current passive approach where dancers are content learning 'set' items from the guru. 'The path that we don't take as young dancers is to explore what we want to do differently. Everyone is mimicking someone else, what with videos and YouTube. Where is our individual voice in this? Where is my life and where is dance? They should be together in my head.'

With regard to music, Wesleyan had influenced Anand profoundly. 'Music as an extension of dance is how I always thought of it. After Wesleyan I thought of it as dance as an extension of music. That gives you the palette that you have. Dance gives you the canvas, but you need the paint.'

Anand wants to 'have dancers become musicians again. I want to sing while I dance because it changes everything. I have become very sensitive to music. The major artistes have their own unique sound,' which their dance is based on. 'So, once you tune your music to the way you want your dance to appear, you're set.'

His friends have advised him not to teach. 'Once you are labelled as a teacher, all the aunties and their children in town will come and learn and they want their opportunities. It is very difficult to then be considered a dancer. Everybody is teaching and learning, it's a little cottage industry churning out more dancers but where are the opportunities?'

In Chennai, amongst the largest concentration of male Bharata Natyam dancers, Anand discovered that, 'It becomes a perilous journey for a straight dancer where you don't know what group you are part of.' In a culture where physical closeness between two male buddies such as 'handholding, hugging, hand over the shoulder, but not anywhere lower' is accepted, it becomes difficult to judge. 'There's a fear among some of the boys that being gay is contagious, something that you can catch by proximity. Or they might have been hit on.'

'Chennai is beginning to open up to who is gay and who isn't. I know at least three boys who are openly gay and dance: "We are *dancers* first, gay later." These gay men are able to outdo the women in their expression of what she would feel for a man. I sometimes wonder what a homosexual *varnam* would be like, because that love is different...but at the end of the day the *atman* is genderless and what we feel for god is genderless. That said, we speak with the language of expression. That expression is going to take on a gender specific form.'

Having thought his way through many an issue, Anand arrives at the most critical one. Performance opportunities and the lack thereof. He is the rare male dancer who has the money to pursue his passion, and who has other options in the larger world outside.

The chief problem is a lack of transparency about how sabhas draw up their lists for the Season. 'Open auditions will clear up the issue. At least it will be more transparent.'

Money power can influence how one is perceived. 'As long as you have the money and time and connections, you can be a very "good" dancer.

I have a lot of friends who have dealt with the worst of the sabha system. People tell me that I *should* pay and get an opportunity to dance. "If you have the money then why not?" they say. I heard of an NRI father who paid for a certain time slot at a sabha for ten years. Not the top ones but a mid-range sabha. They have no qualms about it.'

'That's the myth that the sabhas are running on, that their name alone guarantees you a way of coming up, that's what you are paying for. Because otherwise they do not provide any extra service whatsoever. Equally they cannot guarantee that you will succeed.'

Economics provides Anand with a clue to the future. 'There are very few countries where you have such a ridiculous over supply of artistes. We are constantly negotiating what is the actual currency of an opportunity. Because financially viable performance opportunities are tough to get, we will see fewer and fewer people get interested. Maybe another two generations.'

It is a depressing situation for a solo dancer. 'You have to get your name out there, but you have no shows. You need to get a patron but you won't beg. The Brahmin patrons, as opposed to the Chettiars or zamindars, have their drawbacks. They have a lot of spending power but do no actual spending. You have to get a Government sponsored show but they won't respect you. So the only avenue is to get known abroad. Which you can do with group shows. But then you will be known as a group artiste.'

Back to square one.

Anand is at the crossroads now. He has to make a decision. Should he take a well-paying job at an MNC and somehow manage to dance as well, or should he devote himself to dance, uncertain though the outcome may be?

There's one thing he knows for sure though. Nothing makes him feel more alive and pure than when he dances. 'The minute I wear my ankle bells, I'm a different person. The influence of Chidambaram, of the Dikshitar who blessed my family, of Nataraja, of my grandfather, of temple performances have always energized me and opened some part of my soul that I did not know existed. That has spearheaded or reaffirmed what I want to do.'

49

In 1999, Dhananjayan dreamt the biggest dream of his life. He wanted to start a school for the arts, along the lines of Kalakshetra. It would be in Payyanur; Shanta and he would shift base and live there. The venture was named Bhaskara.

When I heard about it, my heart sank. My beloved gurus were going far away? Leaving their students in Madras? Didn't we matter to them? At that time, my son was a naughty four year old: How would I travel to this remote place with him? Most BK students met this news with varying degrees of dismay but in the face of Sir's childlike enthusiasm and grand visions for Bhaskara, none of us dared say anything.

We had organized a surprise 60th birthday celebration where an elephant garlanded him! There, Sir announced his dream project, asked us to support him in making it come true by donating as much as we could. In the following months, parents, friends, past students, current ones, admirers, fans across the world donated liberally to the Bhaskara Trust.

I remember handing him an envelope, wishing that I could write him a cheque with many more zeros than the one inside. I also wished that I could overcome my scepticism.

One day in class, Sir told us excitedly, 'I spent one whole day visiting many Namboodiri and Nair tharavads looking for a place and was very disappointed. Either they were not suitable or they were quoting huge prices. On the way home, my taxi broke down.

The driver said would take a long time to repair. We were in a remote place and as I had nothing to do, I decided to walk up a nearby hill. My brother and I and some villagers we set off and reached the top. It was a plain rocky hill, and a forsaken place. I could see the setting sun.

'A little further off, I saw a small shrine and the priest said he came there daily only to light the lamp. He told me lots of stories, that it was a very good place, it had a nice tank, like a small lake, which never dried up in summer...cows and animals always had water. But at night people came there to drink and do other things because it is secluded.

'I'm going to make it into a very beautiful place!' His face lit up as he spoke. 'And then all of you can come there.' We knew that once Sir set his mind on something he would achieve it. This chance discovery of the site just confirmed that providence was helping him.

Time passed. We heard that buildings were coming up, that classes had begun. But as further time passed, there was more silence than news about Bhaskara, except for the annual dance camp held there. I never made it to those camps, so I did not see what had become of my guru's dream.

But there were rumours that it was not quite the success Dhananjayan had envisioned and some of those who had attended the camps complained about how remote the place was and how basic the amenities offered there.

In 2001, came the breach in all our lives. It was a terrible tragedy that took place near Bhaskara. The son of a mridangam player, B. Rajesh Kumar grew up rolling mnemonic syllables off his tongue. Since his father, N.V. Balakrishnan 'Adyar Balu' accompanied many senior dancers, Rajesh imbibed both music and dance. At a very young age he learnt his basic *adavus* in Kalanidhi Narayanan's school. However at the time he was not very serious about dancing nor did he sense any great talent within himself.

Soon after he joined BK, in 1996 I saw him dance in a supporting role that barely lasted minutes. While he stood out due to his height, there was nothing to suggest that in a brief span of five years he would become the most promising solo dancer of his generation.

It was a combination of a conducive environment, a ripening of his own talents and blistering hard work. Rajesh spent most of his day at BK, practising his *adavus*, learning new items, rehearsing for the many programmes he was increasingly involved in and soon, teaching juniors. At a time when Satyajit had abdicated, Rajesh was moulded to fit his spot.

Not only was he part of the Bharata Kalanjali troupe, he also danced *with* Shanta and Dhananjayan in their Bharata Natyam performances, which resulted in accelerating his growth as a performing artiste. He had the added advantage of being able to handle the cymbals with aplomb while our gurus danced.

At his debut, Rajesh danced in a manner that delighted everyone present there. He turned every member of the audience into a 'rasika', one who tastes, savours, enjoys the feelings created in her by the dancer. I remember watching him dance with joy and abandon and artistry, cheering him silently, grateful for being taken on that winged journey. It was a debut performance like no other.

Here, finally, was a male dancer who excelled in *abhinaya* as much as *nritta*; who had the elusive '*it*'.

My last conversation with him, in April 2001, was an animated discussion about Krishna in the *Gita Govinda*. Rajesh wondered whether he was at heart a one-woman man, devoted to Radha, as Dhananjayan saw him, or an incorrigible flirt, incapable of committing to only Radha, as Kalanidhi Narayanan saw him. Rajesh's own portrayal of Krishna in the *ashtapadi Maamiyam Chalita*, where Krishna rues the fact that he has hurt and angered Radha, would depend on his understanding of Krishna's true nature.

Rajesh never got to performing *Maamiyam*.

The next time I saw him, barely a month later, he lay fresh faced in an open coffin, covered in rose petals.

A guru's dream and a student's steadfastness; it was a strange case of entwined destinies. When Dhananjayan envisaged Bhaskara,

Rajesh Kumar

Rajesh was the only one who supported his guru, promising to help him in whatever way he could, committing to stay in that remote place if required. He kept his word to the very grim end.

The annual summer camp at Bhaskara had just been completed successfully. The last night of the camp, Rajesh danced Kathakali like a seasoned artiste though he had never trained in Kathakali previously. 'He danced so well! Both the Kathakali gurus Sadanam Balakrishnan and Kalamandalam Gopi praised him. He had learnt a very difficult *padam* in just a month. It was as though someone envied him so much, they cast the deadly evil eye on him,' said Shanta, narrating the events of that fateful day, 13 May, at Bhaskara.

'He did not know how to swim. The previous week, when we took the kids to the river nearby, he jumped in suddenly...the wrong way, feet first. We were so scared. I scolded him. He was not supposed to go swimming but he did. And he must have done the same thing. They had opened up the dam that day.'

Talking to Dhananjayan I pieced together what had happened. 'That morning we were planting trees on the campus. Rajesh said, "I am going down to the house of a music student living down the hill, to have tea." I said, "Don't go." The previous day, Rajesh's cousin had got married in Chennai but he preferred to remain at Kaithapram. Had he left, then he'd still be alive...it is all fate.'

Dhananjayan sighed heavily. 'Without my knowledge he went to the river. He always had a fascination for water. Without knowing the depth he jumped. He was with another dancer Pradeesh. Pradeesh told him "Don't! Sir will be angry," but in spite of that he jumped in.'

'When he surfaced, waving, they thought he was fooling around. Then Pradeesh realized it was serious. Rajesh was so heavy in the water he could not pull him to safety. He ran to get help and other boys from the campus came. A very strong swimmer found him underwater. By the time they pulled him out, found a jeep on a Sunday, a hartal day, and took him to the hospital twenty minutes away, it was too late.

'Only then did they call me. They said, "One of the students is here." I thought someone was sick. They did not tell me who it was. When I went to the hospital I realized it was Rajesh. It was a big big shock.'

Shanta added the pertinent detail. 'He died of choking, not drowning. Maybe he hit something underwater, or had cramps. He was a very slow eater, I always used to tease him about his food pipe being very small. When they pumped him only food came out. He could not breathe because of food choking his windpipe.'

Pradeesh accompanied the body of his friend, as they returned by road from Kaithapram. Having weathered a nightmarish twenty four hours, he walked like a zombie alongside the coffin into Rajesh's newly constructed home, and collapsed. Many eminent Bharata Natyam gurus and dancers filled the house, a testimony to just how much everyone liked the young man.

It was a reminder to everyone present there that one could have talent and fame and money, genius even, but without a pulse, without the deep rapid breaths that a dancer takes as he powers through an exacting piece of *nritta*, it comes to nothing.

Eleven years after his death, no male entrant at BK has matched Rajesh in his completeness.

It was bad publicity for Bhaskara.

Months after the accident, Dhananjayan seemed to have changed. He was spending far too much time staring at the computer, a faraway look in his eyes. He wrote letters to the editor on many a subject, believing that his art alone is not sufficient involvement in society. He engaged with the world around him and tried to change it in certain aspects, whether it was the facilities provided by sabhas to artists or the perception of male dancers. He expressed his thoughts on various subjects, always forcefully, at times bluntly. If he was able to talk in minute detail about a particular aspect of Bharata Natyam, he was also able to stretch his mind to issues such as the linking of rivers across India.

He had strong views on the role of artists in promoting social change, bemoaned the unwelcome changes that have crept into Kathakali, felt that Tamil ought not to be neglected and pointed out the defects in our educational system. He did not hesitate to talk about the disorganized garbage collection in the city long before it was contracted to private organizations in Madras. If he was upset about people smoking in trains or the quality of food provided on certain sectors, he immediately wrote about it to the railway authorities.

I was jealous of this machine that took him away from us, away from class, where he belonged. Over the years, I'd learnt an extensive repertoire from him, feeling in every class a great elation. I thirsted for more, but he did not teach as much as before. When he did, he did so without the earlier displays of temper. A class in which Sir did not scold me? Unacceptable!

Clearly, his mind was elsewhere, as the worries pressed upon him.

Two years after Rajesh passed away, BK lost another dancer Ravi in a far more sensational way.

Short, curly-haired Ravi arrived at BK, an important letter in hand. What he thought was a recommendation letter was actually a message from the Principal of Kalakshetra enquiring if Dhananjayan could help the boy who could *not* be taught dance, in some way?

On hearing that he belonged to a poor family, and had left his small town impelled by the desire to learn dance, Dhananjayan felt for the young man in his late twenties and asked him to start coming to classes from the very next day. In a couple of years, Ravi was not only teaching the junior classes but also participating in the Bharata Kalanjali productions. When Shanta, in a rare huff, decided to shift many personal possessions to Bhaskara, it was Ravi who loaded the truck for her and drove it all the way to Kerala.

Ravi had an impishness about him and spoke with a casual familiarity. He also had a very tangled personal life. But Ravi seemed unfazed by it, practising breezily in class at BK. 'He would involve everyone in his problems. Dump them at someone's feet and run away. He was very good at escaping a mess of his own creation,' said Ravi Malamakkavu, Dhananjayan's secretary.

All of a sudden Ravi hit big time. A friend wrangled a government grant for him and overnight, he hired a huge bungalow in Anna Nagar and started a dance-school: Ravi's Naatyopasana. Veritably a Pied Piper, he seemed to have no trouble attracting students.

The last time I saw him, astride a new expensive bike, a thick lava of self-satisfaction emanated from him. Weeks later, on 29 October 2003, he was dead.

Murdered.

An unemployed man had befriended Ravi, and over the five months of their growing friendship had observed his sudden riches. Using the knowledge gained from a previous job with a chemist, he ground sleeping pills into Ravi's favourite chutney and as he ate, pretended to eat it too.

Leaving Ravi unconscious, he rode all over town in a drunken state only to have his bike impounded when the police caught him. At dawn he made his way back to the bungalow where he found Ravi struggling for life. He fed him pesticides this time. Collecting a gold bracelet, mobile phone and ATM cards, he left the house through the open back door.

Withdrawing 60,000 rupees from Ravi's bank accounts, his murderer stopped by at the police station to pay the fine and reclaim his bike.

When it was time for the morning class, Ravi was found dead. Those who saw him said he lay in a perfectly composed way, kurta unruffled and hands and arms aligned like a doll's, symmetrically. Rumour spread that he had killed himself and not many came to mourn him.

On November 3, inexplicably, perhaps thinking he had gotten away with it or out of a sense of guilt, his 'friend' arrived to condole with Ravi's family. When the police interrogated him, he confessed and was charged with murder.[48]

With Rajesh and Ravi gone, a pall of mortality hung over BK. Other male dancers too left in search of greener pastures and there was a void.

More time passed.

Then, in 2010, came the news that it was all over. The sun had set on Bhaskara.

50

Recently, Dhananjayan was in an introspective mood and I dared to ask him about what went wrong with Bhaskara. Sitting in his newly-renovated drawing room, the many brass artefacts gifted to them displayed on a side table, he talked about the cost of achieving his dream.

'People had been asking us to start something in Kerala, contribute to my village and North Malabar. I thought that since these people were interested, they would also help. A great percentage of Kalakshetra students are from Kerala. I thought instead of coming to Madras they can come there, it would be easier for them. With that idea, I explored the possibilities.

'I wanted to offer a place with art-integrated education, like a gurukulam. I wanted it to be like Kalakshetra, a school and arts training side by side...prayer here, amphitheatre there. I learnt too late that Rukmini Devi had lots of people, especially Shankara Menon, who helped fructify her vision. He gave up a job to come to Kalakshetra for half the salary. In those days things were not so commercial. I thought the world is still like that. That was my mistake.'

What was Shanta's reaction? And that of Sanjay and Satyajit?

'From the beginning, I had opposition from Shanta and my sons. Shanta was not very keen but I thought I would be successful. And so, we started everything with good intentions and it progressed well.'

This was a surprise; Shanta's support in anything he did was a given. While she had publicly helped him with Bhaskara, she had hidden her misgivings from us.

'As you know, I came across this hill in a remote place near Payyanur and wanted to build Bhaskara there. People dissuaded me from buying it, in fact they did not even know who it belonged to, but I was adamant because of the hill and the atmosphere I envisaged. Finally, some of the villagers came to meet me and said, "Take it. A society registered long ago owns that place." I liked the idea that the money paid to the society would go to help the temple. Originally they said there is no value but by the time we fixed the price it came to about 6 lakhs which was a lot of money for me, at that time. Fortunately, we found that there is a lot of water beneath the ground, good water, so I was encouraged by it. It was a good sign.

'I formed a trust called Bhaskara and T.N. Seshan laid the foundation stone. I had to invest a lot of money to develop the area. We planted trees, the villagers helped. Things started moving very well when I found a good architect, and we built the classrooms.

'To my shock, nobody sent their children because they thought Bhaskara was old fashioned. Some children came and enrolled themselves, but they were from other villages. Even my being there, my life as an example…did not work. The local villagers wanted the "secular" English education which I am against.

'For one year, I struggled to run the institution. It drained my resources. We employed teachers for music and dance and about 15 students came. That part was running well but we were not getting enough money, not even the fees. Meanwhile, the students who wanted to go to Kalakshetra continued to want to go there, for the name.

'The teachers too, they did not stay for long, they left. I had selected 3 or 4 boys to help, taught them and trained them but they also left. I got 85 children from the local elementary school to come and learn for free, but after one or two years they would go away to the sixth standard elsewhere. When we started introducing fees they did not want to pay even 10 rupees for the art course; my bank balance was getting lower. I could not run it like this forever. It was such a big disappointment.

'All my brilliant ideas fizzled out. I thought the workers in the Gulf, NRIs, would appreciate Bhaskara but no NRIs sent their children. The Gulf people wanted a modern kind of school, they did not want the gurukulam type. I saw some very sophisticated schools functioning in Cochin, that is what Kerala NRIs want. So in fact I thought of offering this place to some of them to run, but Bhaskara was in a far-off place and they wanted it in a town.'

It was the first time I had heard Dhananjayan ever admit to defeat. I remained silent as he continued, not wanting to break the flow of his narration.

'So, with a heavy heart, I decided to close it. Some parents wanted to file a case but I found their children schools elsewhere. I offered the place to Kannur University, to run their music BA and MA classes. While they conducted the classes on our campus, they did not give me any rent. But that worked out well for them, and all those students were from outside Payyanur.

'Meanwhile, the villagers had been giving trouble. They wanted to be in the committee, they wanted some money out of the whole thing. They started filing small cases...like when we wanted to put a road, they blocked that. That is the way in Kerala, anything you want to start there is opposition. Even to good things.

'My children and Shanta also wanted me to close it. It was telling on my health...the tension of dealing with these people, going up and down every week, handling small court cases...it was too much.

'Still, we conducted annual summer camps for which a lot of my students came from abroad. That is when calamity struck. One of our teachers Rajesh went for a swim and drowned. The villagers immediately spread rumours that this place is unlucky because he died here. He did not die on the campus but still...I was very upset because of the incident.

'After that, I had a lot of problems, and litigation and finally managed to close Bhaskara in 2010. Now, a new problem arose. The villagers put a stop to my selling it. Give it back to the temple, they said. They have no locus standii, but the case is still going on. Meanwhile I found a college nearby, they wanted a place and said they would deal with the case when it comes up. That is how I got rid of the headache. It was a very bad time, according to my horoscope too.'

Some of the people who had contributed, or raised money for Bhaskara, wondered where it had all gone. 'A lot of students contributed money...' I said and trailed off.

'The trust is still there, but it was a big loss for me. Of course all the students contributed but it was not sufficient, maybe 15 to 20 lakhs, but I sank my life savings. I spent 1.5 crores from our savings! When we sold it, we got some back. Land prices rose and thanks to me, the whole surrounding area got developed. In one way, I was protected in that it did not affect our career or BK here. Other funds came in, so we had money to live on. It was my big failure. That is the story of Bhaskara.'

Shanta happened to walk in, looking radiant in a maroon sari with a mustard blouse. The mustard blouse is a bit of an in-joke because she wears it so often with her jewel coloured saris. I asked her why she hadn't tried to stop Dhananjayan from going ahead.

'From day one I was not for it. I did not think it was a good idea... we were settled here. But my mother and my aunt were for it. In fact, at one point when things were going bad, he said, "I'll stay in Payyanur and you stay in Chennai and look after BK," and my mother and aunt offered to shift there to look after him! After a while I felt bad, I saw he was doing it with so much enthusiasm, I stopped telling him. But I had a great fear, *Oh, can we do this? We have to shift everything there. How?* One day I was so upset, I said, "Let's go." Whatever I could see in front of me, books and things, I put into a truck and sent to Bhaskara! By then, without completing the building, they started functioning. In the rain. When I look back, I don't know how we did it. The first camp, no infrastructure but a 100 students. I was so tired. Lots of work. I was drained.'

This was a rare admission from Shanta.

'For instance, the kitchen was not a model kitchen, made do with what they had. We had to arrange for gas, so difficult. Huge cauldrons for rice were made every day. Village school children would come and eat in great quantities. Sir would say, "Give, give, let them eat." I have seen a five year old polish off ten huge idlies. Great food, and we spoilt them for all that. I was not only teaching dance at the camps but dealing with laundry and the toilets! Even though we paid three women for laundry, there was a big mound of clothes by evening, and the students had to hunt for their clothes. I had to do all this. Some nights I would cry, I couldn't say anything to the students. I would wake up in the morning and teach. When Sir got help from other people, it was for what they could get out of it…not for Art. They massaged his ego for their own gain. While he was idealistic at every stage there were so many difficulties. When he gave the building to be used, that became a big headache. Phone calls at night from his brothers, "What to do? What to do?" All our life savings through our hard work went into this. I used to pray, *Ishwara, if we come out of this I'll be grateful.*

'Even here at BK, we could not let our students down. We had to teach as though nothing has happened. The whole thing was like a bad dream. It took ten years of our precious life. And throught it all, everything was going on…classes, performances, travel. And while we were having our own problems, students and our children were also having their problems, all simultaneously!'

I thought of Shafeek who had profited from the mirage of Bhaskara. Training at a highly advanced level in Bharata Natyam had travelled from Madras to reach him in a remote village in Kerala, an inversion of the journey Dhananjayan had undertaken so many moons ago.

It was in 2000 that Shafeek read with about Bhaskara and a camp to be held there, in a newspaper. Months ago, he had seen Dhananjayan dance at Payyanur. 'I was speechless when I saw Sir. I was a beginner in dance. But when I saw him I knew the possibility of how it can be! It engraved itself in my heart.' He watched him dance again at the

Malabar Mahotsav but was too shy to introduce himself. And now, this newspaper promised him the opportunity of learning from him.

'I reached Bhaskara one day after the camp began. I went the way I usually dressed, wearing a baggy pant with pockets here, there, down the leg, buttons and zips all over and a T shirt! All my clothes were like that. Sir looked at me up and down, and asked brusquely, "What do you want?"'

A rattled Shafeek explained that he wanted to join the camp.

'Sir agreed, and then he scolded, "Hmm. What sort of dress is this? Go change."'

Shafeek dug around in his bag and found a single veshti, to his immense relief.

There were two other boys at the camp, Rajesh and Ravi, so he had company.

The camp ended. Shafeek joined Kathakali classes being held at Bhaskara. It took him two hours to travel there from his home. 'In the beginning there were ten or fifteen children. Then they dropped out. There were only four of us left so the classes were stopped.'

By now Shafeek was in his second year of college, working towards a B.Com degree. When Dhananjayan asked him to stay on at Bhaskara to teach in the evenings, Shafeek readily agreed. He returned home only on the weekend. In his final year, he left college. His parents 'were not bothered. I had joined college for my own sake.'

The final year was about to end when Shafeek had decided he wanted to make a career in dance. If he was going to do it, he would do it well. With two months to go, Shafeek attacked his books, spent a month catching up on all that he had missed and sat for eight exams one after another. He cleared all eight papers with good marks, better than when he was a regular student. 'That was how I could join Madras University in 2004 for the degree. MA Bharata Natyam, first batch!'

In Chennai, attending classes at BK whenever he could, Shafeek wished he had come to the city earlier – he would have learnt so much more. For Shafeek at least, Bhaskara had proved to be a boon. It was all about being in the right place at the right time.

Satyajit poked his head in the door, wanting to know the schedule for the evening. While his parents conferred, I asked Satyajit his views on Bhaskara.

He summed it up. 'What was his intention to start Bhaskara? Why do something like a Kalakshetra? He wanted to contribute to the arts like Rukmini Devi, to be on the same level but her era was over. His intention was wrong. It was to make a big academy, not to train genuine artists therefore it could not flourish.'

Dhananjayan tried to be philosophical about it. 'I learnt a lot of lessons about human behaviour. How people can be crooked and venomous. Like the *chakravyuha*, I got into it, met shady people, lost money but not ourselves.'

He had the faraway look in his eyes again. 'I made a beautiful campus. Have you seen it?'

I hung my head, feeling very guilty.

'*No?* Even my own niece has not seen the place to this day and I thought *all* of you would help!'

If only…

If…

51

One opportunity that has developed for male dancers is that of 'freelancing' in the productions of other dancers. If a production requires a certain number of male dancers, or a dancer of a particular ability to play a part, then freelance dancers, who may not necessarily have trained in the same style as the other dancers in that particular production, are hired.

Both Narendra Kumar and Shafeek benefitted greatly by being freelance dancers. I first caught up with Narendra Kumar to ask him about the challenges of being a freelance dancer.

Looking at the self-contained young man in jeans and faded khadi kurta, a lone rudraksha worn around the neck, one would never guess that he has danced his way across many countries – Germany, Malaysia, Singapore, Korea, Japan, China and at least ten times in the USA. In China he had to rely on his drawing skills, drawing a hen and an arrow pointing to the egg beneath it, in order to get something fit to eat. Looks *can* be deceptive, I thought to myself.

Narendra began to freelance around 1999, accepting opportunities that came by word of mouth. 'I started earning a little.' The first thing he did was to spend 350 rupees on a bus pass. 'I could travel anywhere in Chennai, twenty-four hours!'

When Anita Ratnam invited him to participate in a contemporary dance production, it opened a fresh phase in Narendra's life. He joined a group of dancers who would spend hours watching an ice cube melt and then try to capture that through movement. Or, the feel of water splashing onto the floor from a jug. It required a different kind of mental preparation and physical fitness. Narendra loved it. 'All classical dancers should go through some modern training to understand their body better.'

He discovered the spontaneous, wild side in him that came to the fore in contemporary dance. It takes a certain temperament that submits to all the rules of the classical arts in order to find the unlimited freedom held within. Narendra, by nature, likes to be in the unrehearsed moment, fearless and confident. 'In contemporary dance, there are no rules, no walls, the earth is mine. I can do what I like, I'm like a bird set free!'

Yet, classical Bharata Natyam remains his first and abiding love. 'Bharata Natyam is like living in a family where there are rules and regulations that you follow. I try not to cross the boundaries. Only where I feel it can be enhanced. Be it classical or contemporary, it is *dance*. When you do modern dance, it is a good workout but in classical Bharata Natyam, because there is a spiritual element, the feeling takes you elsewhere.'

Soon, Narendra got a lot of opportunities to 'choreograph, travel, perform and grow. I did a lot of freelancing in Bharata Natyam productions.' Wherever men were needed in a production, Narendra accepted the role, earning 750 or a 1000 rupees per show. Disappointingly, he got very few opportunities to dance solo Bharata Natyam. 'Freelancing helped me earn, whereas if I danced solo I was out of pocket.'

Many tours abroad came his way, the first being one to America in 1999 with Anita Ratnam. Working with Mark Taylor, at the Dance Alloy Pittsburgh, exposed Narendra to a different way of treating the body-as-instrument. 'Mark Taylor was primarily concerned with the body, dance and choreography came later. When I was showing him all the *adavus*, he was aghast. "How do you do this?" When I showed him the *mandi adavu*,' – where the knee often strikes the floor with a thud – 'he exclaimed, "Such a shock to the limbs!" To him the body was like a glass *objet d'art*, to be protected.'

As a freelance dancer abroad, Narendra's chief problem was loneliness. While a dancer's life revolves around rehearsals where one forgets the passing of time, it was during his off hours that he was at a loss. 'Back home, there's a tea shop every so many yards. In America, even if I set out for a walk, there'd be nobody on the streets.' Not fluent in spoken English then, he had trouble with the accent.

Being invited to perform in Saraswati Sundaresan's musical *Annamayya*, touring the US and Canada in 2000, meant that Narendra came into proximity with the great Carnatic musician Balamuralikrishna. Though he had never had formal training in Carnatic music, Narendra discovered he had an ear for it. He honed that skill by listening to Balamuralikrishna singing Annamacharya songs as the eponymous hero.

'I learnt so much from him. How much one can do with music... He would do new things every day. I got inspired. It showed me that classical artistes have the freedom to change.' Earlier, Narendra had spent a lot of time listening to singer Rajesh Vaidya. 'I was also very taken by the way O.S. Arun sings; the way he blends feelings and the grammar of music.'

Travelling with many groups abroad, he noticed that some hosts were extremely mean with food, contrary to the fabled Indian hospitality. He knew dancers who had to stagger through long rehearsals having had just a single slice of bread for breakfast.

Narendra spent eight years with the Arangham Dance Company and credits Anita Ratnam with having opened his mind to different ideas and ways of movement. 'I got a space in which to experiment. There I really grew.'

That growth was to reflect in his own productions.

Once, experimenting with a certain movement of the chest, Narendra decided to do it lying on the floor, and voila, moved like a snake, a ripple running down the length of his body. It was to star in his maiden choreographic venture, the *Kalinga Nartana tillana*. He required many dancers for the *tillana* but had no troupe. What he had though was a wealth of friends. 'They came in the pouring rain to practise. They were from different schools of dance but they all danced in it.'

In 2001, when he presented the very innovative *Kalinga Nartana tillana* at the Abhai Annual Day, it was a tremendous hit; with that he had 'arrived'. Narendra had boldly broken the rules of a conventional *tillana* while remaining within the classical ambit. Was he not scared to present it in front of the doyens of Bharata Natyam?

'When it comes to dance, I have no fear. Right or wrong, I just want to do it. It spills out. I just did it for fun.' It is this passion for dance that keeps Narendra going. 'As an artiste all I want to do is put on my makeup and mount the stage.'

Recognizing talent when she saw it, Mrs Y.G. Parthasarathy, gave Narendra a lot of opportunities at her sabha, Bharat Kalachar. Unlike other dancers, Narendra says, 'I never went to "apply" to sabhas. I did not know this is how it operates. If people invited me I would go and dance.'

He developed a certain bravado; a complete lack of stage fright and an ability to adapt to different styles of dance and turn the lack of resources into a triumph. In 2001, asked to present the story of the *Dashavatar* at Bharat Kalachar, Narendra had only enough money to pay one musician when the quorum is four. At the same time, he could not afford to relinquish the opportunity.

'I went to Keshavan the mridangist and said, "I have only enough to pay you. Please help me." We had not rehearsed together, but I went on stage and danced, just me and Keshavan, for *one hour*. The audience was spellbound and I got a standing ovation.'

What was even more remarkable was that Narendra's preparation had only consisted of flipping through an *Amar Chitra Katha* comic book narrating the story of the ten avatars of Vishnu. Remembering the visual progression of images, he had combined movement and *abhinaya* and body language to tell the story without song or music.

If there is one thread that recurs in Narendra's life, it is his ability to make friends and inspire in them a generosity towards him. Narendra met John Britto, a Chennai-based contemporary dancer, while running summer camps for children in a school. In a gesture unheard of in an intensely competitive environment, John first suggested to Narendra that he approach 'corporates' for well-paid shows and when John could not accept an assignment he passed it on to Narendra.

'I did not know that this world exists.' Narendra was to become adept at conceptualizing shows for events held by companies. 'They want to see a group dance, a nice group. First I got the show and then made a group. All my friends across dance schools and styles came for the sake of friendship.' And in 2000 the Anusham group was born.

Otherwise unmindful of his clothes, 'hundred rupee jubbas will do,' Narendra learnt to dress in branded trousers and shirt when meeting organizers. 'If you wear Indian clothes, kurta-pyjama or veshti-jubba, they don't understand where you are coming from, our pride in our culture.'

Over time, he invested the money he earned in making a publicity package replete with visiting cards, brochures, photographs, website, DVDs of performance excerpts and carried a laptop to presentation meetings. By 2001, he was zipping all over town on his TVS Scooty, weaving in front of the very buses that had once been his lifeline.

With his can-do attitude, he was soon choreographing shows that ranged over all sorts of themes. 'The organizers give the theme. Spirit or Hope or Energy.' Performed mostly at star hotels, Narendra was to find amenable working conditions. 'They build whatever you need. I hire the lights. I learnt lighting design and sound engineering because I am very particular about winning audience interest.'

Sometimes the requests were seemingly impossible. Once a company asked for something to be done in just 40 seconds, as a curtain raiser. Narendra obliged. 'We did something very fast, like crackers exploding on stage because the theme was Energy.'

Branching out into this area was lucrative; at least Narendra was not out of pocket as in the performances for sabhas. 'They pay depending on their budget. The highest we earned was Rs 50,000 and when we did a show out of town we got a lakh. We get money, but we also have to spend on costumes, on lighting, the dancers and travel.'

Ganga, Shakti, Mrita Sanjeevani are just some of the names of his innovative productions with a classical base. '*Shakti*, on the mother-daughter theme, earned back the investment in costumes and music etc, and corporates liked it a lot.'

Times have changed. Unlike the days when we students danced for Dhananjayan for free, believing it to be a privilege, now dancers expect some renumeration, even at BK. 'I pay all my students,' says Narendra with quiet pride. 'To those who are professional dancers, I pay a little more. It can cost 500 rupees for ten rehearsals to and fro by bus. Why should they be out of pocket? If I get money, I must pay them.'

He underlines the inconsistent nature of earnings. 'Sometimes I may get 30,000 in one show, and not get anything for another. It averages out.'

One would think that his early days of penury would impel him to save money. Instead Narendra ploughs back whatever extra income he has into fresh productions. 'I do not save. I got a fellowship from the German government in 2009 for *Shifting Grounds* presented in Cologne. I used that money to create and record the music for *Jungle Book* with lyrics in English. Now, I can go ahead and choreograph it.'

He explains, 'People earn but do not plough it back into their work. They wait for a sponsor. God has given me the energy to work. By god's grace, I do earn. For my hard work I am getting the rewards. I don't feel I am 37. Time has just flown by.'

When Narendra started teaching, there was one social prejudice that he had to overcome. 'Ajith acted in the movie *Varalaru* as an effeminate dancer. So the public thinks that all male dancers are like that. I tried to train fresh new boys, but they didn't want to learn. I offered myself as an example. They said, "Maybe you are okay but the others are not. We will become effeminate if they learn." I could teach only four poor boys, who are very good dancers today.'

Narendra is vexed by effeminate male dancers. 'I have a friend who dances like that, I scold him. He says, "It makes me happy to dance this way." What can I say to that? If Dhananjayan Sir does a female character, you can see a girl there, but he is not effeminate ever. It is communicated through eyes and *bhava*.'

Further, 'You cannot say that effeminate dancers are all gay.' Gayness per se does not interest Narendra. 'It is their personal business. There are so many doctors or engineers who might be gay, so why focus on whether or not male dancers are gay?'

Looking ahead to the future, after *Jungle Book*, Narendra's dream production would be to do Kalki's famous Tamil novel *Ponniyin Selvan*. Another dream, currently unattainable, is to, 'Start a home studio to record music for my productions. It will cost 15 lakhs. You just need a sound proof room at home!'

Home is a tiny flat in Adyar, for which Narendra is still paying loan instalments.

Shafeek too became a freelance dancer, in order to fund his studies.

The fees at Madras University were Rs 25000 and he had 15000 saved. He thought he would bridge the gap. Unfortunately, just before he was about to leave for Chennai in 2004, his father fell ill and Shafeek had to spend his savings on medical treatment. 'My bank balance was zero.' Shafeek borrowed from friends and paid the fees.

In Chennai, 'I got a merit scholarship for music and dance.' That helped him pay for his share of rent and food.

Luck favoured Shafeek in the form of a classmate at the University, Archana, who introduced him to Anita Ratnam. She cast him in a production. And thus began Shafeek's career as a freelance dancer. 'The rehearsals were early in the morning, at 6 a.m. I would take a bus or even walk, every day, finish rehearsals, and then go to college.'

Shafeek did many shows as a freelance dancer: 'Any show, anybody who called me, I danced.' He earned just enough to pay back the 25,000 he had borrowed. The next year, another 25,000 was to be paid. Again he borrowed to pay the fees. 'I did not think about money then, I don't think about it now. I have a degree, I could have gone to the Gulf but I cannot sit at a desk morning to evening. I like doing this. This is what I want to do.'

In 2006, Shafeek got an opportunity to go to London, and this trip highlighted the ignominy a freelance dancer risks. In most situations, there is no emotional bond, unlike in one's own guru's troupe; nor even a prior acquaintance with the person. Although the terms are clear, and it is a verbal agreement to dance for a certain renumeration, very often offstage they face contempt and unprofessional behaviour.

A well-known London-based dancer needed boys for her production, and Shafeek and Kalakshetra-trained Vikas travelled from India to stay in London for three months. They were to be paid Rs 85,000 but there was no contract. The lack of empathy began even before they reached. 'She said we have to buy our own insurance. I had to borrow the money for the visa as well, and she promised to reimburse it on arrival.'

On reaching London, there was no orientation, no welcome. Rehearsals were to begin the next day. In the evening, a messenger was sent with metro passes. Over the weeks, the dancer would keep tabs on them by checking where they had gone in their free time using the metro pass.

'She felt she had to squeeze work from us because she had taken us there. The local dancers would make many mistakes but she would want all of us to start from the beginning. The only correction she could come up with was that I had to straighten my arm. But the number of repetitions...!'

Ten days passed and Shafeek was not reimbursed his visa money. 'So one day I said, "Either you pay or I am going home." At once she took it out of her bag and paid me.' She took everyone's passports but Shafeek refused, knowing that to do so would be to relinquish all control. He sent the money home to repay the loan; his honour was upheld.

London is an expensive city. The dancer expected two grown men to survive on 25 pounds a week for food. But a trip to Scotland taxed this meagre allowance further. The cherry on the icing was when they participated in a competition. 'Out of 200 competitors, we came first. It was a very tiring 15 minute number, with lots of speedy *jatis*. *We* danced, *she* got 29,000 pounds as the choreographer but she did not give us a pie. For Diwali, grudgingly, she gave us 50 pounds.'

He was supposed to leave on November 26, and the shows ended on the 22nd. Shafeek thought they would have time to sightsee and shop. On the 22nd he was told to leave the very next day. 'Thank god I had used the metro pass to see some of London!' He took back Rs 85,000 less hefty taxes.

'If you have money, you can dance. That's what I learnt from that trip.'

In 2008, Shafeek jetted off to New York, to dance at the Carnegie Hall, this time as part of dancer-guru C.V. Chandrasekhar's troupe. It was a much better experience, 'He gave us full freedom. As long as you rehearse properly, you are free to roam around in your spare time.'

Meanwhile, his destiny was to bind him even more firmly to dance. Asked to choreograph a *varnam*, Shafeek had arrived in Trichur to discover that the school was run by a Muslim lady. 'Their home was not like a orthodox Muslim's home. Only the name was Muslim. Then I saw Shebana, her daughter.'

Shebana was eighteen. 'I was twenty-eight, there was a big age difference, so I did not see her in that light at all.' Still, enquiries came his way and people who knew both of them seemed to think it was a good match. 'It was only after we got married in 2010 that I watched her dance. Then I took class for her every day early in the morning and knocked the kinks out and corrected her style.'

When they danced together in Mysore, Shafeek had a nagging ache in his leg and could not dance as well as usual. 'The papers said "Compared to Shafeek, Shebana has a higher standard in the Kalakshetra style!" I was thrilled.'

Life as a dancer is difficult. 'I go walking to sabhas and ask for shows. Narada Gana Sabha and Brahma Gana Sabha, they are unfailingly polite. "Next time, next time" they say. The others ask for money to give me a platform. When I get the rare chance to do a solo show, I'm ecstatic. But then, I have to raise the money to pay the musicians.

'I am not earning that much, some months I can't pay the rent of Rs 3,500.' Shafiq lives in a small room in a congested part of Thiruvanmiyur. 'I do not ask anyone for money. The only way out is to teach. Because the money you get there, you use to pay for your dance shows.'

However, in order to teach one needs a studio space which Shafeek does not have. For now, he is a freelance dancer who spends the week in Chennai and returns to his wife and one-year-old baby in Trichur on the weekends.

Doesn't he get disheartened? 'If I think about it, it *does* seem bleak. But until now I have not thought about it. Now that you ask me, yes it is difficult.'

53

What does it take to be a successful male dancer? Is there an additional factor that overrides the common requirements they share with their female counterparts? I asked Dhananjayan.

'Men have to have a certain calibre and the necessary physique if they are to compete with women who have the natural advantage of their physical beauty and attractive jewellery. Unless a man is totally involved in his dance, it is very difficult for him to click. He should be attractive in every sense of the term. Apart from technical prowess, the gods need to bless him with lots of luck and that something extra.'

Who were the dancers he admired?

'In the generation older to me, I admired Guru Gopinath. Of course, Krishnan Nair, and my own Asan, Chandu Panikker, though he was not in his prime when I learnt from him. Closer in time, I greatly admired Durga Lal. He and his brother Devi Lal...they were like stars. The great Birju Maharaj. Singhajit Singh, he's very dignified, you look at him and you see the dance personified. Raja Reddy, he has a strong personality. He is a very successful male dancer. Somehow, I was not enamoured by Kelucharan Mohapatra's dance. I could not relate to the exaggerated *tribhangi*, the feminine curves of the Odissi style, in his dancing. There are not many male dancers in Bharata Natyam that I find riveting. I like Sridhar of Bangalore, and Kiran Subramanyam.'

At one time in BK, there were as many as thirty boys enrolled to learn. Over two decades, Dhananjayan presented many well-trained men. Other dance companies which did not have their own male dancers began to hire them as freelance dancers. By the 21st century, this resulted in a demand for trained male dancers. Thus the Kalakshetra and BK boys found themselves jetting off as 'contract' dancers, participating in various productions across the globe, not in least because the training given ensures uniformity of technique and the ability to synchronize perfectly.

'I used to send my boys to other troupes. Most of them are from lower middle-class families. They needed money so I encouraged them to take part elsewhere. They make good money as freelancers. They do a lot of private shows for company launches or promotions. They are given air-tickets and stay in five-star hotels, something we, even though senior artistes, don't always get.'

The one undeniable fact is that while there are many good dancers, not all are successful as solo artists. More so the men. 'The freelancers don't get any satisfaction from that work. They get the chance because of their Bharata Natyam training but they are not known as Bharata Natyam *solo* dancers. So they earn there and want to spend here, to become known as soloists.'

Dhananjayan talked about giving timely advice to his students. 'The main thing is separating the ones who could make a career of it, from the rest. Not everyone can become a performer. One boy wanted to become a full-time dancer, but we discouraged him. Now he has his own business, and is very successful. He uses his money to encourage theatre and school boys. Similiarly, Selvaraj, the painter...Bharata Natyam helped him in his painting. Learning dance movements helped him evolve his style and he's known as a painter now.'

Dispassionately, Dhananjayan enumerated the long list of male dancers he had trained, identifying the few that had it in them to be successful solo artists. 'Very few people have that star quality. Satyajit had it, but he left. Rajesh Kumar had that capacity, and he was completely dedicated.'

For more than twenty years, each January when the national awards were announced, I would eagerly scan the papers for my gurus' name, only to be disappointed. With each passing year, Bharata Natyam artistes younger than them, with not as many achievements to show, their artistry itself a matter of debate, became Padma Shri. It was galling, but Dhananjayan took it in his stride.

'Most of the dancers got it because of Delhi connections. After some time I said, "I will not accept Padma Shri, only if it is something higher." We had a lot of opposition. Some of our own community of dancers who were members of the selection committee, they objected saying I am not a Tamilian, I am a Kathakali artiste. My Kathakali training was held against me, that I am not qualified to do Bharata Natyam! My own colleagues stood against me. And Shanta also lost, because if they gave her, then I could ask, "Why not me?" The deliberations which are meant to be secret, are always leaked. Others on the committee would tell me, "So and so said this about you"... referring to some top artistes here.'

Meanwhile people made their own assessment. Invitations to perform would arrive addressed to Padma Shri V.P. Dhananjayan.

The Government of India is the biggest patron of the arts. It sends artistes on tours abroad, chiefly through the ICCR and organizes inter-state exchanges through the zonal Cultural Centres. It offers grants to serious students and scholars of the performing arts and every year, it considers artistes from different fields for the Padma awards.

In practice, given the lack of publicly declared criteria and a transparent selection procedure, those with the most influence have a greater chance of being selected. Given that key government cultural institutions are based in Delhi, those artistes who live there automatically gain from their proximity to power.

Artistes living in Madras, the hub of Bharata Natyam, have to make many trips to Delhi to meet bureaucrats and other functionaries in Delhi, if they wish to remain in the reckoning. I remember a remark made about a dancer who suddenly shot into the limelight 'Oh, she has a budget of a lakh set aside just for networking trips to Delhi each month.' Though born of jealousy, the remark did have the bitter ring of truth.

Dhananjayan was certain they lost many opportunities by choosing not to move to Delhi. 'We never wanted to move out of Madras. Had we been in Delhi, our fame and status would have been more. We would have got more opportunities. In spite of that, I went on my own abroad, without the Delhi influence or the ICCR or government. I have no connections but people recognized our talent, and invited us. There were times when we were undercut by people with influence. We were invited on a tour and then suddenly told someone else is going. At least foreign organizations send a letter saying sorry, so and so is coming instead. In India they will not tell you.'

He continued heatedly, 'The Culture Department is totally corrupt, regardless of which party forms the government. Money is swindled with the connivance of touts and officials, so it is not reaching the artistes. Whom to approach? Everyone is corrupt. If we complain, we are blacklisted. I have publicly stated that we are representing India with bad dancers. ICCR tours have become a kind of foreign junket for the family of the artistes.

'Breaking into the Delhi clique is very difficult. There is favouritism and a major share of tours used to go to Delhi-based artistes. Now it is worse, every one wants to be empanelled, to go abroad on an ICCR tour. Hundreds of applications are sent to the ICCR, but who has the time to read them? But if you have influence, then you can ensure that your DVD will be seen by the selection panel. The more you talk about yourself, the more publicity you create, it helps – never mind that you are an average dancer.'

It is a fact that none of us, the students of BK, have surpassed our gurus in dance. Therefore, every award or recognition they receive becomes a matter of pride. We share in those moments with them, and there have been many occasions for celebration, such as the time they got the Sangeet Natak Academy Award.

Dhananjayan talked candidly, as always, of what it entailed. 'Recognition wise, Delhi has not given us much. Take the Sangeet Natak Academy Award. In 1995 I accepted it, provided it was jointly with Shanta. It was a bad decision. One award gets split between two people, even the money. So we got the same amount, Rs 25,000 but we both got a medal and shawl each. It's a wonder they did not make us split that!

'The SNA panel membership came out of the blue and again I was branded a troublemaker. There was lots of pressure and recommendations for undeserving cases. They wanted to give the award to some children, calling them prodigies. I made a recommendation that these awards should be given after 60 years, because in our arts, artists mature with time. Those who try to rise very fast cannot sustain it and fade away soon.

'Needless to say, my term was not extended. The same thing happened with the Finance committee, Ministry of Education. In the first year itself I gave my report, that there was no accountability on the part of grant-winners. Grants were being given to undeserving institutions. These were 'letter-head' institutions, if you went and actually looked at them, they were not even functioning. There were touts who promised a grant for a cut. The Secretary at that time, an IAS officer, appreciated my report but could not do anything. It was disheartening.'

To Dhananjayan's embarrassment, artistes started approaching him for favours.

'Only when I got the SNA post did I learn just how people use influence. Dancers and musicians would come home, I would not entertain them. I'd say "This will be a disqualification, please leave." Junior artistes would call, undeserving people. Some new entrants, young kids in the limelight at that time, their parents and grandparents came to lobby on their behalf. Imagine! When artistes much older had not got their due. Even today, very well-known dancers approach us saying, "Please nominate us," because Shanta and I have two votes.'

Dhananjayan bemoans the fact that despite our wealth of cultural and artistic traditions, India does not have a National Troupe of the 'best of best' dancers, unlike so many other countries. Coupled with bureaucratic favouritism, this results in shoddy presentations sometimes by troupes sent abroad.

He is particularly incensed by artistes who are elevated to the Rajya Sabha and then 'waste' their term by not achieving anything concrete for their fellow artistes across India. 'Lata Mangeshkar rarely attended!' he fumes. Although invited to perform all over the world, the prestigious Music Academy remained the last bastion. Dhananjayan traced the history of his association with it.

'Once T.T. Vasu, President of The Music Academy, openly said, "Who will watch a man dancing?" I was so annoyed. I argued with him...*Men have been dancing from time immemorial. Without understanding the provenance and divinity of our arts, the so called patrons talk like this.* If people did not watch me, a male dancer, I would not have come to this level. So I stood my ground and fought for male dancers, even my contemporaries or seniors who did not have the limelight. I paved the way for them too.

'It is only during the past decade that The Music Academy started inviting us to perform, *with* proper renumeration. In 2004, they recognized me with the title Sangita Kala Acharya.'

In 2009, overdue by years, the Dhananjayans were finally given the Padma Bhushan.

'I tell people it came walking from Delhi...that's why it took so long,' joked Dhananjayan. 'We do not have any godfather or influence, it came on its own. That too without the advantage of living in Delhi.' Never one to pull his punches, Dhananjayan added, 'And there are no privileges given Padma awardees. I thought we might get a free air pass around the country or at the very least a free rail pass. Nothing!'

In April that year, when Dhananjayan turned 70, the BK students past and present joined together for a joyous lotus-themed celebration held at Kalakshetra. We had not only witnessed but been the lucky recipients of their relentless hard work and dedication.

54

To find out if living in Delhi offered an advantage to dancers, I travelled there to meet Navtej Singh Johar. In his early fifties, Navtej's beard is flecked with grey. His long hair is drawn back in a knot. As he chooses his words trying to articulate what is in his mind, his deep comfort with himself becomes apparent. He attributes it to yoga. 'Yoga gives me an experience of being self-contained and to be able to stand on stage with that feeling. It gives me the confidence that I am here, I am fine.'

Navej made his way from Delhi to Kalakshetra in 1980. He was twenty-one years old, the youngest of seven children, and had travelled hours by train following an impulse deep within him. It was not an easy thing to have done.

It all began when Badal Sircar, having mentored Navtej in a workshop on street theatre – 'the first most intense moment, the turning point of my life', told him to study dance. Until then, Navtej had a vague idea of what Kathak looked like but had never seen a Bharata Natyam performance.

In those days, the general perception of dance in the north, and in Navtej's community in particular was of '*nautch*...work relegated to prostitutes. I was very afraid. In Punjab, we had not heard of anybody dancing. Economic security...there were many issues.' Navtej began to put out feelers to his parents. He was in his second year of college.

'All hell broke loose. My father didn't even know that I was doing theatre. *Men* don't do this...Theater, dance...it's wrong. We had huge

Navtej Singh Johar

fights. That was a pretty traumatic time for everyone especially my mother who was stuck in between. It took me about a year and a half to let them know that I'm very very serious. And then my father said, "Be a painter. *Paint.* Don't dance," and sent me to Delhi to learn art.'

There, Navtej saw a Bharata Natyam performance by Padma Subrahmanyam and he was floored. 'She was fantastic and I knew instantly that it was what I wanted to do.'

Navtej's father, having locked horns with his son on the issue for months, now gave him his blessings. 'He said, "This is your calling.

You must do it." He told the whole family to accept his decision. I was a good boy, a very sensible kid, I didn't rebel so he discussed it with his friends and let me go to Kalakshetra. I had only begged him to let me go for one year. He said, "No. If you are going, go for the whole course."' Navtej's uncle, an informed and very well-educated man, told his father that he was sending his son to "the scum of the earth."

Arriving in Madras, where Navtej did not know a soul, he made his way to the Music Academy. There he got talking with Shyamala Mohanraj, one of Balasaraswati's disciples, and at the end of an hour had become the best of friends with her. Shyamala advised him to try Padma Subrahmanyam or Kalakshetra. Still carrying the train's rhythm within him, Navtej took a bus to Kalakshetra.

'It was June. There was no outer boundary to Kalakshetra in those days. I loved the place, it was like an enchanted wood. I just spent the entire afternoon there, lying on the sand, sitting by the pond, leaning against the vast banyan tree, wandering near the adjacent crematorium.'

When he did eventually enquire at the office about the beginning of the term, he met Chinna Sarada Teacher, who casually joked about his beard. Most male Bharata Natyam dancers avoid facial hair as it can obscure one's *abhinaya*. However for Navtej: 'I grew up with a beard. At that age I had no compunctions about being a dancer or having a beard. It did not cross my mind that it can't be done.

'Whether a Sikh can do Bharata Natyam, or a man…if I am a dancer in my heart, if I feel that I can dance, I identify with a free space and it is from this free space that my sense of expression comes. I cannot nitpick there that I am a man, a bearded man.'

While it now defines Navtej's appearance as a dancer, it has also brought its share of curiosity and dismissal. 'People ask me all the time how I dance with a beard. I could not care less. I don't buy into their standard of aesthetics. People keep saying, "Oh! He must have been such a rebel." I was not! It was so smooth, I just followed a path.' Abroad, the director of a prestigious festival looked up and down at Navtej's appearance and dismissed his abilities with a single word: *You?*

'I've had this kind of response, that's fine. One has to learn to deal with it.'

Navtej both loved Kalakshetra and felt loved there, even though the training was so gruelling, half his batchmates dropped out in a month. 'I had no idea how difficult it was so I had no struggle with the form. I got it immediately. But after a while, reality dawned: *Oh my god, this is what I'm going to do for the rest of my life!* I got scared. No one else in my circle was doing it.'

The real suffering though was related to food. The strapping Sardar brought up on a diet of wheat 'couldn't stand the sight of rice after a point. There was not a single place in Madras where I could get roti. I wrote in my diary *Soul suffers, body suffers*. I was constantly hungry all the time. I was always a little sickly in Madras and I had very little money too.'

On a parallel track, Navtej had also joined the peerless T.K.V. Desikachar's Yoga Mandiram as a student, learning yoga at the same time as dance. 'My life in Madras was very rich. I would finish at Kalakshetra at 4 p.m., have tea and head to the Mandiram. I get goosebumps when I think of it.'

But, 'For the longest time, dance and yoga were completely at loggerheads in my head. I loved yoga from day one. Yoga took me inside and dance used the same body to project outside. But when I danced, hungry, I used to feel that all the beauty I created in my body through yoga I destroyed when I did *tattadavus* because I felt I was hammering it out of me.'

A year and half into his course, Navtej's father died and, 'all my support came crashing down. Chiefly, my mother wanted me to be closer geographically.'

So Navtej left for Delhi, where after a gap he became Leela Samson's student in 1983. It was to lead to other changes in his appearance on stage. 'Leela akka was the first to put me on stage. I did a *shabdam* with a simple patka covering my head. Then I started working with Chandralekha. She said just do your hair in a top knot like a rishi.'

Navtej completed his training, did his *arangetram*, and then '1984 happened. The day Indira Gandhi was shot, I was on the last bus from Delhi to Chandigarh. Leela akka put me on the bus, said "*Go!*" My father was no more; my mother was petrified. She could not sleep, she wanted me to get out of the country. I could not come up as a Sikh male Bharata Natyam dancer, it was too dangerous. I knew I had no future in dance at that point in India. So I left for America.' Years later, Navtej would return to Kalakshetra to finish the course.

'I love Delhi,' states Navtej who chose to settle in the city on his return after ten years, from America, with a graduate degree from Tisch School of the Arts at New York University. He 'spent six months trying to decide. Madras *can* be opressive, closed at times. Delhi is very stimulating because of the kind of people who go through Delhi...I get to meet artistes, people from all over the world and have some very intense interactions in Delhi which would not be possible in Calcutta or Madras. There is a vitality here. Bombay has no dance energy, but Delhi is very exciting.'

As for proximity to patrons, whether bureacratic or otherwise, Navtej says, 'I don't walk through the corridors of power. It is very easy for a woman to wear a pretty sari and go and smile at these men and get a show. It gives the female dancers an added confidence. I don't have that sort of confidence to walk into someone's office, unless they know me and like my work. I don't seek. It is not part of my temperament. I don't have the confidence, *because* I am a male dancer. The public perception of Bharata Natyam is a pretty girl. I can't be that. Yet, I believe in what I can do, so it's okay.' However, he does like 'the sense that I could go to Mandi House *if* I want to, even though I don't.'

Delhi as a city has allowed Navtej the space to express himself through contemporary dance.

Early into his time at Kalakshetra, Navtej was aware of what he responded to and what he abhorred. 'From day one, I *wasn't* impressed. I loved the dance, the technique but when I saw Bharata Natyam on stage, apart from that first time I saw Padma, I was not enamoured of it. There were lots of things that did not appeal to me. The female dancers were too bedecked. They were almost grotesque to me, I did not find it beautiful.'

In his second month in Kalakshetra, 'The way they spoke, presented themselves, the way they did *abhinaya*, it seemed false to me. I *loved abhinaya* but I believe there are things you cannot show such as the relationship between the *atman* and *paramatman*. The dancers do not feel it, they do not live it. It's all from the outside. It was not present in them. So it is a sham.'

Given his background in street theatre, he always knew that he would not stick to classical Bharata Natyam but would explore other opportunities that involved dance and movement.

'The turning point was, and I resisted it, was when I began to see how Bharata Natyam was an artificial construct, it wasn't really like this even 50 years ago. That came to me as a shock. I started studying about devadasis and similar agents in different cultures, shamans for example. The only unique thing we had post nationalism was culture and therefore this great pressure on culture, on maintaining culture. In Kalakshetra we are brainwashed to think that we are god's own people.'

It was in Delhi, in the 90s that Navtej tried to crystallize his voice, his work. 'I was happy with the direction but wasn't satisfied with the work. When I did my solo works I made lots of follies. I was experimenting, trying to find a language. My head was full of the Bharata Natyam crowd, Kalakshetra, they were very critical of what I was doing. There were lots of eyebrows raised.'

While he loved Bharata Natyam, 'It is a beautiful format and there are some things that I can *only* express with Bharata Natyam,' it did not express everything that he needed to say.

His first contemporary work, about the anguish of a tramp, done on a bed with a four string symphony and a vocalist singing a *padam*, was well received in Chennai. 'It was a very slow work but the audience liked it.'

It was in the past ten years though that Navtej's voice in dance acquired a clarity and direction.

'*Fanaa: Ranjha Revisited,* which premiered in 2005, was a defining moment. I am a north Indian, I am Punjabi speaker who loves the language. I am also a Bharata Natyam dancer. I love both languages and both cultures deeply. I wanted to debunk the idea that Punjab is agriculture, Tamil Nadu is culture. So I put them side by side. I was trying to put two things together that were close to my heart.'

In the version of *Fanaa* I saw, homoeroticism seemed to have been given full play. Navtej and another male dancer, dressed in gathers of translucent white cotton, explore not only space but also each other's bodies, giving the audience the sense, as poet Sudeep Sen describes it, of 'deep-felt nerve-ends – electricity waiting to spark'.

'That was an accident!' exclaims Navtej. 'Originally it was performed by a trio, one girl and two men. The whole idea was that there is no male no female, no south Indian, north Indian. My focus was fluidity and interchangeability in Sufi thought. Then there were difficulties with the girl, and so we stopped performing the piece. When I got an offer to do it in a big festival, Anil Panchal thought we could do it, just the two of us. There is so much physical work...with just two bodies we had to remake the whole piece.'

However, Navtej does believe in blending eroticism into his work. 'Eroticism is beautiful. It can be spiritual. Dance is far freer than we have made it. It is beautiful because it is free. The beauty of eroticism is that it is free of gender boundaries. It is beyond morality, beyond many things.'

A dancer must have 'a very resolved sense of sensuality. Doing those *padams*, the devadasis' sense of sexuality was different from ours.' To get to that point requires 'a personal journey, a rigorous self reflection which many classical dancers don't embark upon because we are trained to be like that.'

I asked Navtej if *Fanaa* could be read as a statement about gay identity. 'It's not an issue. The same way that I am a Sikh and I dance. I don't push it in my work.'

After *Fanaa, Mango Cherry Mix* 'was an antithesis where we stay far away from each other.' There Navtej was 'working with a familiar other. The West does not understand the nuances of Indian dance. Hiroshi Miyamoto was an Easterner, his sensibility was very distinct and we had a very smooth collaboration.'

Navtej describes his work as one of 'juxtaposition, putting two things together side by side, not meshing them. For example, in Charumati Claire Singh I juxtaposed the life of a French maid, a bit of Jean Genet's play *The Maids*, with that of a devadasi. All my works end up back in dance, where I find my answers. The musicality of the *padam* or a thumri, the eroticism, the dialogue that the *padam* evokes, *that* is central. The last couple of times, I have sung a thumri on stage. It is important to be a singing body. In face, my latest collaboration with the German, is the only work where the *padam* has not been the central piece.'

As to the realities of earning a living, 'I do make my living doing yoga. I would have to work very hard to make a living from dance. I would have to be very aggressive.'

Navtej did open a studio to teach dance but could not deal with the expectations of both the children and their mothers. 'It is soul-destroying to teach. I have a few select students whom I work with, but I would not teach. Something is hugely flawed. I think dance is in crisis, it comes from how we are taught and how we teach.' His income comes from various sources, 'teaching yoga, performing or through dance assignments. But I do make a decent living.'

Navtej had little patience with the idea that male Bharata Natyam dancers must explore the male voice and experience in dance, an issue that a younger generation of dancers such as Anand seem to be grappling with.

'They are missing the point. It is not about men and women. It is about the human condition about being incomplete and in the Indian tradition, that is the feminine. I have no problem that I am a bearded man going on stage and being a woman because I am a *dancer*. You are killing it by making a statement that because I am a man I cannot do this. I am expressing the longing of my soul and that is a feminine voice.'

It would profit a male dancer more, suggests Navtej, if he were to ask the question: What is the requirement of dance, within Bharata Natyam?

'Bharata Natyam expresses the feminine voice of the human condition in the most beautiful manner possible. Sufism expresses it one way, Vaishnava poetry of all kinds, Gurbani expresses it, folk songs, folk tales...they all do. If you are a male expressing it, then your identification is with that voice. It's not the form, the costume, the jewellery, that's all secondary...the core is the *voice* of this dance. Which is that of beauty, longing, eroticism, human incompleteness. If you don't get that and say I will only do this as a man or not, then stay at home.'

While Navtej doesn't disrespect a straight young male's anxiety of being perceived as gay, he believes: 'You are not there to prove a point about your sexual identity. This is dance you are talking about. It is bigger than being mistaken for a queen. You are not a woman, you are not homosexual, you are a man and you want to dance, you must have resolve about it.' In his experience, 'If they are straight they want to be heroic. And if they are gay, they want to be better than the women. It defeats the purpose of dance. That is not the space for you to do that. How you deal with homosexuality will affect how you project yourself. If you are cool with it and you are straight then you are fine on stage. If not, then you will be uncomfortable in your skin. It comes with the turf, you have to deal with it!'

About the stance of a male Bharata Natyam dancer, 'The form is empowered and you have to be able to carry it in its vitality and strength. It does not allow a limp body. You can't be limpwristed. You have to be strong. I would not want to watch either a male or female dancer who is limp, floppy.'

Above all, 'Everybody is individual. Two men do not have the same level of masculinity. Each person carried their own honesty of who they are. It is about being honestly present on stage the way you are.'

Coming back to the subject of living in Delhi, it was here that Navtej discovered his aim really is 'to reach out and connect and have a dialogue with the rest of the world. In our dance scene, we are constantly patting each other's back. We are self-aggrandizing, self-flattering. Our dialogue is incestuous. I wanted to step out of that dialogue.' Therefore he sees himself as a 'bit of an oddball because I am between the classical and the non-classical. Even though both parties are my friends, I slip between the cracks many a time.'

55

First the gods tested me with one barbed question – 'So, you've stopped dancing?' – posed by any number of people, and delighted in the awful sensation it produced. It hurt. The answer, rallied with great effort of will, 'No, I dance every day, in class,' was no answer at all. The silent question is, *Why have you not made it?* And the unstated sentiment is, *We are elated by your misfortune.* There was no way I could convey to them the radiant contentment wrought by adhering to my own inner truth.

Then the gods forgot me for a while.

One day, they opened doors I did not know existed.

A friend decided that I would be the right person to perform for a group of executives visiting India from abroad and fixed it up without asking me. It was in another city; I had not performed in five years; I had already made plans to spend a week in Kolkata with my family; was not free the day of the show and even if I were to accept – flying from and returning to Kolkata – how would I rehearse with the musicians in Madras? '*No!*' seemed the right answer, but then I would be letting my friend down.

So, having rehearsed a week in advance, my musicians and I converged just hours before the show began. For the first time in my life, I was nervous. I had not had time to withdraw into myself, fresh images of the verdant countryside of Bengal were crowding my head, I was trying to centre myself, suspicious of this unexpected luck, but still felt off-kilter as I did my makeup.

There was a distance between me and the girl in the mirror, a woman now really, a mother. Not even the process of wearing my costume seemed to help. I was heading for disaster.

And there it was, the zero hour, one minute backstage, the next on. Everything I had planned to say vanished from my mind, but other words came instead. And miraculously, as the music began, every little nuance that had been absorbed and had been a-pickling streamed out, glittering. The strength of my training, the experience built incrementally over the years held me afloat that evening.

It was the first of many shows of a kind, in-house, for high profile visitors. They offered everything that a sabha performance often lacked, an attentive audience, substantial payment and a setting that allowed for a greater rapport both with my musicians and those watching.

But of course, the gods had not stopped their play. Since these were private performances, and not reviewed anywhere, I still had to face the question: 'So, you've quit dancing?'

Only, it did not matter anymore.

56

The darkened auditorium is filled with people, in a city that has such a surfeit of Bharata Natyam that many performances go unattended. They have come thirty minutes early to ensure good seats and as the hour draws near, their attention is focused on the curtain, anticipating its rise.

Suddenly, there is the sound of men singing, the evocative sound of bhajan cymbals ringing afar. The music travels from the back of the huge auditorium and everyone turns in their seat, neck craned, eyes searching the darkness. An audible buzz of excitement begins when they see a man dressed in a simple dhoti and cotton headgear moving down the aisle followed by a group of disciples. It is Dhananjayan, already immersed in his role as Thyagaraja, ardent devotee of Rama, the revered poet-saint of Carnatic music.

I am his student, I have seen the show umpteen times but I too fall for the theatrical entry; I have goosebumps.

Just as he has descended the sloping aisle, an old woman, overcome by the sight of Thyagaraja, slips out of her seat to bend herself double on the ground at his feet. I worry that my guru might not see her and trip, as his gaze is directed heavenwards, and I admire the adroit ease with which he moves around her, both accepting the obeisance while still in character and dealing with the unexpected as a seasoned dancer.

There have been many such touching instances of the way people have responded to his art. In Varanasi, a Muslim boatman told him that he had seen Allah through him; in a remote village in Andhra

Pradesh, a poor farmer hesitantly held out a tattered five-rupee note on his soiled palm in a wordless gesture.

On stage, Dhananjayan is visibly an elderly man – he refuses to dye his hair – but also a dancer who at seventy-three is remarkably agile. There may be certain postures and movements he will no longer attempt but that does not detract from his dance. It is one of those instances when his age matches perfectly the character he is playing. Some say *this* is the role of his life.

In his sixth decade of performing, he now commands the stature to dance alone on the stage, his beloved Shanta to his side moulding the flow of music to his requirements. It was not always so; this is a space he has achieved where none existed.

Dhananjayan as Thyagaraja (r), from left, sitting: Ramakrishnan; standing: Krishnakumar, Vijay Viswanath, and Satyajit

Thyagaraja sees Rama everywhere, in everything. The only thing he longs for is the blessing of actually seeing him in all his radiant glory. Rama teases him, perversely keeps him waiting because he enjoys hearing the soul-full music produced as a result of Thyagaraja's longing. Thyagaraja is most unworldly. When the king sends him gifts and gold, wanting to appoint him court musician, he sings the immortal *Nidhi chala sukhama*, weighing the benefits of pleasing the king in a court versus serving the lord in his temple. Here, the dancer stretches out both arms, like the scales of a balance, considering which is heavier in worth. Of course Rama wins over gold and his right hand descends lower as his face registers the happy realization. When his brother, furious at his spurning all the wealth the world has to offer, throws his beloved idol of Rama in the river Thyagaraja is bereft. After days of sorrow, he miraculously finds the idol in the waters and cradles Rama in his arms. Placing him reverently back in his shrine, wiping the water off him, enquiring if he caught a cold, he tenderly sings *Nannu vidachi*, telling Rama not to leave him for even the fraction of a second for even the thought of it is unbearable. So deeply embedded are Thyagaraja's songs in the southern psyche, people to my right and left are singing softly every familiar song. Many eyes are bright with tears.

The stage is a prayer room and his dance all prayer. He is elevated. In experiencing Thyagaraja he gives us the gift of being able to *feel* Thyagaraja; one forgets oneself.

I see that my guru's *abhinaya* has acquired an even greater clarity and simplicity over the years. He can communicate the most difficult of thoughts simply, cleaving the shortest direct way through the words... now the poet-saint envisioning his divine poetry, now the mortal man caught in the throes of worldly existence.

There is nothing he cannot say with his face.

It is this face that I have watched from childhood, registered every emotion that it expressed including mockery and flammable exasperation at me, it is this face that draws me into every emotion the poet-saint feels, longing for Rama, joy in picking flowers for Rama, the anticipation of awaking Rama the next morning after only just lovingly putting him to sleep, the shock of losing him, the desolation that blights his life, the incredible joy of finding the idol, resuming his daily conversations with Rama, and finally, the tearful ecstasy of seeing Rama *and* Sita *and* Lakshmana *and* Hanuman.

The audience rises to its feet; the ovation lasts several minutes. Gratifying yes, but he is in a trance, a place of enchantment and great peace. All the travails of life are held at bay. People swarm him backstage, offering him their tearful adoration, but he is aloof. None of the praise percolates through. It takes him time to become his normal self.

The next morning, grey hair freshly shampooed, he enters class at BK dressed in a simple white veshti and cotton jubba. Part of him is still with Thyagaraja; there is a remoteness about him. He's caught a cold.

Not knowing how to tell him just how superb he was, we burst into spontaneous clapping.

This is my continual good fortune; *that* lord of dance whom I beheld yesterday is my guru.

Notes

1. *Rukmini Devi Arundale, Birth Centenary* Volume, Ed. Shakuntala Ramani, The Kalakshetra Foundation, 2004, pg 83
2. Ibid, pg 37
3. Ibid, pg 38
4. *Kalakshetra Rukmini Devi, Reminiscences* by S. Sarada, Kala Mandir Trust, 1985, pg 4
5. *Rukmini Devi A life*, Leela Samson, Penguin 2010, pg 98
6. *Rukmini Devi Arundale, Birth Centenary* Volume, Ed. Shakuntala Ramani, The Kalakshetra Foundation, 2004, pg 41
7. I am grateful to scholar V.A. K. Ranga Rao for both translating and sharing with me his understanding of Kshetrayya, Annamacharya and Sarangapani's padams.
8. Ibid
9. In an 1981 interview (*Bharatanjali* by Sudharani Raghupati, Doordarshan) she explained, 'If you take a really good Kshetrayya padam, first of all you have to select the right songs, because what may sound right in poetry may not sound right in actual gesture by the human flesh and form…These songs were composed by divine inspiration. They had actually pratyaksha, vision, of Krishna and they saw everything in a divine form and they put that into the music into the poetry. What we have to do is to interpret the same spirit in our movement. But being purely physical, and it is movement, we have to convey it through movement and through expression of the eyes and so on. If you bring it down to the level of the flesh, then you are not keeping it at the level at which the composer composed it. Therefore we are not even interpreting it in the right way.'
10. Translated by V.A.K. Ranga Rao
11. *Sruti Magazine*, Vol 8, 1984

12. Sudharani Raghupati's series *Bharatanjali*, Doordarshan 1981
13. Ibid.
14. *Rukmini Devi A Life*, Leela Samson, Penguin 2010, pg 18
15. Dhananjayan prefers the word *natya* to be used instead of the generic 'dance' to distinguish it from say Bollywood-type dance or contemporary dance
16. *The Hindu*, Thiruvananthapuram, August 5, 2005
17. Attendance, Ed Ashish Khokar, 2009/10, pg 15
18. *Times of India*, 30th April, 1973
19. Yatho hasta tatho drishti, yatho drishti tatho manah, yatho manah tatho bhavo, yatho bhavo tatho rasah. Abhinaya Darpana by Nandikeshwara.
20. *Sruti Magazine*, Vol 2, 1983
21. *Times of India*, Bombay, Nov. 2, 1983 S.V. Vasudev
22. *Midday*, Bombay, Nov 8, 1983, Sumitra Srinivasan
23. *The Indian Express*, April 17, 1971
24. My first novel, *Meeting Lives*, Niyogi Books, 2008, was a fictional representation of motherhood and the dancing self.
25. 1975
26. 1981
27. 1977
28. 1998
29. *Indian Express*, Dec 19, 1983
30. *The Hindu*, Nov. 5, 2003, V. Gangadhar
31. *Statesman*, New Delhi Nov 8, 1986
32. *The Sunday Observer*, Feb 5, 1984
33. *Indian Express*, Dec 20, 1983
34. *Statesman*, Nov 8, 1986
35. *The Hindu*, Nov 14, 1986
36. *Raga Mala*, The Autobiography of Ravi Shankar, Edited and Introduced by George Harrison, Wecome Rain Publishers, New York, Sept. 1999, pg 253
37. Ibid., pg 254
38. *The Indian Post, Bombay, Nov.* 22, 1989, R. Sridhar
39. *The Independent* Oct. 5. 1989, Jan Smaczny
40. *The Guardian*, Oct 5, 1989, Tom Sutcliffe
41. *The India Today*, Dec 15, 1990
42. *The Plain Dealer*, July 29, 1995, Wilma Salisbury
43. *The Beacon Journal*, Nov 6, 1996, Elaine Guregian
44. *The Beacon Journal*, Nov 10, 1996, Valerie Thorson
45. *The Plain Dealer*, Nov 11,
46. *The Plain Dealer*, Nov 3, 1996
47. 1996-1997 Northern Ohio LIVE Awards of Achievement brochure, Sept 22, 1997, pg. 16
48. *The Hindu*, June 4, 2000

Select Bibliography

Raga Mala: The Autobiography of Ravi Shankar, Edited and Introduced by George Harrison, Wecome Rain Publishers, New York, Sept. 1999.

Rhythm in the Heavens: An Autobiography, Ram Gopal, Secker and Warburg, 1957.

Rukmini Devi: A Life, Leela Samson, Penguin Books, 2010.

His Dance, His Life: A Portrait of Uday Shankar, Mohan Khokar, Himalayan Books, 1983.

Rukmini Devi Arundale: Birth Centenary Volume, Edited by Shakuntala Ramani, 2003

Kalakshetra Rukmini Devi: Reminiscences, by S. Sarada, Kala Mandir Trust, Jan 1985.

Sruti Magazine archives

From Sacred Servant to Profane Prostitute: A History of the Changing Legal Status of the Devadasis in India, 1857-1947, Kay Jordan, Manohar Publishers and Distributors, 2003.

Balasaraswati: Her Art and Life, Douglas M Knight Jr., Tranquebar by Westland Ltd, 2011.

Acknowledgements:

My gurus, V.P. Dhananjayan and Shanta, for giving generously of their time over the months it took to record their life-stories. For providing open access to their entire archive of papers and photographs.

Anand Satchidanandan, Navtej Singh Johar, L. Narendra Kumar, B.K.Shafeekuddin, C.P. Satyajit and Charles Ma for sharing their journeys in dance with me.

V.A.K. Ranga Rao, for the most informative sessions on Telugu, and other, poetry.

C.P. Satyajit, for shaving off his rather dashing moustache and beard to pose for the cover photograph. For taking the cover photograph with such care.

Nandita Aggarwal, for commissioning this book within seconds of our meeting, for the first time, in 2010. For her firm editorial touch that saw the book through to completion.

Mini Krishnan, for her warmth and friendship, always.

Sudeep Sen, for graciously permitting me to quote from his poem 'Almost a Touch', from the collection Fractals: *New & Selected Poems | Translations 1978–2013.*

Ravi Malamakkavu, for helping me navigate my way through the numerous files and photographs that document the dancing years of the Dhananjayans

Monisha Mukundan, for the space she gave me in *Namaste* magazine to explore a certain kind of non-fiction writing.

Dipa Chaudhuri, for friendship, and sage advice readily given at unearthly hours.

My mother Seeta Badrinath, for the gift of dance.

My son, Chinmaya, for being mine.